A Tale of a Soul | Samuel Refaeli

D0663947

Producer & International Distributor
eBookPro Publishing
www.ebook-pro.com

A Tale of a Soul: A Soul's Journey Throughout Human History
Samuel Refaeli

Translation: Yossie Bloch

Contact: srafaely@gmail.com
ISBN 9798749808353

This book is dedicated to you, dear readers,
with the sincere hope that you may find your way
to the good and the love within you
to the soul that you are.

A Tale of a Soul

A Soul's Journey Throughout Human History

SAMUEL REFAELI

CHAPTER ONE

The Woman in the Cave

Silence.

A divine silence settled over the land.

All the members of the tribe stood in a circle, quiet and awestruck, surrounding her still-warm body.

The news of her passing spread like wildfire. More and more people joined the circle. For a few days, the air had been suffused with the sensation of the end of an era; many people, even from other, more distant tribes, had dropped everything to see for themselves. Could it be true? Could the sacred healer really have passed?

Silence.

Nature itself seemed to have been silenced. The birds had stopped singing, the wind had stopped blowing, and even the morning clouds scattered and allowed the sun to peek through and to wonder... Could she really be dead?

She had been a holy woman. She had always been accompanied by people gripped by fear of the gods; now, as she lay in the center of the circle, the feeling of closeness to the gods intensified. It was almost as if they themselves had joined, hovering around the circle, without the assembled people being aware of it.

The clearing in the forest's hilltop stretched to the cave where she had lived for many years. It looked far off, to the tops of the green trees in the surrounding woods, to the streams and the paths. They all appeared to be shrouded in silence. The people trod along the paths on their way to her as if in slow motion, as if something had muted the whole world.

Everything was hushed. Some people from the crowd audaciously entered the circle to sit down around the body, sobbing inwardly, shoulders shaking, eyes tearing – but not even the slightest sound was audible. No one dared rebuke them or move them away. They owed her their bodies, their spirits, and she seemed to draw them nearer, to receive, at the last moment, one more gift of goodness, of provision for the coming days, for when she would no longer be bodily present.

Large men stood around, fur-clad hunters who seemed insecure without their weapons. The holy woman had not allowed any man to come near her or seek her help while they were armed, even for the sake of her own protection. Now that she was gone, they didn't have the courage to violate her command, so they left their weapons at the edge of the clearing.

A small murmur went through the crowd when the healer's husband, an elderly man, appeared at the entrance to the cave; their offspring stood behind him.

The tribal chieftain emerged from the crowd, passed by the body of the holy woman, stopped for a moment, and then continued reverently towards the old man. When the chieftain reached him, he kneeled and bowed his head.

At first it appeared that the old man did not notice him, but he suddenly stood erect and began to speak. "The voice of the children, on that cruel and violent day, still echoes in my ears. The cries were not of joy or of play, not even cries of anger or apprehension. They were the subdued sounds of fear and terror – the fear of a great catastrophe about to befall us."

He spoke softly, as if he were telling the story to himself or to his children, but with the vast silence all around his words could be heard – powerful and sharp, clear and precise.

"There were just a few of us, chopping up the bear we had hunted. The others heard nothing, but I noticed a subdued sound. I ran to the cave entrance, as if the bear had returned to life and began chasing after me; I ran as if death itself were chasing me, and I burst into the cave. I could not see anything; the light outside had left me blind, and the only light was that of the flickering fire. The sound of someone being beaten told me what had happened. She lay on the ground, bruised, curled up. She was like a worm curling in on itself, and he, evil incarnate, stood there, kicking her and beating her with a club. She was soaked in blood, her own blood, but he had a smile on his face – a smile of satisfaction, a smile of joy and delight.

"I don't remember how it happened, but suddenly I was on top of him, pulling him off her, beating, screaming, hitting until he fell, but I kept on kicking, slashing, tearing at every exposed inch of his body. Then suddenly I heard her saying, in a voice that emerged from crushing pain, 'Enough. Leave him alone.'

"I looked at her in astonishment. 'Leave him alone? He won't leave this cave alive!' I screamed. But she said to me, her eyes shut and covered in blood, 'We will not be like him.' I stared at her, shocked. She was lying there, unconscious, her lips pursed in pain, but a soft, delicate voice came from her mouth, whispering, 'Let him go.'"

The old man stopped speaking. Tears welling in his eyes, he looked at her for a split second and then continued. "It wasn't she who spoke; it was the gods speaking from her throat. I knew it, and I suddenly understood that my life was about to change. I understood that my wife was an emissary of the gods, and I was her servant. I would serve her with great love and subjection.

"She had been a beautiful young woman. My old friends can testify to that. She didn't look then as you young people see her now. But her injured face remained twisted, as her broken nose never fully healed; her broken legs never fully healed either, and she limped for the rest of her life. The scar that split her right cheek never faded, and the bulge on her forehead from that last clubbing remained as a memory seared into flesh. Although the body was broken, a new woman was born, a woman I had the privilege of serving throughout my life.

"Many days passed as she lay in the cave, unconscious, dissociated, in agony. Some days she had a raging fever; on others, she shivered with chills. Sometimes she curled up in fear, and sometimes she slept in peace and security, but never alongside us. Good women helped us take care of her, watching her and the children, even bringing a nursemaid to feed the baby, but it was if she were in another world. She couldn't see us, couldn't hear us, he couldn't respond at all. The healers who came to treat her said that it was a miracle that she was still alive, that I ought to prepare for burial rites. But she was detached from all this. I lost hope; I couldn't understand why the gods were not helping her. Each night, I went to sleep at the other side of the cave so I wouldn't disturb her.

"Then one night, while I was still deep in sleep, I heard her. She called me. I couldn't believe my ears, but she called to me again, so I took a branch from the fire and approached her."

Some of the old men in the community remembered that day, and they shook their heads to acknowledge the great wonderment of the miracle that had occurred – as if they still hadn't processed its magnitude until that day. Others, who were hearing about it for the first time, looked at them in astonishment.

"'I have returned,' she said. 'I have returned, and I have much work to do.'" The old man smiled as he remembered that night. "'Wait,' I told her, in utter disbelief. 'Wait a minute. How can you go to work now? Don't you need to recuperate first?' But she put her hand on mine, asking 'How long have I been like this? How are the children? How are you?'

"So I told her. I told her about those good women who had so selflessly dedicated themselves to helping, I told her about the children, I told her about everything that had happened to her during that time, but when I tried to go back and tell her about the events of that cruel, violent day, she refused to listen. 'He was an emissary,' she said. 'He came to link me to my destiny.' What can I say, my friends?… I didn't understand a word of what she said, and I certainly did not believe what I heard.

"The children heard us talking, woke up and came over to us. One of them went to wake up the women. The cave quickly filled with people, and the sounds of laughter soon echoed throughout the cave. Since that day, the sounds have not ceased."

A soft murmur ran through the crowd as an old woman stepped forward and said, "With your permission, my dear friend, I will continue the story. I was a young girl when all this happened. I was afraid of the ugly, scarred, limping woman who emerged from your cave. In particular, that bulge over her right eye terrified me. I was worried that she would harm me or my siblings, so I always followed her so I could see ahead of time the bad things she was likely to bring.

"When she went out ot the fields, I did as well, surreptitiously, so I could keep an eye on her. When she went to the forest, I would track her and hide among the trees. Little by little, and much to my surprise, I discovered a special woman. I saw her plucking leaves, but not the leaves we collect to eat. I watched as she went down hidden paths, petting animals and feeding them various things she took out from beneath her garments. As time passed, the animals began to recognize her, and they gathered around her without fear. Sick or injured animals would come up to her, put their heads on her and wait for her to treat them using the leaves she had picked.

"She didn't have an iota of evil in her, and I felt ashamed of my suspicions. For many hours, I stood and watched her in amazement; I was naïve enough to think that she wasn't aware of my presence. Then came the day that changed my life forever. She met my mother and began to talk to her. I was a bit taken aback, like a child caught red-handed. But when they saw me, they smiled and beckoned me to come closer.

"My mother looked at me and said, 'I have heard good things about you from our neighbor. She wants to take you under her wing, to teach you all the things she does. I don't understand exactly that means, but the woman radiates such an aura that I trust her to take care of you – but only if you agree.'

"If I would agree? If I would agree? How all the gods shared my joy! All I wanted to do was jump and shout for all to hear my 'Yes!'

"Since then, for years now, I never left her side. I learned from her, I was her apprentice, I saw how people learned of her abilities and how her reputation grew and spread far and wide. All of you know how many people came to this clearing, patiently waiting for her to return from some rescue mission she had embarked on. She never refused. I had the privilege to be present during those magic moments of happiness – when she helped people, and during the hard times as well, when she knew how to caress, to embrace, to console.

"I mourn her passing; it is a deep loss for us – for our tribe, and for the surrounding tribes. As for our future, who can say what will be?"

The old woman sat back down, and another man came to tell his story. He was hesitant, embarrassed, but he told about his magical encounters with the healer. After he was finished, the dam burst as men and women rose to tell their own stories, relate their experiences, the miracles they experienced when they were near her – but it was all done with exceptional quiet and order.

And so, as if they didn't want their last encounter with the miracle worker to end, they kept on telling their stories as the day faded and the chieftain signaled for them to arrange themselves for the funeral rites. It was an empowering experience for the tribe. The tales were destined to pass from parent to child, and generations of their descendants would be raised on the stories of the miracle worker, told with the great respect she had earned at the time of her passing from the world.

However, none of those present knew the full import of the story. How could they? They were flesh and blood, mortals not exposed to other, hidden dimensions of the universe. If any one of them might have mused about where that miracle worker went, they would have believed, perhaps even have been aware, that the gods had taken her; this would have provided a bit of comfort. However, the entirety of the story would still have been unknown. None of them knew that I, the soul of that old woman, was hovering over them all that time.

I looked down, observing them with interest, but without understanding what was happening to me or what was taking place there. I was perplexed; something had happened to me, to the woman lying there – something fundamental, something accompanied by a strong sensation of irrevocability.

I simply hovered above their heads. The images seemed blurry and bizarre. My beloved husband appeared younger than his age, while some of my children seemed older. The opening of the cave seemed a bit different. As for the crowd, the forest and the animals, they seemed at times to be in motion and at times to be frozen in place. The background was different, obscure.

The place was certainly familiar to me. I had spent long periods of my life there; I had traveled from there to far-off places in order to heal people, and I had returned. I knew every path, every rut and jut – but now it was different, as if it were no longer mine.

I floated above them for many hours, back and forth, but I couldn't solve the riddle. I didn't hear what they were saying; I only saw their lips move. I swooped down along them, going into the cave and coming out, looking for my loved ones, my family.

I saw my young granddaughter with her finger stuck in her mouth. She didn't understand why they were all sad, why they all kept shushing her. Her mother sat on my bed, her legs crossed beneath her. She cradled her youngest, uncovering her breast to feed her. I descended to embrace them, but they didn't sense my presence. Here, as I saw my daughter feeding her daughter, I began to grasp the reality: My life in this body had reached its end.

Something new was supposed to happen to me, but I didn't know what. A new adventure awaited me. The desire to stay, to avoid the change, was extremely strong, and it was clear to me that I wanted to remain there, to be with the people that I so loved and cherished, and to continue taking care of them.

Would it even be possible? I toyed with the idea for a bit, until I saw them taking my body to burial. I almost felt it as those clumps of earth; the earth I loved so much, hit my body and pained me, as they covered the hole, but then I understood that this was it. It was over. I soared to the cave, waiting for them there. I wanted to feel them, to touch them, to cry with them, but I knew that I could not embrace them, only depart from them – a leave-taking that I, and only I, would be aware of; they, on the other hand, would not see or be aware of me.

Night fell. They all went to their beds. I couldn't sense anything, except for the crackle of the fire and flickering shadows on the walls. I floated among them, making sure each of them was at ease, that they were covered up, that none of them was cold; after all, this was what I had always done. However, when I descended to adjust the blanket on one of their sleeping bodies, the new reality slapped me in the face – I could do nothing! Fortunately, he turned over in his bed and sighed as he covered himself, as if he didn't want me to remember him shivering in the cold.

But what now? What am I to do? Where am I to go? Is this it? From now on am I to be left to my own devices? Am I to have no companion?

I soared outside, into the open skies, moving to and fro without any direction or destination, not wanting to distance myself from the cave. I only wanted to stay in the area. The hours passed, and there I was, above the tribe that slept peacefully, as a question ate away at me; What now?

Then suddenly, as if of their own accord, feelings of great acceptance and joy suffused my innermost being. I felt that I was being swept in a direction I could not define, a new dimension of love and comfort. I had a growing feeling of returning home, accompanied by great happiness and longing, towards something that I could not name. I found myself advancing towards a long, illuminated corridor, without fear; I let the light draw me inside with increasing speed. I knew that many entities were waiting for me at its end. I heard the joyful calls, feeling as if loving hands were extended towards me. I felt great delight.

I was returning home.

I invite you, my readers, to join me on this wondrous journey, a journey that began in other places, in other spaces, many years before the miracle worker was born. Let us be secret travelers, as we accompany her spirit, her being, her consciousness, her soul, and let us see what fate has in store for her. We mustn't worry that we are doing something forbidden; she knows that we are behind her, watching and wondering.

CHAPTER TWO

Birth of a Soul

My journey began thousands of Earth-years ago, before the miraculous healer's life story began. I was a new soul then, a soul that had just been separated from the infinite Source of Creation as a new, curious, vital, energetic being.

This is how it all started. The moment of my formation I remember quite clearly, the very first moment, that fraction of a second in which I burst forth into the universe, becoming a new soul, distilled from the infinite, beginning a long passage of learning and cooperation with the worlds of spirit – and, eventually, with the material world as well.

When was this? It's difficult to estimate this in human chronology. All I can say is that there were periods in which I was aware of the secrets of Creation and of the Creator; I also went through various eras, each of which served as a basis for the next, during which the experiences that shaped all my basic beliefs, patterns and insights were poured into me.

You could imagine this as a kind of light that suddenly bursts forth at the top of a cone, emanating from the Creator Himself, a soul that appears as a shining star that has begun to make its way through the space of the cone, along a path that it builds itself, changing all the time, as it advances towards the broad, open side. Its progress is accompanied by infinite decisions about new directions which pour its character into it; in its development, it experiences various "leaps" and various levels, which lead it to a new plane, a new "era."

Every plane of the cone is further from the Creator, but it is also broader than its predecessor. With its progress, the soul experiences, to a great extent, the splendor of the Creator's greatness and power, alongside the growing possibilities of learning. On each plane, the soul experiments with lessons to assimilate feelings, thoughts, and beliefs within it. In every era, it forms itself into a vessel whose purpose is love, as it decides its goals and where it will want to achieve them after it departs the path of formation in the cone.

On its way through the planes, the soul experiences many cosmic influences and encounters various spiritual entities, and it does not always complete the full procedure of processing the different lessons. Throughout the process of its development, it travels down paths that require focus so that the general perception of the expanse is narrowed, much as when a pair of binoculars focuses on a certain area at the expense of the "big picture;" thus it narrows the pure and complete consciousness of the infinite. All of these greatly influence the shaping of the soul, but also minimize the degree of its connection to the Creator. Despite this, this is a wondrous system that ultimately allows the new soul to be revealed in all its might – unique and unlike any other soul.

When I completed the passage through the eras, I decided to be incarnated in the material world, on Earth and among humans; however, not all souls choose this. I knew my goals, and my destiny was clear. I had a long way before me. Certain lessons throughout the process of my formation had not been fully realized and assimilated within me, so I remained a deficient vessel, without the capacity to contain the full cosmic love, a deficiency that would be expressed in various and sundry ways as I would be incarnated among humans. At this early stage of my formation, I did not yet know how these deficiencies, these wounds, would influence me in many different ways, such as damaging my feeling of self-worth, causing a lack of confidence, and dissuading me from taking responsibility. However, there would also be times in which arrogance would be my undoing and cause me problems in relating to people and doing my work, among many other "soul wounds."

Every soul is formed with these soul wounds, each with its own wounds; this is what causes such great variety to be found in the human race, and its great beauty as well. "Healing" these wounds allows the soul to increase the capacity to connect to the divine light that drives each human being. Thus we souls are reincarnated, again and again, until we have healed everything. When this process is complete, we achieve a wonderous unity with Creation, in its entirety.

As I look back on the long period of passage through the eras, within the cone, and preparation for a life in the material world, I can tell you that this was a unique period that is difficult to describe in human language; all I can say is that it was glorious and that it imparts to us souls the one feeling that we share: love.

When this wondrous process reached its end, I was like a newborn baby taking its first breath – a baby who looks like other babies, but who carries within it its uniqueness. I then moved on to the company of souls right for me, to begin to become familiar with them and their worlds.

I was then a baby soul. A great deal of patience was required of my Guide as he revealed to me the many worlds of spirit, their unity and their variety, the hidden entities, and the servants of God as well as those whose path towards absolute and infinite good and light was just beginning.

In this book, we will follow together "the chronicles of my existence," the path I took; we will go through the healing of my soul wounds, the healing of the traumas I experienced throughout my years as a human being, and we will reveal the topics that I wanted to study. Here, in the spiritual world, whenever I want to share an experience with my soul friends, I need only desire it, and they immediately understand every thought, idea, or feeling. But for your sake, dear reader, I must attempt to find words in human language, as our languages differ so greatly from each other. Whichever language I pick to explain what's happening "among us" in the spiritual world would always be deficient because – and please don't be offended – the physical world is so limited...

You are matter. And we? When we are realized within matter, it becomes living; when we depart a living body, it goes back to its basic state – matter. So what are we? People love to use the term "energy," as this is the closest a word can be to describing what we are, and perhaps because this is a word you can comprehend; but just between the two of us, reader – you can admit that you don't know what that energy is, right? You're familiar with heat, you know what electricity is – obviously – but which energy are we? In what form is this expressed? You have no idea.

For you, it's all physical, and you know that. But did you know that the same is true of us? You have four dimensions to your physicality, right? Three of those are the spatial dimensions of length, width, and height – and then there's the dimension of time. For us, it is far more complex, greater, broader – but at the same time, excessively fine. If only you knew how many dimensions we have... Your high school students study hard to understand your limited physics, so just imagine their experience were they to study here. But don't be dismayed; I'm not saying that you are ignorant or uneducated, just that this knowledge is beyond your ken.

In our course of study, we discovered different processes in the development of the soul, learning about its various goals and aims; we came to understand the division of labor in this world, a division that can best be described by the word you have in your language – "hierarchy." Still, this is an imprecise definition, one that misses the egalitarian character that exists among those who carry out various functions – whether they are experienced veterans or unlearned novices. We also learned about the various tasks and functions that souls fulfill, in addition to the realization in the human body at the time of their incarnations.

Incarnations? This is a word I recognize from my "prenatal" period. Then I had known that a material world existed, but it had been only theoretical, while now I could reveal its essence.

And what did I find? I found a complete universe, different than anything I recognized or had imagined – a strange universe, with abilities not extant in our world, abilities that emerge from its very existence as matter. A universe divided into different and strange celestial bodies, star systems that have a relationship between them, some of which orbit around the others. When these systems are organized in galaxies, even though everything is based on three dimensions alone, they succeed in creating fascinating, vibrant life – i.e., life energies that exist as mineral, vegetable, and animal.

Then we discovered Earth, the life on its surface and then – what was initially scariest – the human being. We came to understand that we were part of it, and that we were the ones who maintain its consciousness. We learned that integration in the human body provides us with a fantastic lodging-place, a home in which we could develop, a home in which we could heal our soul wounds, a home that could serve as a soul academy. But we also came to understand that this is not a unidirectional relationship, as our main aim is to develop human beings by way of what we learn through them.

Does that sound complicated? Absolutely! But that's nothing compared to what we felt when we came to understand the process of being realized in a body. We learned that we "descend" to join a human body only after we have been well prepared for the coming process of life, that we predetermine the lessons we want to learn in that lifespan, that we choose the environment in which we can best realize this, and, in fact, we actually devise a life-plan, a full script that will dictate the life of the human being.

However, we then discovered that... with the connection to the body, we would forget and would not know what we had really wanted to do – not only this, but human beings have freedom of choice that allows them to do whatever they want, and to "cross out" whatever has been planned for them.

On top of all this is another difficulty that emerges from the material character of this world. We had to recognize its limits, the feeling of heaviness and weight, the air all around. Our Guide, who sweetly told us all about this with a smile, said that we would have to practice before we could begin to learn and to plan our first lives as human beings.

Indeed, we were quickly taken to a star in the material world. I cannot explain the transition, how we could pass from the level of energy that includes many dimensions to a limited three-dimensional environment – and to feel it. We stayed there for a long time, which I cannot equate to time in Earth-years, but at the conclusion of the process we could say that it was a fascinating experience that definitely left us with a taste for more.

The climax of our training for the material world arrived, of course, when we at last visited Earth. A beautiful world! We saw the people, the human race when it was still in diapers, as it were – the people, mainly in nomadic tribes, who lived off the land and sought shelter in the caves. We truly fell in love with man, this fragile creature, taking his first steps in the world, achieving amazing things and not even grasping its magnitude.

With this feeling of love for man, this stage of our training concluded, and we became "almost" mature souls. In other words, we could begin planning our first life cycle, if we so wished. My reaction to the news that we had completed our basic training and were prepared to be realized in a human body was great joy, and I presume that if I were human, it would have resounded with a "Yesss!"

To my surprise, I discovered that although I was eager to get on the road, not all of my friends shared this feeling, and this was one of the first times that I encountered the variance between me and my soul friends.

Then I met my personal Guide, who remained with me through many reincarnations. I waited for the meeting with him with some trepidation, and he appeared as a venerable spirit radiating dignity, but I discovered that he also knew how to laugh and to be very patient with me and my many mistakes.

"The inaugural stage of preparation for your first life," the Guide said, "is to visit the library. Human beings call it 'the cosmic library.' This is the place where you can look for life stories and lessons that you may want to learn in your first incarnation."

But I already knew. Whenever I thought about it, I wanted to live a life that involved the challenges of great difficulty and suffering.

I thought that this could be a successful introduction to my journey among human beings – to start at the bottom and work my way up. In hindsight, I realize that this was the impulse of a new soul, one which had never experienced emotion, which didn't know what suffering was, and certainly had no concept of evil. All I knew was that the process would be difficult and complicated, and from a "childishly practical" viewpoint of the process of development, I felt that it was worth it to begin with "complex" situations and to clear the field. At the same time, there were yearnings reverberating within me to take care of people and to help them, to be a trailblazer, but I didn't know how to reconcile all of this. In fact, I didn't know why I had such preferences, and moreover – why these specific ones? I asked the Guide about it, and he reminded me of the process of development that had formed us, making us so varied and so unique.

"As for the yearning itself," he smiled and added, "slow down, hasty soul, as you do not know what suffering is. In any case, must you entangle yourself in lessons that are so complex already in your first life?"

Rebellious goat that I was, I replied, "Of course. I'm not afraid." Even when the Guide told me that I had a lot to learn first, I insisted, quite like a child. If I had then had human legs, I would have said that I was stamping my feet impatiently. Then he took the trouble to explain to me that without the infrastructure of knowledge and deep experience, I couldn't hope to realize the complex lesson in the best way; practically, it seemed that I would not only miss the true aim of these lessons, but even add superfluous suffering to the life of the human being in whose body I would be incarnated.

This calmed me down, and I agreed to wait. "But only one life cycle," I made it known. My Guide sighed and replied, "Very well. We'll see."

Alas, how right he was! In practice, it would take many

reincarnations and many thousands of years until I came to understand the deep significance of suffering, and until I had the courage and capacity to confront it.

Then we moved on to the library. Perhaps I should explain to you what "moved on to" means. In your language, I don't know how to express it, but the closest I can come to describing our movement is to compare it to an image changing in the blink of an eye. Until that point, we had been somewhere in outer space; but now, merely by expressing our desire, we came to be in the lobby of the library.

Wow, how excited I was when we got there! I was in awe of the glory of the place and overcome by emotion. The Librarian-Guide escorted me on a tour through its labyrinthine rows.

Wow, was it gigantic! And the true wonder? It contained all the books of all the souls. It was explained to me that every soul has its own book, in which all of its incarnations are written, all the lessons it wanted to learn in every incarnation, and all of its conclusions.

The Guide suggested I peruse these books, looking for a tale from the past that I might want to apply to my path. It was an interesting experience. You might call it voyeurism, but it is self-evident that all souls would want to share their experience and tales with its siblings.

In my introductory conversation with the Guide, we both decided that it would be best to begin to study the nature of interpersonal relationships. What is family? Parents? Siblings? Children? What does love mean? Is it concern for another? I discovered that there was a great deal to learn.

Take, for example, love. Ostensibly, what could be simpler? Either you love or you don't. But I discovered that there are different loves – for example, the love for a spouse is not like the love for a parent or for a child. I discovered that to love and to be loved are two entirely different things, and that there are many ways for these elements

to interrelate. To be in love with a person who does not reciprocate is a lesson of one type, while a totally different lesson is when
the beloved not only does not reciprocate, but even loves another
person instead. We must learn the distance between love and mere
affection, or between it and hatred.

In other words, there is so much for us to learn that one incarnation is not sufficient. Luckily, in one life cycle, one may concentrate
on individual topics or various lessons, which may sometimes be
learned in parallel, while at other times they may be distributed
through a human lifespan. And all of this must be planned precisely,
as much as possible.

Reluctantly, I discovered that life is complex, and great patience
is required to study it in a precise manner. After all, I knew what lessons I was striving for, and I had to prepare myself for them properly,
avoiding the trap of haste.

It took me a bit of time, but ultimately I discovered what I wanted
to do. I chose a tribe of nomadic hunters who lived in the hills – the
simple life of a primitive hunter, in the era in which humans began
to use tools, such as stone implements for hunting, fire-starting, and
cutting. I decided to be born as a boy, the son of a hunter who was
young, but skilled and respected.

Because I was a new soul preparing itself for its first incarnation,
I needed a considerable amount of help and support. The Guides
accompanied me through the process, and dedicated groups examined the script I had written in depth, helping me choose the souls
with whom I would pass through this incarnation – those who would
be my parents and my friends, those who would play an important
role in my future life. Once they had been chosen, we conducted a
signing ceremony for the "soul contract" that was appended to my
soul book.

I hope that what I am going to say now will not be considered "condescension" towards human beings, but we have no "ego" here, for our world is run very differently than that of physical life. Ostensibly, I should have been frightened of being made physical in body and of an unknown moment, but that is not how it was. I knew full well that I would never feel alone, that I would always have help. Truth be told, until I was in a human body I didn't know what "alone" meant. A soul may seek solitude when it wants to sink into deep thought or study, or simply flit about through other domains for its own enjoyment, but it is never "alone."

Then the moment arrived! Oh, such excitement! My Guide, my soul friends and many others accompanied me on my way to be linked to the fetus in the belly of she who would soon be my mother – although she didn't even know it!

I was brought to an illuminated hallway. Was I excited? Definitely! I didn't know what was supposed to happen to me there, but despite all the training and all I had been told, I was still excited. I was about to live life as a human being for the first time!

I entered the hallway. The shining light drew me in quickly, and immediately I felt warmth, I felt that I was in an enclosed space, and suddenly I knew that this was it! I was in my mother's womb. Wow, what a thrill! I loved her already.

It's a unique experience to transition from being a free spirit to being in a physical and limited body. Suddenly I was in an enclosed space, a feeling I had never had before. There was a feeling of physicality, that I was surrounded by gentle waters. I let myself float and just ... feel. I tried to move my body, and it responded. A unique experience indeed, the beginning of life – in both senses of the word.

Nevertheless, at this point I was still an independent, conscious soul, not a human being in the full sense of the word, as evidenced by my remaining connection to my soul friends, whom I knew were observing me and happy for me. Still, I had not come simply to indulge, and after a time – apparently a few days – I began to organize myself and get to work.

One of the first tasks for a soul when it is linked to a baby about to be born is to be integrated into the baby's consciousness and bodily systems – its DNA, its brain. It must become "one" with the little one. This is a very complicated, delicate procedure in which my Guides revealed their greatness; they were with me the whole way through the deliberate process, until its successful conclusion.

This process was fascinating. There were some moments of boredom, but it was very enjoyable to hear the voices outside – the soft feminine voices, the stronger, masculine voices – although it took a while to realize that this was one of my senses, the sense of hearing. I felt my mother's hands, caressing her belly. I waited impatiently for the moment of birth, the moment when I would draw my first breath – not just the experience of the tiny newborn, but the first experience for me, the soul, as well.

Then the moment arrived. Pressure, slow progress towards the exit, then sliding out, into the arms of the adult woman. She lifted me up, and then came the first breath, the first cry. That was it! I was born!

What a difference. They had prepared me for this moment, but I thought they were exaggerating. For example, I found it hard to believe that I would not be able to open my mouth and speak right away. Still, in describing what I would feel when they lay me on my mother's belly, they didn't exaggerate all – not to mention that a short time later, I snuggled in her arms as I suckled contentedly.

CHAPTER THREE

Hunter

"Roooooo!" the voice roared, wondering "Where the hell has that child disappeared to? If he doesn't show up right this second, he'll have to deal with me!" It thundered powerfully in the center of the camp.

Roo was so excited that he felt weak in the knees and he ran to look for the knife he had chiseled and sharpened for this occasion. He had spent a long time striking it, polishing it, and playing with it, waiting breathlessly for the day he might finally go on his first hunting trip. Now the moment had finally arrived. He picked up the knife, stuck it into his loincloth and ran off. His father shot him an angry look as he shook his head, motioning to him to join the group and load up on a number of tools they would need over the course of the journey, such as clubs, cutting knives, and spears that had been prepared from rods.

Shortly before this, a tribesman had arrived in the camp; with excitement in his voice and motioning with his hands, he described the herd of deer he had seen grazing in the area. Brood, Roo's father, hadn't hesitated but had summoned a number of men to organize themselves into a hunting party. There was urgency in the matter, but they were used to it; sometimes predators would beat them to the herd and scare it away.

They set out soon afterwards. There were six men and two boys, Roo and Rizzen. They moved quickly, and the boys soon found themselves straggling, trailing behind the group and trying their best not to lose it. Brood led them towards the open area beyond the forest. Only there, as they reached an area with sparse trees, did they slow their pace. The children were breathing hard, red-faced, sweating, but they had finally managed to catch up with the adults. The men angrily motioned to them to keep quiet. From here on, they progressed slowly, until the moment at which Brood signaled them to stop as he continued to advance silently, bending behind a tree that stood on the border of the clearing. He peeked out. A few minutes later, he returned, signaled the men to advance with him carefully and quietly; under the cover of the trees, they drew close to a herd of deer.

The herd was grazing on the grass in utter tranquility. The fawns ran among their mothers. From time to time, one of the stags would lift its head, look around, and then regain its calm and lower its head to continue its meal.

The men looked at them and the surrounding area, until Brood reached a decision. He motioned to Roo and Rizzen to come close and whispered to them, explaining precisely what to do. "Flank the herd, at a distance," he directed them. "Then, when you are opposite us but on the other side of the herd, start running toward it, shouting and waving your spears." He passed before each of them in turn, putting his two hands on each boy's shoulders as he looked deeply into the young hunters' eyes and declared, "This depends on you. If you succeed, the herd will be startled and run into the forest, towards us."

How exciting! Roo and Rizzen felt very important as they

understood that the responsibility for the entire tribe's hunt was on their shoulders – a response to their constant complaint, "We're sick of vegetables and plants!"

The boys followed Brood's directions, and the herd was indeed startled as he had predicted; the ploy culminated in two large deer lying in the middle of a circle, the men surrounding them.

It was a formative experience, and the two children wandered around the tribe for quite a while, full of self-importance and puffed-up chests.

Life went on that way for some time. The tribe grew and matured, and as was its wont, continued to live a nomadic life. When the cold of the rainy season began, they would enter the thickest part of the forest; when it ended, they would leave and migrate to other places, all under the guidance of the senior members of the tribe who brought them to places that had game but were free of danger – places in which they could avoid, as much as possible, encounters with other tribes.

As the years passed, and one generation gave way to the next, Roo grew up to be a powerful, courageous man. His mother yearned for him to take Brood's place and assume leadership of the tribe, but she knew that Roo was too adventurous, too irresponsible, and too lacking in the equanimity any person occupying such a position needed. Roo, for his part, was pleased with how his life turned out. He wanted the freedom to do whatever he felt like, at any given moment. He went out on many hunts. He was thrilled by the danger and by finally subduing the animal; he was always interested in an adventure. In practice, his activities often caused conflicts between him and other strong men in the tribe, who recognized his abilities as well as the dangers lurking along the way. Granted, their occupation inevitably involved injury and sometimes even death, and they were used to it; still, they did everything they could to rein in the young hunter.

Indeed, he found himself in difficult situations more than a few times. On one occasion, incapable of waiting for his companions, he had attacked a bear single-handedly. The huge animal had thrown him off with one swipe of its paw, and were it not for his agility, his life would have ended there. The injury he sustained left a scar on his leg, and it would ache through many more rainy seasons; however, this did not change his approach to life.

He was young, handsome, and robust, and the young women of the tribe dreamed about him; their parents discouraged them, however, as they thought Roo didn't have a long future ahead of him. Still, he was very popular among the young women, and spent much time with them. Whenever he approached them, they did not object, as was customary among the tribe. The truth of the matter was that he was happy with this situation – he wasn't built for family life, which would impinge on the freedom of movement he so prized.

Roo's mother looked at him and could not help but worry. Roo was hotheaded, and she was worried that he might get into trouble from which he wouldn't be able to extricate himself. Still, she couldn't stop him, so she just stopped trying. In fact, such events occurred more than once. Roo would find himself in arguments, quarrels, or fistfights not infrequently, but like a wildcat, he always managed to emerge intact and resume his thrill-seeking.

Then it happened, what his mother had been dreading. The tribe was camped in the forest; with the change of seasons, the weather was agreeable. Nature was in bloom, and a feeling of happiness and renewal suffused the air. And Roo? As was customary for him, he was looking for something to interest him – a journey, a good fight, maybe even hunting. He called out to Rizzen, and the two set out for the thickest part of the forest. Rizzen had taken a different path – a mate, children – but he still had a deep and abiding affection for Roo, and he maintained their friendship. This was not the first time that Roo had suggested such an outing; they would often go out to the woods and surrounding areas to look for something interesting.

This time they found a bonfire around which two men and two women were sitting. Roo and Rizzen did not recognize them; apparently they belonged to a different tribe. Mutual distrust soon led to an all-out quarrel, and a fistfight soon allowed Roo and Rizzen to chase away the two strangers. As for the women, who had initially been frozen in place, they tried to escape, but hotheaded Roo pounced on them and knocked them to the ground.

The two comrades did not hesitate for a moment. The excitement of the struggle and the heady feeling of victory over the two strangers that accompanied it caused their lust to surge, and they turned to the women to slake their desire. The women received them with terrifying silence, but Roo paid it no mind until he had finished his business. As he got off the young woman, he looked into her eyes and noticed her gaze. Her eyes, terrified and empty, bore into his very being, and on their way home, Roo was unusually thoughtful and quiet.

Not long afterwards, the tribe was attacked by a group of men who had come seeking vengeance for their comrades. They were not interested in negotiation or adjudication; they merely sought to restore their damaged honor, to scare and intimidate. To their misfortune, they were spotted by a few children from Roo's tribe, who were startled and ran to the camp to seek help.

Roo's comrades had neither the time nor the desire to try to calm things down. If it came to violence, so be it. Thus, as the two sides were aligned against each other, growling and spurring themselves on, a fierce battle erupted. The women gathered their children and looked on in horror at what was taking place before their eyes.

The battle wasn't brief. Neither side was willing to surrender. Men fell and men were injured, but no one would relent. At a certain point, one of the two strangers from the inciting incident recognized Rizzen, and a group of men confronted and closed around him, calling on the two men to take out their anger on him. Roo saw this and, roaring, furiously attacked the group – hitting them, knocking them to the ground, and kicking them in order to get to Rizzen.

Suddenly, with no signal, the strangers fell back and began to flee, leaving Rizzen on the ground. His skull was crushed and he was bleeding. Roo rushed to his side, embracing him and lifting his head; Rizzen breathed his last in Roo's arms.

The events of that day left an impression on the entire tribe. They quickly organized and abandoned their campsite, looking for a far-away place where they could spend the impending rainy season.

But something happened to Roo. It wasn't just the death of his friend Rizzen. True, he was deeply pained by the loss, but death was a constant presence in the lives of his tribesmen, and they were accustomed to it. No, the memory that accompanied him, deeply etched into his consciousness, was the look on the face of that girl in the forest. He could not get it out of his mind.

It wasn't the deep pain that touched his heart, or even the terror in her eyes, but the horrible indifference, the acceptance of the worst of all, that so scared him. He, Roo, had embodied this evil in the eyes, and for Roo this image was unbearable. He was not a man who looked deeply into himself, or a man capable of such an undertaking; none of them was. These were their lives, but something had happened to him, and he had changed.

Slowly he became a serious man, turning inward. He began to keep his distance from the women in the tribe; even though many of them tried to catch his eye, his heart wasn't in it anymore. Every time he met a woman, the eyes of the girl at the bonfire would pop up in his memory, and he would leave. Light-hearted, adventurous Roo disappeared bit by bit. The gregarious Roo ceased to exist. A new Roo appeared in the tribe – "Roo the Recluse." Granted, he still went out hunting, and did not abandon his maintenance work within the tribe either, as he made weapons and utensils for the women in his family. He also continued to attend the tribe's ceremonies, but his *joie de vivre* was gone.

But nature, or the forest, or perhaps the gods themselves, had different plans. Before long, while out on one of the hunting expeditions, Roo stumbled and fell, breaking his leg. He was brought to a woman in the tribe known for her healing powers. She brought him inside, beneath the leather hangings that served as protection from the rain, examined his leg and went outside. When she returned, she had a handful of branches, which she tied around his leg with fibers, setting the broken bone. Afterwards, she brewed a drink which she gave to him, then asked him to rest. The exhaustion of the journey and the pain in his leg overwhelmed him, and within a short time he fell asleep.

When he awoke, dawn had not yet broken. The pain in his leg was excruciating, and he lay there quietly, wondering what he would do now. Then, as if by some miracle, as if an unknown prayer had been answered, the daughter of the healer came over to him to offer him a hot drink, sitting next to him as he sipped it.

The heat of her body, her simple nature, the goodness of heart that she radiated through her actions – produced a warm, pleasurable wave unlike any he had ever experienced. Suddenly he reached out and cupped her curves. She leaned back casually, and he felt the familiar awakening in his loins. Despite his great pain, he drew her to him, feeling the desire and longing for touch. Then, while still erect inside her, he dared to look into her eyes; what he saw there was what he would see from that day forward: eyes filled with hope, love, and passion.

Time, which waits for no man, continued to go on. Roo invited the girl, Murill, to come to live with him, and they established a glorious family. Their children inherited the wildness embedded within their father as well as the depth and goodness of their mother. Roo's life was good until the day on which his hunting party, while trying to battle a boar running towards them, was attacked by a tiger who sneaked up on them from behind. Within seconds, Roo was no longer among the living.

I disconnected from Roo's body and hovered over it. I was a young soul, and this was my first experience of a life's end, a unique experience accompanied by many questions. The transition from a physical body to a soul is not a simple one; even to this day, after so many reincarnations, I can testify that it still involves feelings of detachment and disorientation for a while, and certainly on the first such occasion.

I looked down, towards my body, towards Roo, and I wondered what I was supposed to do. I didn't understand exactly what was happening. I didn't know that on the new plane of existence on which I found myself, the experience of reality was different than the one I was familiar with, that the feeling of physicality was still extant, but a bit different; various objects had, as it were, shifted location, and my perception of time was beginning to warp. I saw, for example, the stone tools that I always used to wear, which had been broken long ago, as if they were still whole. I also saw the tiger that bested me and ran away, but it was still sneaking up on me before it pounced.

Slowly, I realized that this was it, that it was over, and I had just parted from my life. But I was confused. I didn't yet understand that at this point I was already a soul without a body. I simply hovered over everything, considering the area, which now seemed different; I turned to the camp, to my family – who had not learned of my death. I descended among them, in a desperate attempt to speak with them, to take my leave, to give them my love, but they did not see, did not feel, and did not even realize that I was there.

I couldn't leave, but I didn't know what to do. I only wanted to stay there, without thinking too much. There I was, waiting for my comrades to arrive with the game and to tell my tribesmen about my death. I knew it would cause a commotion among my family members alone. The death of men in hunting parties was a common scene, and we all knew the danger inherent in our lifestyle, but we had never stopped to think about it or be afraid of it.

My body was cast by the door of my family's shelter. One of my companions went inside to break the news. I waited a bit more, just to be there for the funeral.

Quickly, I was drawn upwards, although I'm not sure that "up-wards" is the proper term. In the life cycles I passed through, I was accustomed to think like this, but in fact the transition was quite different – not at all dependent on the spatial dimensions of the physical world – but the most convenient way of describing this in terms that humans could grasp would be "upward motion."

An illuminated corridor opened across from me, and I was quickly drawn through it, accelerating, until I reached the gate of the spirit world, which was floodedwith a great light. The feeling of returning home welled up within me, accompanied by great joy. Very shortly, I reached the gate, and on the other side many souls awaited my arrival – my companions from the family of souls, friends, and family members from the physical world who had died while I was among them. There were also souls and spirits that I did not recognize, and they all radiated happiness, joy, and much love. My arrival became a heartwarming welcome, somewhat lessening the pain of being detached from the human world. In the background, the "music" of the upper world was playing, music that I only then realized how much I had missed while I was alive. These were sounds that plucked the chords of the soul, inducing great pleasure, akin to wind chimes playing softly, creating a divine melody that cannot be described at all. Wow, how much you humans lose! But it's not so terrible; when your day comes, when you return home, you'll also "hear" them and recall this great delight.

Most prominent among the welcoming committee was my Guide. He stood head-and-shoulders above the rest in his glorious countenance, his gentle ways, and his encompassing smile. How happy I was to see him! When the welcoming ceremony came to an end, he invited me to accompany him to an area I was unfamiliar with – an area of reorientation and enlightenment. It looked like a VIP section, only quieter.

I would like to share with you what happens at these stages. The soul returns to the world beyond. It is aware of the great difference between the two sides of the veil, and it still feels that it belongs to what it has just experienced in a mortal's body and in human consciousness. This may sometimes be compared to a person's waking up from a dream – that is, the person is aware that what is happening is not a dream, but the story of the dream does not let go. In order to help the soul achieve the requisite detachment, it must undergo a process of therapy, rest, and rehabilitation, a process through which the emotional connection becomes weaker, until it can slowly, but fully, disassociate. It does this in the space of orientation and enlightenment, an area of cleansing. The Guide invited me into this space.

Now, how do you cleanse a soul? This is a fascinating experience. I stayed there in the cleaning room, and a sensation of warm, pleasant light filled me. I felt like someone stepping into a nice hot bath after a long, exhausting journey. Slowly this energy flowed over me, and I felt that I was becoming clean, emerging from the "adventure" that had just concluded, allowing me to shed the constant alertness, the worry, the need to be aware of the happenings around me, and to move on to a state of deep, purifying, calming inner peace.

After this stage, the soul recalls the events of the life that has just ended, but without the accompanying emotions. Suddenly there is no hatred or resentment or desire for vengeance, but this means that the feelings of love and longing also disappear. The soul moves on to a different state, one that may be interpreted by human beings as "torpidity" or "equanimity," but this is simply a different way of existing, an existence that has long-term aims of millennia of growth, a path that will finally develop and improve humanity. Apparently, according to the Divine Plan, this will bring about complete unity between the human race – which will change their physical character and their spiritual being – the Creation as a whole, and the Creator Himself.

I don't know how to calculate, in human chronology, the period I spent in this wonderful place. Some might say that it lasted a year, but I am unsure. Still, when it ended, I knew – simply knew – that I was cleansed and ready to continue my journey, to meet my soul friends and to continue learning and developing. In our telepathic world, my communication with the Guide was instantaneous. He appeared immediately... and we went straight to work.

The Guide went over all the details of the life that had just ended.

Now I could remember all the events, but from an objective viewpoint. After going through the cleansing process, I no longer had my self-righteous bias, nor any need to justify Roo's actions. From a critical and comparative viewpoint, I considered the script I had written and deposited in my soul book.

It was fascinating. First of all, there was the process of recollection. Bit by bit, I remembered the events in Roo's. We went through every detail of it, transcribing it all in my soul book, underlining all the subjects that had been insufficiently learned, subjects that would require more experimenting. Now I understood why Roo had never developed as a leader, why he was so frenetic and curious, why he was so adventurous, trying almost everything – I was the one who had spurred him on to do that. And I was a young, unexperienced soul who had to learn more and more about life. This was not the time to take responsibility for other people, not the time to be serious and weighty, but to be reckless and irresponsible. I also understood the meaning of the Guide's request not to start my journeys in the material world with the script I wanted so much – lessons based on living with great suffering, physical as well as emotional, and even encountering human cruelty.

Had I learned anything? Yes, quite a lot! I learned what interpersonal relationships are; I also learned what recklessness and responsibility are, and what frivolity and seriousness are. I even felt love, although I didn't know what to call it when I was in Roo's body. I could also learn about free will.

The unfortunate event with the other tribe, for example, was not included at all in the script. Roo should have met Murill in a totally different story, and if he hadn't hastily decided to pick a fight with two strangers – against all the rules, in defiance of everything the tribe taught about avoiding conflict with outsiders – that part of the story would never have taken and Rizzen would not have lost his life. This was not in the planning of the script that Rizzen's soul had composed before being incarnated in his body. I know this because in the meantime I had already met that soul.

You see, I didn't conduct this research alone. There were many entities that joined this process. There were those who wanted to listen in order to learn from my experience; there were those who wanted to contribute, based on their own experience, in order to sharpen the scope of my learning, to understand what I had missed and in what I had expanded my nature, what I had not learned at all and what subjects I had learned, even though they hadn't been included at all in my original script. Alongside all this, and throughout this wondrous process, there was my growing desire to return and find form in a body once again.

This is what happened every time afterwards as I tried to plan for the next reincarnation. My first incarnations belong to that era that you humans call "prehistoric man." I would return and find form in a body during this era, usually as a man, because I wanted to complete my studies of understanding people from this unique perspective, until I could understand the world of the material human being in all its depth. This was a fascinating process, in which I was reincarnated in various regions of the world, in different climates, in different field and environmental conditions – and, fundamentally, with the intriguing outlook upon human development between each incarnation. During the periods I spent in the upper worlds, periods that were sometimes quite long, human beings developed and progressed.

In my first incarnation, I lived in a small, nomadic tribe. The tools we used were wooden spears with bone parts embedded in them, stone knives and spears, wooden fire-making tools – and that was about it. Our vocabulary was very limited, capable of conveying rudimentary concepts only. In later incarnations, interpersonal communication became far more developed; we had advanced tools, such as needles made from bone, which women used to sew leather hides, and after many more life cycles, the bow and arrow appeared.

As I followed these developments, I was filled with the lovely sensation that I understood that humanity was developing and advancing, especially because at the time that I was in my body in the world, I was not preoccupied by these changes; indeed, I was not even aware of them. Only at the end of the incarnation could I see the full picture.

And just as humanity developed, I, the soul, developed as well. This was a process based on mutuality. I was reincarnated in human form in order to heal my soul wounds and to learn; my studies allowed me to experiment with greater challenges in the next incarnations, and thus influence my development as a human being. My experiences from previous lives influenced the person in whose body I had been incarnated, even if they themselves were unaware of it. For instance, in one of my reincarnations, the person in whose body I was incarnated was killed when he fell into a raging river. In future reincarnations, I would grow afraid when I approached water sources, especially rivers. There were many other examples.

This distant viewpoint also revealed to me one of the great advantages that human beings had over us, entities of the upper world: the right of free choice. From one incarnation to the next, it became clear that despite the assistance of souls with whom I signed soul contracts, and despite the presence and the involvement of my spiritual Guide in life as he prepared appropriate opportunities for the lesson I was supposed to learn, or piled up obstacles when the path was the wrong one, the person still retains the ability to exercise freedom of choice. This choice caused me, more than once, to go back and try to learn that lesson, but in a different way.

Thus, once many years had passed – when human beings were much more advanced – the periods of migration were reduced. More and more tribes sought permanent accommodations, mainly in tribal caves. As language and interpersonal communications skills developed and family bonds became more significant, I thought the time had come to learn the difficult lesson I had wanted to learn in my first incarnation. In its time, I had thought that it was worthwhile to begin my road of reincarnations at the absolute nadir and work my way up from there; fortunately, the Guide dissuaded me. Today I know that this was the thinking of a "novice," but now I had decided to test that desire as well – the power of cruelty and evil as an incentive to overcome and emerge into kindness and compassion – and I had decided to realize it. I was now enough of a "veteran," with enough experience, to deal with such a lesson. What I didn't know was that this would not be the "lowest" point I was to experience, but I'll tell you about that later.

I already knew that human beings could be extremely violent and it's not an infrequent occurrence that stronger people impose their fear upon those who are weaker, and even enjoy doing so. I knew that male humans considered females to be the weaker sex – which is why I decided this time to do what I had almost never done throughout my human life cycles. I would live this life as a woman.

It seemed to be the right choice, because it allowed me to realize my second aim, which was to learn the lesson of how to give, to help, and to show pity. I knew that by virtue of being mothers, women gave support to their immediate environment, to the family, and even to other members of the community, showering them with affection. I sought a "supplement," something unique and challenging to a greater extent, and after an additional period of consulting and delving into other soul books in the library, I found rare, exceptional life cycles of "wise" and knowledgeable women, who healed both people and animals. I also found a rare case, one in which a woman to whom the sick and injured would flock from great distances. I decided that I would do it. I would learn how to help and support this way.

My Guide "raised an eyebrow" and asked if I was certain and understood the full meaning of such a choice, which was a weighty undertaking. I was confident in my decision.

He didn't doubt this, but he was concerned that I was still too young a soul, and he tried to dissuade me. When I was stubborn, he sent me to the "Council of Elders," the loftier entities who authorize our life stories, but I wouldn't relent. They respected my opinion and accepted it.

This is how the story of that healer began, that "miracle-worker."

I was born, in that incarnation, as a beautiful girl, the pampered daughter of a loving mother, and I grew up to be an attractive, delicate woman who drew the attention of men from all over.

As for my father, he was not pleased by the situation; as soon as I reached puberty, I became an object of desire for many men, who waited in ambush for me around every corner and at every opportunity. More than once I had to flee, and more than once my father had to intervene, forcefully and violently, to get rid of the "parasites," as he called them.

It wasn't long before I found myself married to a stranger, whose cave I moved into. I wasn't alone there; two other women, who were older, didn't hide their hatred of me. I was young and beautiful and drew my mate to me; every time he approached, I could feel the fiery hatred being licked at the back of my neck.

Now you might think that being connected to a man would change how other men treated me, but you would be bitterly mistaken. They still tried their luck; many of them tried to violently force their presence – if not their manhood – on me, and the commotion I caused just grew and grew. And the harder it was to get me, the more their attempts increased.

To my great surprise, my mate was no different than the other men in the tribe, staring at any woman who was in his vicinity, so my presence became a challenge for him. He took me everywhere to "present" me and take pride in me. However, this caused a number of rivals to see his behavior as tasteless provocation, and they tried to teach him a lesson by... hurting me. Thus I slipped between the cracks. I was hated by the women inside the home, while outside the men used force to try to get me. To my dismay, even after a number of pregnancies, I still was attractive to them; in fact, my femininity developed and made me more of an object for them to obtain.

For the most senior woman in the household, my presence was a tremendous burden. She knew that it was no business of hers how many women the man brought to the cave; in the tribal culture and system, this was something positive. But I was too much for this framework. I felt this in her constant attempts to harm me, but I bowed my head before her – simply because she was the senior woman, and this was our way of life. Apparently my approach only infuriated her and enflamed her hatred toward me even more.

Then an opportunity came her way. A nomad joined our tribe, a strange man, ugly in appearance and evil in behavior. We didn't know where he had come from and didn't understand his speech or his ways. However, the chieftain of our tribe found some skills in him that were useful for the tribe, and let him stay with us. The man isolated himself; his unusual, even scary, behavior led him to disassociate himself from all the other members of the tribe.

Except me. He would stare at me, salivating and licking his lips. I was afraid of him. Fortunately, the head of my family noticed him and warned him off. However, the senior woman in the house saw this nomad as an opportunity to dispose of the trouble that had befallen her, to rid herself of the threat she saw in me and in my beauty, so she approached him. She smiled, she brought him food from time to time, and if I hadn't known about the malice that motivated her actions, it would have been possible to see them as true acts of compassion. Bit by bit, she formed a connection with him; she was the only soul in the tribe with whom he felt a bond. He became her bondsman, just so she wouldn't leave him.

As time went on, she convinced him that she, and only she, could help him get me.

She knew how to admit him to the cave and allow him to do to me whatever he desired.

There was only one condition, however. "She cannot remain beautiful. You must use violence, you must use force to hurt her, to injure her. Aim for her face," she told him, "and I'll let you do to her whatever you want."

You already know what happened next. Only after my death, when I returned here, to the spiritual world, did I remember the script and the soul contract. I understood that they all had a role in the story that I had chosen even before my incarnation. Using the Guidance here, I was able to sign contracts with the soul of the woman who betrayed me and the man who abused me. They, of course, were not aware of this, but at the level of the soul, they fulfilled their functions completely. They allowed me to experience the suffering, to study cruelty and crudity, opening a window to another life – to learn and become a healer. Only many incarnations later did I discover the power of this story, when I acquired a unique passion, one that spurred me on as I planned new lives – the passion to care for others.

CHAPTER FOUR

What Next?

From the moment of my creation until this time, many years have passed in earthly terms. And when I say many years, I mean millennia.

To make things easier for you, dear readers, to follow my tale, I will "synchronize" from time to time; by that, I mean that I will explain the situation on a timeline – your timeline, of course – and even use modern names to refer to the locations of places on Earth.

My first incarnation (Roo, rest in peace) was 17,000 years ago, during what your scientists call the Stone Age (in particular, for those of you who are curious, the Epipaleolithic Era). The miraculous healer was born at the end of that period, some 6,000 years later, when people had stopped constantly migrating and began to establish permanent settlements in caves and even in primitive structures.

During those millennia, I experienced about 100 life cycles, as I was reincarnated as different people in different places and climates, and I became familiar with the human race in all of its many streams. I was with tribes in the frigid north, as what is now known as the Bering Straits, between Siberia and Alaska, froze over; I also crossed over with them to the lands of America, and these tribes became the native Indians of North and South America. I was with other tribes throughout Europe and equatorial Africa, but mostly I was in the Middle East.

Throughout these many life cycles, I acquired the experience and knowledge that allowed me to grow and develop, but most of all I learned to be familiar with, to appreciate, and to love human beings for their amazing ability to adjust to various and odd situations, their way of using nature in their environment – not only in order to exist at a given moment, but also to be good to themselves and to develop. I encountered people during movements of happiness and moments of pain, moments of success and moments of disappointment. Sometimes I chose beforehand to be reincarnated in people undergoing complex situations, and in people living simple lives at other times; people who experience social support, and others who experienced isolation or rejection; people who lived in penury or in luxury – and I discovered mankind in the fullness of its glory.

I saw how people acted and conducted themselves in the days before technology, when human speech had not yet developed beyond conveying essential messages, in the era before writing existed, so people could not preserve information beyond the memories in the brain of the isolated person. I watched human beings contend with different climatic conditions, different environmental conditions, in areas made dangerous by disease or wild animals, and I couldn't help but be enthralled by their success in developing themselves in the most impressive manner.

This was not merely admiration for its own sake, but deep appreciation that gave me the motivation to be reincarnated time after time and to become different people. I wanted to be a partner in the process and to experience the life of a human being who learns, under such complex conditions, to recognize their immediate and wider environment and its geography, the forests and the plants, and to use them to obtain the diverse foods that would satisfy all the needs of the body through the various seasons of the year, as well as the zoology of their environment, from insects to large predators – their advantages and their limits. Indeed, I experienced people's looking for and finding ways to maintain their health and integrating this in their culture – for example, by burying the dead, putting together tools for work and for hunting, using fire intelligently, e.g., for warmth and cooking, and even developing a societal culture of tribal hierarchy based on respect rather than on force and violence, creating spousal and familial relationships, even delving into art. I heard about paintings on cave walls, even though I wasn't incarnated in a person or tribe that did so. Beyond all these, they even developed consciousness of god- a consciousness that is aware of a force that directs a system which is not controlled by humankind. And so it is no surprise that my soul friends and I so love you human beings.

The process of reincarnation is wondrous. When I am "up there," in the periods between incarnations, I get a bird's-eye view of human society as a whole. Then, together with my Guides, I determine my aims for the next life, within that societal development. These are new lessons, new targets touching on all the spheres of life, touching on the body, emotions, and mind – lessons by which I will develop.

You might ask, "What does it mean 'to develop,' from the viewpoint of the soul?"

Development, from my perspective, means growth that increases one's "capacity" for love. The loftiest souls, the most developed ones, e.g., the avatars, are receptacles for infinite love, and love is the source of everything.

Among the topics I chose to study are "brief" topics, those that may be learned in one lifespan. Most of the time I chose to study during those incarnations that I knew would end at a very young age, as infant mortality was quite widespread during that time.

However, we usually choose "weighty" topics, ones to be studied over the course of many years and sometimes many lifetimes as well. In addition, there are, of course, the lessons we choose to study but fail to apply while living – mainly due to the freedom of choice man has. However, first and foremost, we must heal our soul wounds, the deficiencies and inhibitions of the soul – i.e., everything that was created and that I acquired during the period of the "eras" before I began my journey of incarnations.

In each life cycle, a topic or two are chosen to be the primary lessons of that life, topics around which that person's life will revolve, which will constitute the central axis that will dominate their conduct. Naturally, these topics are not the only ones; life proceeds according to the primary lesson of previous life cycles as well, topics that have not been fully learned yet.

Over dozens of the last reincarnations, I encountered many primary issues that occupied more than one life cycle. They were not necessarily the main lesson throughout all these cycles; sometimes they were the central issue, but sometimes they were simply one layer within a series of other processes that I had to learn.

For instance, take my training as a caregiver. This developed continually, and was only fully expressed over the course of many reincarnations. Sometimes this was only secondarily, as I was cared for by others; sometimes it was more central, as in the incarnation in which the tribal healer actually saved my life, or the life cycle in which the healer failed to save my mate – during an incarnation for which the main subject was a lesson on loss and pain.

In later incarnations, I already experienced "the caregiver" as destiny. During the life of the aged healer, this was a main topic, and this was also the time at which the consciousness of the caregiver was burned into me, into the soul, and it became a set path in successive reincarnations.

I want to explain something that may not be understood by all of you. Every time a soul is incarnated in a human body, it brings with it memories and experience that have been acquired in previous lives. This knowledge is buried in the human subconscious, and from there it influences the conscious mind. In fact, a kind of precondition for the development of man is created, although they do not at all understand how much their conduct and behavior are influenced by their previous lives.

When it resides within a body, the soul itself is not aware of it; my development as a soul, which in most of its incarnations found form as a caregiver, is a good example. My conscious link to the spiritual world was lost not very long after birth, and it included the plan for this life and the previous memories; nevertheless, I would become a person who was a healer or caregiver. In order to illustrate and demonstrate this idea, let me give you another example.

At a certain stage, when I had been through around 35 incarnations, I decided to address the subject of leadership. Was this compulsion burned into me during my incarnations through the eras? Was it created out of a desire to become familiar with variety within humankind? I only knew that I wanted to study this subject, which lit a fire within me. The Guidance accepted this by consent, the full import of which I would understand only at a later point. "Leadership" was not self-evident at that time, as it preceded systematic organization or the construction of a clear hierarchy within groups; thus, there was unique significance to studying this subject as preparation for future development.

The course of study determined for me was a lengthy one. At first I wanted to experience the influence of strong men on others, but from the perspective of an "observer," and I passed through a number of incarnations in which I was a tribesman under the leadership of some powerful personality. I discovered great variance between these people and their abilities – sometimes it was an authoritative and charismatic person who contributed to the life of the tribe and its success; at other times, it was a person who would direct the tribe at certain moments but without inspiration, without exceptional initiatives or great successes, and the same was true for others – each one with their unique qualities. In terms of the soul's plan, these lessons were always "secondary" in that life, but they constituted a consideration when designing a life path.

Then came more important lessons. In one of the life cycles, the person I was incarnated in took part in action against a person who had made himself tribal leader by using physical might and violence. He hurt many people, including the person in whose body I resided, and many people were alarmed by him and loathed him, until they eventually took action against him – what you would now call a rebellion against authority. There was a pitched battle between him and some of his companions, a battle that ended in his death and my injury – an injury that left me disabled for the rest of my life.

In those times, disability had a heavy toll, which could lead to a life of suffering, of social rejection, and even an early death; it could also exemplify the "miracle" of survival and make a person admirable. My main subject in that life cycle was disability, and it led to pain, suffering, and exclusion, but also to learning how to overcome difficulties. The story of the revolution in that life cycle was a secondary lesson; in fact, I could plan the disabling incident, the main subject, as the result of other circumstances. However, in terms of the lesson in leadership, which was spread over the course of many life cycles, the topic of the rebellion had great significance in later life cycles, and thus was "appended" to the script for this life.

In the first incarnation in which the story of the revolution had a fundamental role, I included an important section on the subject of leadership: avoiding responsibility. I was born and lived as a charismatic, popular man who influenced his friends in a positive way and had the proper skill set to take control of the leadership, but when the proper moment came and he had to make the decision, this man – I, that is – was overwhelmed by fears whose origin he did not understand. His self-confidence and faith in his abilities were undermined, resulting in a phobia of failure in his position and ultimately leading him to flee from it. This event, in the life of that man, made him turn inward and become critical, seeing only the failures of others but doing nothing to change the situation, and cutting himself off from his friends. Only after his death, when I returned home up above, did I remember the rebellion and killing of that leader; I understood that this memory, which was hidden in his subconscious, flooded him with an unconscious fear of ending his life as that murdered leader did. This was what kept him from picking up the gauntlet.

Kungurk

The full study of the lesson of leadership as a primary subject would only be realized in an additional life cycle. This happened in a cycle that took place towards the end of the Ice Age, a number of reincarnations before that aged healer was born. The incarnation began with the birth of Kungurk, the second son of a hunter-gatherer family in a tribe of nomads in Central Europe, a tribe that was large and powerful compared to its neighbors in the area (it is surely clear to you that we did not know that this place had a name, or even that it was a continent).

Living conditions were harsh for the areas that bordered the ice-bergs at the center of the continent and in its northern reaches, but the tribe grew familiar with the area and its wildlife. The tribesmen learned to freeze food for the difficult times, managed to produce sewing gear for the fur-based wardrobe, and even developed animal traps. Due to this, they never suffered from lack of food, fur, or bones from which to make tools.

Kungurk, whose leadership skills had been recognized even in his youth, had grown up to be a robust man, popular in the tribe, and a family man. His youth seemed routine, but life apparently had other plans; shortly after the birth of his second son, the forces of nature demonstrated their might. Upheavals in the weather caused harsh ice storms, and strong, unending winds blew for a very long time, preventing them from going out to hunt. Massive chunks of ice rolled down and destroyed their stores of frozen food; but the most terrifying event of all was when the path leading to the system of caves they lived in was blocked, allowing no one in or out.

Kituyu, one of the tribesmen, who by virtue of his charismatic personality was placed at the head of the tribe in times of crisis, understood the gravity of the situation – a lack of food, water, and fuel for the fire – and he resolved in his heart to stand up and do something. This was not the first year in which they had faced a dangerous natural disaster, but now the situation was worse than ever and he understood that the tribe must change its lifestyle and migrate southward. As was his wont, he didn't waste any time; he told the members of the tribe, and ordered them to organize for their departure. Kituyu was an authoritative person, a man on whom it was easy to rely, and the eyes of all looked to him. Thus, while the people were still organizing for the journey, he summoned Kungurk and two other strong youths. Together they went out to look for an alternative route to get out of the area.

This was no simple task. They spent a lot of time in the field, exposed to danger, investigating alternative routes, which they eliminated one after another; they even had to deal with an angry, hungry bear that blocked a seemingly promising path. After three difficult, challenging days, despair began to eat away at them. Kituyu decided to go back and reevaluate a trail that they had previously rejected; it led the party among soaring walls, white and cold, forcing them to climb over chunks of slick ice and putting them in serious danger of slipping. There, in the middle of the path, suspended between heaven and earth, they were surprised by a powerful gust of wind that sent them tumbling downwards as slivers of ice glided in their wake.

They realized the magnitude of the calamity only when they came to a stop. A long time passed before Kungurk managed to recover from the fall and raise his head. His entire body was painfully bruised, but he got up to help the others, finding two of his companions injured and in shock – but Kituyu wasn't with them. They found him only after an extensive search, lying upside down among the icy rocks, his head crushed beneath one of them.

It was a gruesome scene, and it took them a while to come back to their senses and begin to digest the meaning of this blow. They knew that no one in the tribe had the stature of Kituyu – that is, someone who could lead the tribe to a safe harbor. There was no leader in which the members of the tribe could put their trust. But there, next to his body, among the slivers of ice, they would have to come to a decision.

The other two members of the party fixed their eyes on Kungurk. He was used to it. In times of crisis, he had often been cast as a savior, but now the fate of the entire tribe rested on his shoulders. They had to find a safe passage and get back to the tribe, and he knew that aside from him, no one in the tribe could deal with the challenge and lead the people. He understood this as he stood in the overwhelming cold, feeling the pain from his fall, and with a sensation of utter loneliness.

This was a crucial moment in Kungurk's life, a once-in-a-lifetime occasion, a juncture at which his next move would have an impact not only on his life, but on the lives of the entire tribe; the magnitude of the role and the responsibility filled his entire being. Yet instead of determination or even joy at the opportunity – and the idea had crossed his mind at some point in his life – he felt fear and a tremendous flood of loss of faith and self-confidence. He realized that it was all a mistake, that he was not the right man, that he would inevitably fail and drag the whole tribe to the brink of the abyss with him. He felt his body shriveling, betraying him as he lost control; his muscles were weak, and he began to shake all over. He wanted to get up, but he didn't have the strength to do it. He simply closed his eyes; all he wanted to do was to disappear, to flee.

Thus, as the three of them stood there, in stifling silence, something was awakened in his inner being. A small voice, deep inside him, ordered him to open his eyes and consider the situation. He saw that his two companions were looking at him with worry and impotence, and suddenly their eyes reflected his two young children. In the eyes of his spirit, he saw his aged parents; without understanding why and how, he stood straight and looked up, feeling a powerful force streaming into him, an inner voice calling him to rise and take responsibility.

Kungurk looked down at his two companions and said to them, "The ice has fallen, so let's see what the path looks like now." He didn't notice that his voice was different, that he was now girded with a certain authority; only later could he internalize the realization that upon him lay the task of protecting the tribe, that he could not, and perhaps did not want to, abandon his role, that he was not prepared to let his inner fears overwhelm him and control him.

And that is how it happened. The collapse had opened a path for them, out of the dangerous area. They quickly returned to the worried tribe; Kungurk gathered all of them, and in a strong, authoritative voice told them about it and announced that he would take over leadership of the tribe.

The lesson about taking responsibility in this life cycle ended in great success. How did it happen? When Kungurk had fainted and was lying next to his two companions, "something was awakened in his inner being. A small voice, deep inside him"– and where do you think that came from? This was the Guide who accompanied me throughout this life, waiting for the opportunity to present to Kungurk the two choices – resoluteness or weakness – and Kungurk's ability to lift himself beyond the paralyzing terror emerging from his memories of past lives, and his success in overcoming this emotional impediment, constituted the culmination of the lesson that I had descended into his body to learn.

The lessons, direct and indirect, of the soul plan that emerged from this topic had all been learned. His success concluded a long process that was spread over a number of life cycles and required the precise, coordinated planning of many reincarnations reinforcing each other, knowing that the people who experienced the elements of this plan were unaware of it, but their success in bringing the plan to fruition allowed me to grow and develop as a soul. As I have already said, development is the expansion of capacity to contain more love. When I am more developed, I can be reincarnated in more complex lives, allowing people to experience fuller and more interesting lives. The more souls there are that develop and grow, the more we are able to influence the direction of development for all of mankind.

CHAPTER FIVE

What a Mess...

I had experienced 150 reincarnations since the time of the aged healer, and I was deep into planning my next life. I'd like to share the process with you.

I had just finished analyzing and documenting my last life, and had already consulted my soul friends – primarily my twin soul. I had already visited the cosmic library and sat with my Guide to determine my upcoming goals. Now, we were already putting together proposals for scripts that would encompass these targets as well as others that remained from previous cycles.

Composing such a script is a very difficult, complex task. The life circumstances are calculated with a precision that you cannot imagine. Every process, every act, is part of a great, complex tapestry that requires supreme attention; these include the various subjects that I want to be challenged by, the lessons I will experience, the primary subjects, and those that are part of lessons and subjects that have not yet been completed. There are other questions that are no less important, such as where will the next life be, who my parents will be, which people will influence this life or be involved in it. – and of course we must reach agreements concerning their role in my life with all the souls who are to be incarnated in these people (what you would call a "soul contract"). Naturally, this includes all of the hazards and obstacles, the risks that a person must take in their life, and countless other variables. These all require the most fundamental effort, and you must know that a not insignificant number of lofty entities and the most developed souls, who are trained in this field and whose task it is to calculate and devise the plans for these lives, wrestle with the problem.

At the end of this painstaking process, the plans are presented to me. At that point, it is my fervent hope that the human being in whom I am to be incarnated, and through whom I will have to realize all of this, will not make a bad choice, wrecking this, beautiful, precise strategy.

Please join me as we land in the area of Jericho, 8,000 years ago. It is a time when the human race is undergoing a great, revolutionary change, i.e., giving up the freedom of nomadic migration and beginning to gather, settle in villages, and devote itself to agriculture. Join me, in the era in which people begin to build square houses containing multiple rooms, abandoning their round mud huts, as they learn how to plaster their houses, and even begin to mold and form the first utensils for cooking and food processing.

My main aim in this life is to learn a lesson about accepting frameworks, self-esteem, and openness to change. By the way, the high Guidances involved in determining the course of my life take into account my level of development as a soul, deciding to take advantage of my reincarnation for a broader need, beyond the life of one lone human – but that is a topic we will soon return to.

Will the person in whom I am incarnated endure these simple tasks, or will their desires make them veer off the path? Come, let's see.

Brashita

Brashita, her two daughters, her two friends and their children were all on their way back from the spring, holding jugs and waterskins. The spring was a spot to escape the pressures of home, and the group enjoyed the place, without paying attention to the passage of time or the growing darkness. Brashita had to urge them to hurry home.

On moonless nights such as this one, moving through the desert was unpleasant, and the dangers were well known and obvious. They had a long way to go, so they walked quickly, despite the weight of the water, and without chitchat.

Brashita had a bad feeling, a familiar fear in the pit of her stomach. Indeed, a few minutes after they had set out for home, they heard the howling of distant wolves. When the howling got closer, they were gripped by panic, and they sped up their pace even more. Brashita, the oldest in the group, was intimately familiar with desert life, so she began to prepare herself and the others for the anticipated encounter. From her sack, she took out the fire-starting tools she always carried with her, then looked for kindling, asking her companions to grab branches for themselves as well.

The wolves were quick. The dark night kept the women from seeing them, but they could hear them coming close, and before they could set themselves up to light the fire, the first of the terrifying wolves arrived. The women broke into a run and screamed for help, but the wolves were faster, and they drew close to the group, howling ferociously. Suddenly Brashita stopped, and in an authoritative voice told the women to stop and gather around her. As they huddled against each other, she attempted, with shaking hands, to light the branch, but it stubbornly refused to ignite.

The situation was challenging, but the experience, which was terrifying as well, was not foreign to them. They didn't lose their composure; instead, they threw stones at the wolves, shouting at them to scare them off. This blocked their advance, and the attack was halted. However, although the creatures' progress had been stopped, the wolves would not leave. Bit by bit, a circle of wolves, teeth bared, assembled around them; then, bit by bit, the wolves closed the distance, howling all the while. Despite Brashita's great fear, she managed to get the fire going, and by boldly waving the flaming branch, managed to scare the wolves, who retreated somewhat. The women passed the fire from one to another, and with a bit of confidence began waving their hands at the wolves, even throwing the flaming branches at their predators.

From her experience, Brashita knew that they had to stall until the men of the village could hear the commotion and show up. Indeed, in the silence of the desert, their cries could be heard far away, and it didn't take long before Brashita's spouse arrived along with some neighbors, all holding torches and bows. Two or three flaming arrows shot towards the wolves alarmed the creatures, and they ran for their lives.

Brashita knew the area like the back of her hand, for she had been born there. She would hike from the river in the east to the salt sea in the south. West of her, tall, awe-inspiring mountains towered, but traveling north was more comfortable and enjoyable for her, and she was accustomed to going there from time to time, to the spring and its surroundings, to hike with her children and pick dates and other fruit in the orchard. There they would gather various herbs to cook with or to be dried and preserved for the trying times of illness or injury. They would take the goats, two females and one rebellious male. She discovered that the sheep gave more copious – and better-tasting – milk when they ate the flora that grew among the trees by the spring.

She had another reason to love these hikes. Her spouse was accustomed to releasing all the frustrations of his workday on her. When the cutting stones were dull, she paid the price; when the water she brought each morning was insufficient, or leaked or spilled, her spouse poured out his anger on her. He was no longer that darling boy she had met many years ago, a happy young man who'd had no concept of worry or responsibility. Village life and family responsibility did not sit well with him, and he struggled to face their challenges. However, she could not complain about him. Physical force and violence were a way of life, and the other women also suffered from vicious beatings at the hands of the men. They knew nothing else.

Still, Brashita, unlike the other women who were her friends in the village, found it difficult to accept this lifestyle. She knew her physical limitations, she knew the boundaries and her place in the social fabric, and she did everything in her power to keep everything tranquil, but a strange fire burned within her. Unlike others in the village, she noticed mistakes made by others and understood how life could be managed better. When she saw it in her spouse, she could not remain quiet, even if she knew that she was the one who would suffer afterwards. She simply understood, via her intuition, how things could be done differently. She knew, for example, that it was better to split the ground before sowing, as opposed to simply tossing the kernels into the wind. She knew when the best times for reaping were, but that was a man's job. She was aware of this reality, and she struggled with the paradox.

Her friends in the village warned her every time she complained or raised ideas about how to do things differently. They valued her intelligence; more than once, she had offered them suggestions about maintaining their households, advice that had been proven to be sound. Still, her ideas were frightening; no good, her friends knew, could come from them. A woman had to know her place, they thought, even if they did not always say so.

Brashita's house was always in order and her housewares were the best. This was because she was good at molding utensils, so the items in her house were nicer, bigger, and more numerous than what was in the others' homes. Still, the most important thing Brashita knew was her place. She understood life differently; she would have acted differently, if only she were able. But she was a woman, not a man, and this was something she could not change.

From her youth, Brashita was different from her friends, and her mother worried about her. She was stubborn and opinionated, or as her mother put it, "If I didn't know better, I'd swear she was a man..." It was no wonder that the family sighed in relief when, despite her mother's concerns, she found a man who wanted to take her as a mate. She quickly built their home, and were it not for others' reactions about her involvement in the construction process, and were it not for his own thoughts, her husband might have enjoyed her contribution. But his response was a different one, a very violent one.

When they returned home after "the wolf adventure," and after he had expressed his anger and explained her mistakes to her, and after she had put the rest of the family to sleep and arranged the straw in the goats' corner, Brashita went to sleep. In a bizarre counterpoint to the anger and shouting that had just filled the house, she felt great satisfaction from the exciting experience of their encounter in the desert, and did not even protest when, later in the night, he came to her.

This was Brashita's life. There was only one thing she could have her way in – raising the children. She raised them to do things differently than in the conventional manner, even explaining the ramifications. Not all of her children adopted her ways, but some of them indeed did. Mainly it was her firstborn son; although his societal worldview was much like that of his friends, he understood and accepted the utility of innovative practices and perspective that diverged from the conventional wisdom of the times.

Her life could have continued like that for many years were it not for the fateful day when her husband became involved in a violent quarrel with their neighbor. It began with an argument over the precise boundary of their property, an age-old dispute about a patch of land that was no wider than two or three paces but was particularly fruitful. That year, her husband had decided to scatter wheat kernels in this patch as well, and when the neighbor discovered this, he became furious. The argument devolved into a shouting match, then threats, then physical contact. When her firstborn son arrived at the field running, he saw the two facing off, one forehead against the other, their hands behind their backs, roaring and screaming. He stepped in between the two to separate them, but the neighbor's son, who had arrived as well, attacked him; now it was a four-man mêlée. Fists were raised, stones were thrown, and it was not long before Brashita's husband was on the ground, stabbed in his chest. He died within a short time.

Such events were not rare. The era of nomadic hunter-gatherers freely moving from place to place, eating the fruits that nature provided, and avoiding territorial conflicts, was over. Permanent settlement and agriculture brought into their lives quarrels and fights that became the daily bread of the men of the village, and death in violent circumstances was widespread.

The family began the funeral process according to the ceremonial rules. They dug a pit in the courtyard, dressed the corpse and put it in the proper position – the fetal position. After some time had passed and the body had decomposed, they would open the grave and perform the skull-plastering ceremony.

Brashita had no time to mourn, but the loss did lead her to intro-spection. There was a lot of room for worry. She needed someone to protect the family plot of land. Who would work it? Who would sow and reap? Her firstborn son was still too young for such a task. In addition, Brashita herself was a woman at the height of her power, a subject of desire by lustful men. She understood that the new lifestyle imposed on her was beyond her abilities; like all her female counter-parts, she would need a man to agree to take her under his wing. Still, something in her could not accept this method. Was it worry for the future? Was it the realization that she didn't want to live as her friends did? She struggled to come to a decision. The friends who came to help her did not understand this. They argued that this was the way of life, that a woman had to be part of a man's household. Since she had been left alone, she had to find another man, they even added, winking that her exceptional wisdom and beauty might make the men compete for her hand.

But Brashita wasn't like them. She knew that no one would under-stand what she was talking about, and she had to make this decision by herself. Then, one morning, without thinking about it too much, she called her children together. Not by way of explanation, even to herself, she told them that she planned to maintain the house as if it still had a man in it. She didn't want to take shelter under another man's wing. When her firstborn son would come of age, she told them, he would be welcome to choose a woman and bring her into their shared home.

This was an amazing declaration, particularly in light of the various proposals for a husband that had already come her way. All the villagers thought that she was making a colossal mistake, undermining the very foundations of the societal structure; she, however, felt a newfound, glorious sense of freedom, one she wasn't prepared to surrender.

But in the heavens... if only she had known what pandemonium she caused! The Guidances had to admit, once again with great perplexity, how little they knew about the twists and turns of the human spirit.

Brashita, of course, was not aware of her own soul plan. How could she have known? She didn't know that I, the soul incarnated within her, had reached a high level of development, allowing the Guidances to determine that she would be born with mental capacities far beyond the average for that period, due to the perspective of Creation, pushing man towards development and progress. She was an unusual, exceptional woman, who would raise and educate her children in a more progressive way, allowing evolution to do its work.

Recognizing the value of oneself was a primary focus with which I had been incarnated for several reincarnations. This was a weighty subject that was not the result of my curiosity or inquisitiveness, but the trauma I went through in more than one reincarnation, which went deeper; it penetrated and created a sort of "soul wound," a type of distress that manifested itself in low self-esteem.

In a number of my previous reincarnations, I tried to fix this. The Guides helped me a lot, but the people I was incarnated in (mostly men) didn't have the courage or the moral fortitude to overcome feelings of inferiority.

This incarnation was an additional attempt to learn the lesson. The woman born as Brashita, in whose body I was reincarnated, was full of self-esteem, the product of her great mental abilities compared to all her contemporaries and everyone else in her environment; the script was meant to take advantage of this for the sake of repair.

The plan written for this life was to bring about a situation in which Brashita, who maintained a high sense of self-worth despite her marriage, would, after her spouse's death, marry a man who would try to deflate her. She would experience a fall from the heights of her self-regard that would change her lifestyle.

Then her moment of truth would arrive, an event requiring her to act in a way diametrically opposed to that of a person who self-minimizes. This event was detailed in the script, requiring soul contracts with others, and was designated to present her with the opportunity to make a different choice and take action. If she could transcend, she would learn her lesson.

The script we created together indeed progressed – until her spouse died. Then Brashita used her freedom of choice, and in deciding to remain alone, she unknowingly veered off-track from the script, which of course had to be altered. The first attempt was to make it difficult for her to choose independent life and cause her to adopt social conventions nonetheless, i.e., the life she did *not* want. If not, not only would the lesson fail to be learned, but the Guidances would also have to undertake drastic revisions, because her decision to remain independent violated the social contracts signed with others.

I, the soul, was connected to Brashita's consciousness the whole time, and detached from the world beyond; thus, I could do nothing about the matter. However, my Soul Guardian saw, my Higher Self knew, and they were connected to the lofty Guidances. They tried, to the best of their ability, to change Brashita's decision, and they did this in two ways. First, they made her life as an independent woman difficult, and second, they sent her a man to attempt to "get her back on track." But what happened? Let us continue to observe the life of this brave woman.

At first, her decision was of no interest to the villagers. Each person had their own business, their own work, and their own battles, but Brashita knew that anyone interested in her property or in her would not leave her alone, and the matter would not go unnoticed. She rejected everyone, all the proposals, and she threw out of the house anyone who tried to impose his will on her. But she had to maintain the house and the small field, and she needed to employ the entire family in this endeavor.

Knowledge about a strange woman who acted like a man slowly spread through the village, and its residents – the male ones, of course – saw in her a real threat to their way of life. They harassed her, even forbidding their wives and children to be friendly towards her or any of her family members. Even her parents and siblings were angry with her. They were worried about the reputation she and they had acquired, and they were certain that she would fail, as there was no way a woman could live and act that way.

But Brashita pursed her lips and would not surrender, and it seemed that she was making it through this period, despite the difficulties. These were good days for her. The hard work didn't bother her. She was accustomed to it, and her reward – knowing that she could do whatever she wanted – proved to be greater than she had anticipated. She saw her firstborn son grow and develop a way of thinking that differed from the other men of the village; she also saw her daughters growing up differently, and she was gratified. She knew that when the time came, when she grew old and was not able to labor anymore, her children would honor her, and she would know no deprivation.

Time passed, and the season of her husband's death came again. Brashita called her children and asked them to join her for the skull-plastering ceremony. Together, they opened their father's grave, exposed the skeleton, and gently plucked the skull from it (leaving behind the lower jaw), then closed the grave again.

Brashita began to deal with the skull. The plastering process had to be done gently and with great care. After she had thoroughly cleaned the skull of all remnants of the grave and from the rocks and sand that adhered to it, she began to get ready to plaster it with clay. Her aim was to recreate, as much as possible, the face of the family's dead father, and she invested a great deal of time and patience in the endeavor. After she had finished and was satisfied with her work, she used loam to stick two shells to the eye sockets; then she decorated the skull with a red rim.

Once the clay had dried and become hard, Brashita invited her neighbors to come to her house in order to affix the skull in a prominent place in the structure. This ceremony had great importance, as the plastered skull symbolized for them the tradition of the father, publicly displaying the honor and respect he felt towards the family.

Brashita was not surprised to get the cold shoulder from their neighbors, but it grieved her to see the disappointment on her children's faces. In her heart of hearts, she had hoped that time would heal all wounds – in this case her fellow villagers' wrath– but the reality was quite different. Many of them interpreted her declaration of independence as an invitation to harm and steal from her; they saw the lack of an adult male presence as a personal affront. She discovered, more than once, that her work tools had disappeared, that people had trespassed on her plot, and she once had to face off against two boys who attempted to steal one of her goats.

Brashita didn't realize that she constituted a threat, nor did she know that as long as time ticked by and she survived, the threat against her only grew. From her point of view, the situation was different, and in fact she even managed to find moments of pleasure, moments she understood as generosity of spirit. This was expressed by a man who had been close to her husband; he began shouldering her burden, helping more from time to time. His presence, although not constant, helped her more than once to withstand the vandalism and the malice. The truth of the matter was that she was not at all surprised when at one point he proposed that she join his family, to become an additional wife to him. It was an enticing proposal. Since the death of her husband, her brave decision had lost some of its luster, in light of the anger and harassment directed at her. In her innermost being, she felt that this was it; she had proven that she was "capable." It would be best to take advantage of the opportunity, which ought to bring peace and tranquility to the family. Surprisingly, the harassment increased, and after more violence against her by the men of the village, she was ready to accept the proposal.

In heaven, they smiled in satisfaction because she was returning to the track of the original script. However, Brashita's independent consciousness proved to be stronger than they were. Shortly before she gave her final assent to the proposal, her well-developed sense of independence, her progressive thinking, asserted itself, and she decided to investigate.

Without consulting her prospective husband or receiving his permission, she initiated a meeting with the other women who lived in the house. What she saw chilled her heart. The man of the house was just as violent as the other men in the village, oppressing and hurting his wives; yet they, like all the other women in the village, saw nothing unusual in this situation. But Brashita? A wave of self-worth and acknowledgement of her own ability, washed over her, which switched her to "active" mode. She digested and internalized the fact that she faced two difficult choices – one a relatively comfortable life to be paid for by suppressing herself and surrendering all of her beliefs and desires, and the other a dangerous and difficult life that would allow her to maintain her independence and sense of self-worth.

Naturally, Brashita didn't think of the situation in terms of self-esteem or self-confidence, rebelling against societal conventions or other such concepts of which she had never heard. She only knew that either way, her life would be a challenge. The only difference was whether she could rely on herself and her discretion or not – and she made her choice. She rejected the proposal. It was no great surprise to see his expression change before her eyes; fortunately, she was agile enough to dodge the fist he then threw at her and escape.

Thus the years passed. Her son grew up and became a strong, brave man, deliberate in his vision and actions, just like his mother. After he had found a wife and brought her to their house, he was established as "the man of the house"; left with no choice, the villagers had to accept this strange family. At last, Brashita's life was one of peace and tranquility.

As was her wont, Brashita could not rest on her laurels. As the onus of household maintenance slipped a bit from her shoulders, she found herself attracted to the field of healing and caring for others although she couldn't explain why. As with everything else in her private world, she delved deeply into the topic. She became a successful healer and caregiver, known throughout the surrounding area.

When she died, all her children and grandchildren gathered around her bed, along with more than a few villagers. A year later, her son plastered her skull; even though it was against their traditions to do this for a woman, a great many people came to attend the ceremony.

And I, when I went back up to the world beyond, felt that the lesson of self-worth had been fully learned, even if the path had diverged from the script.

CHAPTER SIX

Evil. What Is It Good For?

Existence in the spirit world is comfortable, easy, and simple. We exist on the level of pure consciousness; emotions are not part of our nature, and they have no influence on our conduct. Our environment is one of pure love, and our development is expressed by expanding our capacity to contain love. As I have said – comfortable and easy.

Still, there's a fly in the ointment. The absolute love that presides here prevents us from having learning experiences. We don't experience incidents of success or failure, and there is no fear or frustration, there are no likes or dislikes, there is no euphoria or misery. However, in order to develop, to grow, and to change, "to expand the vessel," such situations are necessary, as are various experiences that may be, to some degree, difficult. We have to go through processes of struggling and contending with emotions, encountering complex situations that may at times be unanticipated. None of this exists in the world beyond.

If changes do occur, they happen languidly; we remain with our soul wounds and traumas, which cannot be easily healed. Finding form in a body and in human life gives us the opportunity for all those emotions and experiences, and the conflict that allows fundamental, rapid changes. Therefore, until we reach full rectification, we maintain the path of our existence while being incarnated in a body, going through processes that may be easy or difficult; then we return to the world beyond to rest and relax, to prepare the path of the next life, after which we are reincarnated. Indeed, through the process of my existence, I acquired great experience; many of those soul wounds I'd had at the beginning of my journey had already been cared for and healed, many of the experiences that I had within the incarnations were absorbed and learned, lessons were concluded, and even the moments of crisis that left their impression on me after that incarnation were dealt with and resolved.

As you have already seen, we dedicate the time after our return home to rest and recuperation from the events of that life. Only afterwards do we turn ourselves to analyzing the life cycle that has just ended, to learn its lessons, and prepare for the next life. We are not required to do this immediately. Our time is in our hands, without any pressure; however, we enjoy sharing our experiences with our friends from the family of souls and participating in their stories.

Lest you think that this sums up the life of a soul in the spirit world, let me correct you. Existence here is fascinating, and we are involved in an assortment of leisure activities that enable us to experience pure happiness. Aside from all this, there are additional roles for which we volunteer, such as positioning ourselves by the gate of the spirit world to receive those who have just completed an incarnation – we welcome them, and we enwrap them with love and happiness until they reach the recuperation and rehabilitation area. I volunteered for this position more than once, arriving at the gate especially at a time when a soul had just experienced great hardship. When a life is cut short with abruptness, cruelty, or suffering, this leaves an impression on the soul, and great spiritual powers are required to calm, embrace, and accept it. I do this volunteering with great love, and it is motivated by an inner need to learn as much as possible about humanity and the processes of the soul incarnated in it. I consider humanity to be one complete organism that develops over the years. As you may recall, in my first incarnation, in Roo's body, people lived their lives in nomadic tribes, with their development at the most fundamental level. Thousands of years later, Brashita was living in her village settlement, based on the first iteration of agriculture. The story of the next incarnation I want to share with you requires us to jump forward another 4,000 years, bringing us to the beginning of the Old Babylonian Empire, the days of Hammurabi's[1] Dynasty (1800 BCE), when people had already "invented" the wheel and changed the face of humanity. They no longer needed to drag heavy loads along the ground or on sleds; now, they bound oxen to wagons, to carriages, and even to war machines. Writing had just recently been introduced. Even if it was used mainly for lists of inventory and quantities, it was developing; at that time, it also transmitted messages for the government, such as transcribing laws. No doubt this was a major development.

These changes allowed settlements to grow and develop, people to establish political and military organizations, and this was when

---

1   Hammurabi is famous mainly for his Code, inscribed on a stele that is currently in the Louvre Museum in Paris. Researchers discovered the scope of his activity as king and the influence he had on Babylon's place in history. His name is the Akkadian version of Ammurāpi. This led many researchers to identify him with the biblical King Amraphel of Shinar (Shinar is identified with Babylon in Scripture), the first listed among the four Mesopotamian kings who wage war against the five kings of the Jordan Valley. They kidnap Lot, Abraham's nephew, so Abraham goes out to rescue him. He defeats the four kings and rescues Lot (Genesis 14).

the empires began to take their first steps. From my residence in the world beyond, I observed these changes, seeing them and rejoicing over my role, together with all the other souls, in this development.

Since the days of Brashita, I had experienced about fifty more life cycles, in which my character as a caregiver and healer was fixed. Still, over my last few incarnations, I began to feel that I was missing something. I was accustomed to being incarnated as a "positive" figure, compassionate and caring, but something still seemed lacking to me. I spoke to my Guides about this a lot, and I was astounded to learn that this was no surprise for them. I also got the impression that they were waiting for this feeling to float to the surface. Then, before the incarnation I am going to tell you about, the topic came up for discussion. The Guidance proposed that in the next life, I would be incarnated in a person occupying a position of power, holding a high office in the military hierarchy, someone who needed to make difficult decisions that would have an impact on the lives of human beings.

Even though I had already experienced incarnations in which the topic was leadership (then I did not even understand why the Guidance pushed me towards them), the topic of hierarchy had not been important at all. In the era of nomadic tribes, this had no meaning; the issue arose only later, when villages and local organizations began to be established. Now, with city-states a given, and with the first empire[2] already behind us, I was tempted by the idea of integrating into these new spheres of human life. However, this suggestion was accompanied by a warning. Military men tend to take their roles seriously, using their authority and power for inappropriate ends. It is best for the script to build within the person the desire to join the armed forces, but one must be careful not be drawn into difficult

---

2   The Akkadian Empire of King Sargon.

situations. This can be a moment of truth for the person as well as for the soul incarnated within that human being.

I approved of this challenge, so I "went for it."

Evelit

Egom was a coppersmith in the city of Nippur, and he was famous as an artisan with a good eye and skillful hand. The temple priests valued his artistry, and they purchased many ritual objects from him for the Temple of Enlil and the Temples of Ninurta, god of the city. His reputation became widespread, and the beauty of the items he created earned him fame among the citizens of Sumer and the surrounding cities, especially in Babylon, Ur, and Susa. Egom specialized in the production of strong, durable, bronze utensils as well, and he was known for producing excellent weapons from them for the kings of the area and their army commanders.

Egom's factory, at which many of his family members worked, sat on the Kebar River, which led to the Tigris and Euphrates. He could obtain copper from the tradesmen of Dilmun in the south, who were renowned for it, and he could import tin from the far north to produce these utensils.

Nippur was a holy city; it never had delusions of grandeur or of regional sovereignty. The glorious Temple of Enlil in the center of city served as a spiritual focus for the entire area, with many making the pilgrimage there to participate in the ceremonial rituals. The monarchs from the surrounding cities – the kings of Susa in Elam to the east, the kings of Uruk and Ur in Sumer to the south, and even the kings of Babylon to the north – all respected the site, protecting it and granting many benefits to its residents, as they were neither taxed nor drafted into the army.

Indeed, Egom and his family enjoyed a life of comfort and ease. Their residence in the holy city gave them peace, safety, and economic security, and the future seemed promising. When Evelit, Egom's youngest son, was born, there was no one happier than he. Egom was no longer a youth; this birth earned him great respect from his friends and neighbors.

However, outside the city, a storm was brewing. The news reached them about war against Babylon, due to the rebellion of the city-state of Larsa. The king of Babylon sought out Egom to manufacture weapons, such as swords, shields, and arrowheads, in large quantities and as quickly as possible, so he was among the first to know.

It would take four years to quell the rebellion, and it was conducted with a cruelty that left its impression on the inhabitants of the region. It was dangerous to travel the roads outside the city, and the donkey caravans transporting the copper ore were also in constant jeopardy. Still, no one thought that the brutality would violate the holy city and harm its residents until the horrific,day when, in the early afternoon, a caravan of wagons with a military escort entered the city, sent by the rebel King Rim-Sin of Larsa. The soldiers marched straight to the courtyard of Egom's factory. The unit was commanded by a high-ranking officer, who made a simple demand of Egom, who was standing next to the smelting furnace: "Stop selling weapons to the king of Babylon. From now on, we are your sole clients."

Egom, who by nature was a quiet man given to compromise, could not grant their request. He had strong personal connections to Babylon, and even though as a man of Nippur he was officially neutral, he could not betray the city that had so honored him and his products.

He proposed expanding the scope of his production, allowing him to sell to both sides, but they rejected this. With his refusal, the encounter was no longer a conversation or negotiation; instead, it was a scene of anger and threats. Tempers flared, but Egom – who knew the king of Larsa and his closest advisors personally – begged the officer to take his troops home, consult the king, and then return. It even seemed for a moment that his logical request had been accepted, but then the officer, who would prove himself to be hotheaded, declined. As a military man with troops under his command, he reached a different conclusion. According to him, if there was no consensus, then violence was the appropriate response.

His troops ordered everyone in the factory to gather in the courtyard. Egom tried to appease the officer, making all sorts of offers and presenting tempting benefits, but it was as if the man had become impenetrable, so the violence began. Threatening them with their swords, the troops tied up everyone and began to beat them, drawing blood. Egom's entreaties and explanations, arguing that the city was a holy one and that it was forbidden to commit any violence there, were ineffective; the commander lost all restraint, allowing his soldiers to abuse the bound prisoners and destroy whatever they could lay their hands on.

As the minutes passed, the troops' cruelty intensified. They broke limbs as they screamed that this was the fate of traitors and that the factory would be razed to the ground. A seemingly infinite amount of time passed as the troops took out all of their anger on the factory and its workers, but they eventually tired of it. They departed, leaving behind destruction and injury, but not before forcing the wounded workers to load the wagons they had brought with all the weapons in the factory's warehouse, along with many spoils of war.

It was only after they were gone that the magnitude of the tragedy became apparent. Egom's second son was found dead under a wagon, while other family members and employees were wounded and injured. The entire area looked like an abattoir.

This nightmarish scene was witnessed by five-year-old Evelit, who had hidden between two giant crates of copper ore, silently weeping and afraid to move, his eyes riveted to the shocking tableau. Thus, curled up and shaking, he was discovered by his mother only late at night.

The days passed, the physical wounds healed, and Egom, who was a strong man, recovered. He gathered his men and slowly rebuilt the factory. He did not let fear paralyze him or his men, and within a year they had put it all behind them.

Or so it seemed...

Young Evelit wasn't conscious of the process he was undergoing. The same was true for the others, but the boy closed in on himself, becoming utterly uninterested in everything happening around him. His mother noticed the change and showered him with affection, even convincing Egom to take Evelit on his travels. Indeed, slowly, the child seemed to recover, but something in him had changed. Additional violent encounters he witnessed along the way caused him senses to be dulled to the pain of others. Nothing tugged at his heartstrings when he saw an injured animal, or even when he saw children who were abusing animals. He never felt empathy for the pain of others whom they encountered on their travels. Although his father was greatly distressed by it, Evelit grew up to be an emotionless, insensitive young man.

As the years passed, Evelit grew stronger and smarter. His travels with his father provided him with quite the education, both in terms of his profession and in terms of negotiation. He learned how to read the faces of the traders they dealt with, seeing into their very souls; his incapacity for emotional communication turned out to be a gift, and he served as an excellent adviser to his father.

When he was fifteen, Evelit accompanied his parents on a trip to visit his aunt, who lived in a small village a few hours' ride from the city. Despite Egom's reluctance, the couple's eldest granddaughter, who was Evelit's age, joined them.

It was a difficult time. The winds of war were once again blowing as another rebellion erupted against King Samsu-Iluna of Babylon, Hammurabi's son. Now It was Ilum-ma-ilī, king of Isin, who raised the banner of revolution. The war lasted for a long time, and the tensions in the area skyrocketed.

It wasn't a good time to be on the road, but the widowed sister of Egom's wife had fallen ill, and the family decided to travel to her and bring a healer with them. When they arrived, it appeared that they had missed their chance. The aunt was already on her deathbed, and all the healer could do was reduce her suffering. They decided to stay with her a few days and wait.

This turned out to be a fateful decision.

In the late afternoon, as sunset painted the sky in crimson and ocher, the atmosphere was pleasurable as the family sat down for supper. The aunt even got out of her bed and joined them, despite her pain. Peace and tranquility filled the air. In serenity, they awaited the inevitable.

The dogs were the first to shatter the quiet with their barking, which shockingly became whimpers of pain, followed by a suspicious and terrifying silence. A group of inebriated rebels burst in and demanded food and more intoxicants.

Egom, with his experience, invited all of them in, promising to give them whatever they wanted. The soldiers pushed the diners away from the table, but when Egom surreptitiously signaled to his family to leave the room, they noticed and ordered them to remain.

"We deserve the best!" they roared, laughing and pounding on the tables. The family stood against the wall while Egom and the healer were sent to bring the promised food and drink,

Evelit's mother was worried about her granddaughter, and she tried to hide her behind her back, but one of the drunken soldiers saw her and shouted, "Hey, you! Come here!" The girl hesitated, which set the soldiers in motion. One of them leaped at her and pulled her towards them. In one move, he stood her on the table and jumped up to stand beside her.

With loud cries, his comrades encouraged him to undress her. He smiled and turned to her, "They want me to strip you. But I'm a nice guy, right? I don't want to do that." The fear on the girl's face lessened a bit, but the soldier continued, "You know why? Because you're going to do it yourself! And make sure you do it slowly!" The last two sentences were screamed at the top of his lungs, and his comrades cheered.

Egom and the healer ran back to the room, but they were abruptly stopped by fists and spears pointed at their throats.

The terrified girl was in shock – this only further encouraged the soldier standing next to her, who shouted and smacked her in the face. A cry of "Wait! Stop!" was heard, and the room became silent. Evelit's mother marched forward and declared, "Take me. I am experienced. I know how to give you pleasure." The soldier looked at her and burst out in derisive, almost satanic, laughter. "You? Who wants the experience of a hairy, wrinkly crone like you, with your drooping breasts? Move aside, you tired old hag!"

But the mother would not give up. Out of the corner of her eye, she saw Egom struggling to get free and she yelled to him, "Stop! I still need you!" Egom looked beseechingly at Evelit, but was shocked by what he saw. Evelit lay on the ground curled up, his thumb stuck in his mouth as he trembled, like the five-year-old boy he had been, hiding among the crates of copper ore.

The mother approached the soldiers and dropped her robe. In a quick motion, she slipped out of her underclothes, and she stood before them naked. Silence descended on the room, and the soldier turned to Egom and the healer, saying with a wicked smile, "You have my respect. She is worth something at least." Then he jumped down from the table, dragging the terrified, shaking granddaughter with him, shouting to his comrades, "We're going to have some fun now. We have a full selection!" He reached out and tore the girl's clothing off her. Then he turned to his comrades and said, "I'm taking her," pointing to the girl, "and whoever wants to take the old one, go ahead. Afterwards, everyone can do whatever he pleases." He quickly pulled off his trousers and displayed his erect member. "I'm sure you've never seen anything like this, huh?" He lasciviously gazed at the girl, and salivating from the wine, lustfully threw her to the floor and forced her legs apart. He penetrated her forcefully, as she screamed and struggled.

Without hesitation, a comrade of his – large, stinking, clumsy – jumped on the mother, knocking her onto the table, her back on the surface and her feet still on the floor. He penetrated her and madly thrust in and out. She tried to push him back, to struggle, scratching his face, but he seemed to feel nothing until a mighty tremor passed through his entire body and he discharged all his desire into her. Then he stood back, leered, and bellowed, "She really is something, I swear. Who's next?"

Thus, while the soldiers guarded Egom, the healer, Evelit, and the aunt, the drunken soldiers raped the two women one by one - some from the front and some from the rear, some quickly and some slowly, some with force and violence and some with "gentleness." They didn't stop until they were all satisfied. Only then, as the two women were lying in blood and vomit, unresponsive and glassy-eyed, did the soldiers leave. They shakily walked out of the house, passed the corpses of the two dogs, and disappeared.

The silence in the room was horrific. Egom and the healer tried to rise but stumbled; then they tried again and fell. In the meantime, Evelit stood up; with an impassive face, he covered the nakedness of the two women. He then took his mother into his arms and carried her to the bedroom. He came back and carried the girl there as well. Without saying a word, he turned to the aunt, helping her sit down on a chair outside the room. Then he turned to his father, and in a cold authoritative voice, he sent Egom to his wife's bedside. He looked at the healer, who was in shock, and ordered him to regain his composure. "You have a lot of work to do," he told him. "You cannot save my aunt's life, but you must help these two."

Afterwards, he began to clean up the room, so by the time his father came back, it was already in perfect order. Egom was stunned by the situation. He couldn't digest everything he had witnessed – the horrific abuse, the exceptional conduct of his wife, who had volunteered herself, the look on the face of his granddaughter, and the tremendous contrast between Evelit's behavior when the horrors began and the competent young man who now stood before him.

Evelit was overwhelmed. The unspeakable acts he had witnessed had brought him back to the day that he thought was irrevocably in the past. The stifling, breathtaking fear that had surrounded him at the beginning of the events, and the terrifying change he had undergone while they were taking place, were utterly maddening. The shift occurred at the moment that the granddaughter began to scream and was stifled by a palm clamped over her mouth and a slap. Suddenly, he had felt himself disassociating from the events unfolding before his eyes. It was a scene unconnected to him, something happening to people he did not recognize, from another place. He felt that the emotional pain was bearable, even fading and disappearing. The cries and calls, of the two weeping women and of the soldiers, became muffled background noise. The fear and the horror were cleared out, replaced with a sense of pragmatism and a new, surprising emotion; he felt pressure rising in his loins at the sight of his young niece being raped before his eyes.

When it was all over, he could function and focus. The true terrors would begin only months later, when images of the rape of his mother appeared before him in nightmares and waking dreams. Evelit became progressively closed off from his environment, and he admitted this readily, believing that it was the only way he could still function and the only way to live a normal life. But alongside the emotions that progressively disappeared, there were two new ones: hatred, and the thirst for vengeance.

Two years passed. Egom's factory was still operational, but he was clearly a broken man. He had lost his *joie de vivre*, and his unique creativity and inspiration were forever damaged. His adult sons took over the management and production, and the family lived its life as if a dark cloud hung over it.

Evelit became a dedicated worker in the factory. His own high spirits ostensibly returned quickly, and he was at the core of his young friends' social group, with no event at which he was not the center of attention. He would raise his voice in song, and he was famous for his proficiency in dance; in short order, he became the object of many girls' dreams. However, such a man could not help but notice what was hidden in his son's heart. He saw how his youngest was closed off, his lack of empathy for others, for their suffering, for their pain. He knew that the son would make merry with his friends, but he realized that it was nothing more than a mask. He noticed it when his son abused animals for his own gratification, and he saw how he took great delight in conflict. As the boy grew up, Egom's concern about what might happen became more serious. Thus, he was not surprised that Evelit told him that he was enlisting in the royal guard of the king of Babylon.

There, Evelit finally found his place. In his first year, he and his comrades were sent to carry out policing operations, to escort senior officials close to the royal family, to escort the royal tax collectors to distant villages. They even put down rebellions. Evelit found a place among his comrades, and his commanders found him to be a courageous man who knew no fear, who would never display apprehension, who would never retreat, who would never show weakness in difficult situations.

Evelit's commanders recognized his abilities, promoting him to platoon commander. He became well known throughout the guard, and he loved what he did. Since he had found his place, he no longer needed his mask. Evelit's comrades found him to be unique – a physically robust person who could adapt to difficult conditions with ease, and his intelligence and resourcefulness made him a widely admired platoon commander, even though he was sometimes violent towards his own troops. Evelit would not accept insubordination or argument, and he would subject whoever opposed him to cruel physical punishment. Whippings and floggings were his favorite responses, but there were nasty rumors, whispered *sotto voce*, that he had executed men more than once. Nevertheless, everything was forgiven due to his abilities, his stick-to-itiveness, and his results.

Two years passed, and Evelit was being sent to the most dangerous places, to operations that required ingenuity and brains; his experience in negotiation, which he acquired on those business trips with his father, helped him a lot.

The most important moment on his career path came during the colossal event organized to honor the heir apparent; the prince was the supreme commander of the guard. After the show of force by the soldiers, as the event was drawing to a close, Evelit marched forward, looked the prince in the eye and suggested a contest among representatives of the various brigades – an actual battle to the death.

Needless to say, his commanders did not love the idea, but the prince's face shone with happiness. He asked Evelit if he would volunteer to represent his brigade. With his hand on his sword, he loudly proclaimed, "Of course. I would not let anyone take my place."

And so it was. The participants were selected, although the prince did accede to the commanders' petition and satisfy himself with just four. The first two matches ended very quickly. Evelit finished his contest with nothing much more than one swipe of his sword; he was displeased that the delight of his opponent's suffering had been withheld from him. In the other match, the victor was also known for his combat skills, and he, too, had managed to dispatch his rival speedily and efficiently. Now the two finalists stood across from each other, tense, holding their daggers, waiting for the anticipated command.

Evelit had to admit that his new opponent was a challenge, a courageous, quick combatant, but "Challenge" was Evelit's middle name, and he accomplished his first hit with speed and power. Discovering his foe's weak spot, he began to play with him. The spectator-soldiers cheered him on, shouting and demanding blood. They waited for the *coup de grâce* with bated breath, but Evelit was enjoying every second of the contest. The suffering on his rival's face excited him, and he was having too much fun to let it end quickly. Out of the corner of his eye, he could see the prince; as long as his liege was satisfied, he would continue and stop only when he perceived that the commander-in-chief wanted the battle to end. With one quick dancelike motion, he charged his opponent and thrust his dagger into his throat. He waved his hand in the air, put a foot on his opponent's chest and roared, then drew his sword and with one swipe decapitated the fallen foe. Then he grabbed the dead man's head by the hair, and amid the shouts of approval, approached the prince, placed the head at his feet and proclaimed, "Your Highness the Prince, I would be honored to serve at your command."

A few days later, Evelit was summoned to the prince's quarters and was offered a position in an elite unit under the heir apparent's direct command. Evelit agreed, thus bringing him into the royal family's orbit, with all the privileges that that entailed. Over time, the prince came to respect and value Evelit, and the two became close friends.

As the years went by, King Samsu-Iluna of Babylon returned his soul to the Creator, and the prince ascended to his father's throne, as King Abi-Eshuh of Babylon. His first moves were to establish his rule by taking action on the international front as well as the internal and military fronts; he took steps to forge new bonds and to introduce changes in the forces closest to the throne. In short order, the crown was made secure.

Evelit, whose abilities the new king recognized, became his closest confidant, personally executing whatever the monarch required. The operations that required the greatest secrecy were given to Evelit, who carried them out with great dispatch.

His senior position offered him great freedom of action, and no one dared question his decisions or defy his orders. Stories began to circulate about him, such as how he would cruelly suppress opposition, that there had even been mysterious incidents of slaughter in small settlements – places where thoughts and ideas of rebellion or refusal to pay taxes had arisen. The tales about him spread until he became known as someone it was best to avoid if one wanted to live a long life. Soon, King Abi-Eshuh could rest assured that there was nothing to worry about, i.e., no threat to his throne.

Now, at last, Evelit could execute the plan that had been in the depths of his mind and the pit of his stomach since that fateful day at his aunt's. He secretly sent his agents to hunt down the commanders of the villains who had raped his niece and his mother. It was no simple task, since the years had covered their tracks. Still, he did not stint on the resources he expended, from enticement to bribery, alongside threats and intimidation. Within a few months, he found the two commanders in the village of Ursin, far away in the southern reaches of Sumer, not far from the city of Ur.

Evelit arranged a "tour" of the southern districts. He took the two men who were closest to him, along with a small platoon of warriors to keep them safe on the journey. About two weeks after their departure, they reached the home of one of the two men he had found. Evelit sent a few warriors to the home of the second to bring him and his family. He entered the house with his two companions.

He knew what he wanted. The images had been in his imagination for such a long time that he had no need to hurry. Vengeance would bring him tranquility, and vengeance ought to be exacted slowly and coolly.

His entrance made quite the impression. A tall officer, resplendent in his uniform, he announced in a grave, authoritative voice, "We are exhausted. We need food and drink. Will the master of the house consent to honor us?"

He immediately recognized the face of the man of the house. Many years had gone by, but his features were burned into Evelit's memory. It was the man who had seized his niece and violated her on the table. The man and his wife (he had other wives in another house) couldn't hide their apprehension as they said, "Of course, my lord. Whatever you desire in this modest house is yours!"

Evelit glanced at them, and with a wave of his hand sent them to get something. While the two were in the kitchen area of the house, the second man came in. He, too, had only one spouse with him, and the boys joined her. Evelit lost his breath and his heart almost stopped.

It was the bastard who had raped his mother.

He called the two from the kitchen and ordered them to sit. They all sat on the floor, leaning on the wall, as three soldiers were standing across from them. Evelit felt a rising sense of pleasure within him, and in a cold, emotionless voice, told them, "We have not come here for food or drink." Then he fell silent for a moment, continuing in a slow, calm voice, "Instead, we came here to toy with you." The fear on their faces developed into full-blown terror. His intent was inescapable. Coldly, he called in the troops who were outside. He ordered them to tie up the two men and the children. When they finished and left the house, he looked at the two women, and in a chilling voice he ordered them to strip and get ready to be mercilessly violated.

The women were so terrified that they didn't know what to do – they could only stare.

Evelit grinned and glanced at his two friends, as if to say "What should we do? It looks like they don't care for you. They aren't going to help you."

His companions, who had been waiting for his signal, approached the two women, dragged them to the middle of the room, slammed the table against one of the walls and lay them down one alongside the other, one's head next to the other's legs. They quickly and forcefully ripped off their clothing and began torturing them. Professional and proficient in their equanimity, they totally ignored the weeping and screaming of the two women. They ruined their beauty, leaving scars and cuts on their cheeks, breasts, and thighs. They enjoyed their "creation," as it were. Whenever one of the women fainted, her torturer would wake her up with a slap or by pouring water on her face. Only when they grew tired of their game did they violently rape them, before the eyes of their husbands and children.

Evelit just stood there and observed. When one of the husbands or children tried to look away, he whacked them with his sword to force them to take in the scene. Their pain and suffering gave him great joy. When one of his companions seemed to be "going soft," he spurred him on by yelling encouragement.

But this was not enough for Evelit. Once the two had satisfied their sadistic and sexual desires, he called the soldiers who had been waiting outside to "join the party." Then, when they had all finished and were about to leave, Evelit discovered that one of the soldiers had not entered the house and had refused to join in. Evelit summoned him into the house and told him to drop his trousers and take part in the rape.

The soldier faced a great dilemma. He did not want to participate, but his cruel commander terrified him. So he took his clothes off, but to his great embarrassment his body would not cooperate. The soldier stood naked, pensive, hanging his head as his member drooped. Evelit looked at him and with mocking laughter said, "Don't worry. We'll help you." He approached one of the two women, forced her to sit up on the table, and he ordered the soldier to approach her. He ordered her to help the soldier with her mouth. The traumatized woman couldn't even understand what he wanted. Evelit took this as a refusal, so he turned to one of the boys and asked, "Who among you is her son?"

"I am," one of the children answered quietly.

Evelit unsheathed his dagger, put it up against the child's face, and in a cold voice asked the woman, "Which eye do you want me to poke out first?"

This horrific shock woke the woman out of her frozen state, and she whispered, "No, I beg you. I'll do what you want." And so she did.

But the author of this nightmarish scene had other plans. The unspeakable event had so traumatized the solider that his manhood would not respond, despite the desperate efforts of the poor woman holding it. Evelit felt his anger swelling within him, grabbed the soldier from his spot next to the woman, stared into his eyes, then drily and coldly said, "You are an embarrassment to the crown, to the royal guard, and to me. You have no place among us!" To the amazement of all, he took his dagger and plunged it into the soldier's neck; he immediately crumpled to the ground, wallowing in his blood.

Evelit gazed at his dead soldier, spat on him and kicked the corpse. When he had calmed down a bit, he stared at the two husbands. "I have not sated my lust, but I will stop here nonetheless – not simply out of compassion, but mainly because I am tired of it. My comrades have worn themselves out from enjoying the pleasures your wives granted them so generously. Still, the two of you ought to understand why this is happening. After all, it is you who are the guilty parties." They stared at him, glassy-eyed, as he continued, "It was more than a decade ago, in a small village outside of Isin. The two of you brutally raped my mother and my niece." He stopped for a moment to gaze at them, waiting for the memory to float to the surface. "I swore then that I would take revenge on you." Then he looked at the boy, the son of the woman, and said, "I would never have harmed your eyes. I want the pain to be etched in them every morning when you open them."

As they left the courtyard and turned north, Evelit found himself experiencing a strange sensation. He thought that once he had taken his vengeance, he would feel some relief, but it was not to be. Vengeance had long ago become a challenge, a call to action – but nothing more. Cruelty was now an inseparable part of his constitution.

A few months passed, and to Evelit's surprise, the secret got out. The story of the cruel emissary of the king became known in the cities of Sumer, making it all the way back to Babylon. The reports arrived at a particularly bad time, as the king was right in the middle of forging a political union with the four districts of southern Sumer – without involving the military. The king knew Evelit well and was ready to accept his missteps, but this time Evelit had gone too far. As much as the king loved and valued his commander, he knew how dangerous it would be if such an event were to be tolerated, and he had to get rid of his man. He summoned Evelit and, looking him straight in the eye, said, "You are hereby relieved of your duties, and of your position in the royal guard."

Evelit left the palace, feeling betrayed. Within him swelled disgust and disdain towards his monarch. He resolved to take some time to figure out his next move, and thought that for the time being it would be better to return to his parents' home.

The next day he saddled his horse and headed south, to Nippur. Leaving Babylon, he was accompanied by some close friends, but a short way down the road, they parted ways, and he continued alone. When the sun began to set, he got off the path, pitched a tent, lit a fire and soon fell into a deep sleep.

He woke up in the dark, feeling a sharp blade at his throat. Out of the murk, a figure said to him, "I have been sent to kill you, and nothing would bring me more joy. You hurt me. You hurt the love of my life. You ruined my life and the lives of others without batting an eyelash, without feeling any pain." The figure continued, "It is not happenstance that brings me here, and it wasn't luck that helped me find you. Your good friends, the ones you relied on, the ones who escorted you – they told me which way you were riding. Yes, like me, and like so many others, they, too, will rejoice in your death. Enjoy your trip down there, to the netherworld below, to endless suffering."

Great tranquility enveloped Evelit. He recalled something from his childhood – the horrible day, when he was just five years old, curled up in his mother's arms. A massive wave of sadness washed over him. "What a waste of a life!" he thought to himself. He looked at the man standing over him, his killer, and said to him, "You should not be angry or hateful. At least you experienced the taste of love. Do your duty and don't hesitate." He closed his eyes, and from his throat burst forth a scream that echoed through the mountains. Some say that it made it all the way to Nippur. "M o m m y !"

I had never experienced such a feeling.

I got to the gate of the spirit world very quickly. I didn't even take the time to look down, to see, and I didn't even attempt to watch what happened next. All I wanted was to escape. I didn't even stop to try to understand why.

At this stage, we souls are on the lowest "plane of existence."[3] Even though we are no longer physical, we still retain some physical sensations. I was enveloped by feelings of fear, the sensation of a nightmare; more than anything, I was harshly disappointed by what I had done when I was a part of Evelit.

---

3   It is convenient and conventional to divide the space of existence into a number of planes. The plane closest to the physical level is the "etheric plane," and it represents the aspects of the physical body. This is where the soul arrives as it completes its life cycle and leaves the body. The level of energy density in this plane is lower than in the physical plane, but the difference is not great. The soul still experiences objects as material, and time in this plane still has real meaning. However, the universe containing this plane is no longer the physical universe, and this is reflected in the behavior of time and space, in which consistency and limitations are lost, creating "distortions" compared to the physical perspective.

When I reached the gate of the spirit world, my Guide already knew about my state, and I suddenly felt a wave of peace, tranquility, and strong love wash over me and I could stop. None of the difficult feelings disappeared, but I suddenly felt that at least I could stand myself. If I were a human being, I would have cried, I would have cleansed myself with tears; but alas, I am a soul, and we do not have access to such a wonderful tool... We simply disassociate from any human emotion, and we see the story as if it is a picture, as an array of data points that allows us to analyze the events. However, at that point, I was far from that state. I still felt pain, shame, and – more than anything – anger over being in a body that had done everything it had done. I was not yet in a position to analyze, to try to understand, to explain, to see and perhaps even to think about how to fix it. All I wanted then was quiet.

The Guide brought me over to the area of orientation and enlightenment, and this was exactly what I needed. I had been tossed and turned violently by this life, and what was weighing me down had to be cleaned off or I wouldn't be able to proceed. As a soul that had already been reincarnated many times, I had a unique nature, a special essence of mine that, in most of my incarnations, directed me to find form in a person whose life was filled with compassion and emotionality, and so I often found myself as a caregiver or healer. When I was a human being, I certainly experienced moments of difficulty, moments of physical or emotional pain, but I accepted them as part of my life at that time. This was not so during Evelit's lifetime. In his body, I was cruel, devoid of emotion, even enjoying the suffering of others. Evelit's cruelty was exceptional, even relative to that period, and so I felt a need to stay in the rehabilitative area for a very long time.

Indeed, I stayed there for far longer than was usual. Bit by bit, I remembered the conversations I'd had before this incarnation, the warnings about finding form inside such a person. We spoke then about the danger of being in a body making its own choices, difficult decisions diverging from the script, and the enticement inherent in a position of power that can put a human being, as well as a soul, to the test. In retrospect, I could think of nothing other than my apparent failure, and this was not a heartening conclusion.

The reorientation clinic – I choose to call it "clinic" because that's what it was for me during that period – proved to be the right place for understanding, for insights, and for cleaning out the emotion that prevents accurate analysis.

It's nice in this area of healing – nice in such a way that would be difficult to describe in human language, but it did its work. The process may have taken longer than usual, but eventually I developed the ability and desire to move on. As always, as soon as I felt that I had taken full advantage of the opportunity and began to think about the next step, my spiritual Guide appeared. I was happy to see him, and together with him and a few others who had joined, I went on to the next stages in my journey ending my time in that body, the phase of analyzing and documenting that period in the cosmic library. When it all ended, and when I felt strong enough, I happily returned to my family of souls, to the friends whom I had missed terribly.

However, something had changed within me. A heavy burden had been created and accompanied me. It was not a matter of healing; rather, something had changed in my very nature, in my essence. It was clear to me, and my friends here all agreed, that clearing out this trauma could not happen here in the world beyond, in the stable and quiet realm. The only way to do it would be through another reincarnation in human form. And so I started to plan my next life, a life in which the human being I would inhabit would have to face a challenge posed by evil itself, to confront it and to conquer it. Only in this manner, I understood, could I come clean.

I didn't want to wait longer than necessary, and I felt that it was worth it for me to experience my next reincarnation in the same era of life on Earth. The change in the social structure, which had brought about the ascension of nationalism and the creation of empires, also led to the development of armies and technologies employing innovatively destructive weapons, allowing a great opportunity for abuse to raise its ugly head. These were the days of monarchs and militaries getting drunk on power, and there was no problem finding a time in which I could be reincarnated in such a person.

Indeed, after a period of preparation, I felt the excitement of rebirth growing and swelling within me. Thus, about forty years after Evelit's death, I was born in a farming village near the Hittite capital of Neša.[4]

Ammunas

Ammunas was a full-bodied boy who intimidated his friends; when he grew up, people recognized him as a character to avoid starting anything with. As a sixteen-year-old, he was drafted into the army of the Hittite King, Hattusili I. He moved through the ranks quickly, and he soon joined the king in his new capital, Hattusa. Ammunas went to battle throughout the Anatolia region, all the way to Zalpa on the shores of the Black Sea. He went through many upheavals in his life, but the destruction that he sowed along with his comrades, and the unnecessary cruelty that he used against many people, did not sit

---

4   Today's Kültepe, located about 250 kilometers southeast of Ankara, Turkey.

well with him. A few times he was very close to deciding to abandon war and return home, but peer pressure stopped him in his tracks. Ammunas met his end in one of those battles, and his commanders paid him homage and respect.

But for me... as I returned to the world beyond, I felt like a failure. We had built the plan and the personality of Ammunas so that at the moment of truth, he would have the strength to overcome the challenge. We created a person whose point of origin was forcefulness, but within his innermost being, there was a seed of softness and compassion. I hoped that at the moment of truth, this seed would bloom and flourish, building within him the power to abandon the path of his comrades, to withstand peer pressure and the pressure from his commanders, to overcome the fear of the appearance of "betrayal." But this was not what happened.

When I ascended again, I was no longer in the difficult emotional state that I was after the death of Evelit, and this bothered me. I was concerned that evil and cruelty had become part of my character, and I felt that I had to try one more time. So I embarked on a further mission. First I examined my contribution to the "failure," as well as the contributions of my friends. Of course, I knew that human freedom of choice overruled all of our plans, but I began to suspect that perhaps we, the souls, had missed the mark. Could it be that while I was *in utero*, I had failed to precisely prepare the personality of Ammunas? Perhaps one of the souls I signed contracts with for this life had not done what it was supposed to do?

After that, we planned the course of the life of the person who was to be born. The "Council of Elders," a senior group of entities who proposed and outlined the script for this life, suggested returning to the environment in which Evelit lived and was active, to that lifestyle. They thought – and I agreed with them – that the greater the similarity to my previous experience, the greater the potential to cleanse my trauma by overcoming evil.

I wanted to make sure that any act I would have to carry out would be accompanied by my Guidance's criticism and counsel, so I turned to the lofty, experienced Guidances, who fully committed to the matter. I ascertained that my twin soul would be with me in this incarnation, in a pivotal role. I very carefully chose my parents for this incarnation, and I did this at the last moment, when I was absolutely confident that I had done everything in my power to make this incarnation a success.

I presume that in your eyes, dear readers, this process seems very human, orderly, and simple, but I assure you that it was a very complex matter requiring delving deeply into the processes with the assistance of very lofty entities. Action itself, as you already know, is carried out here very differently from how things are done in the material world. The only reason the description seems so simplistic and orderly, almost schematic, is that I must explain everything that happens here in your language, in human terms.

The preparations were at an end, the time for reincarnation had arrived, and here is the tale of Savium.

Savium

Savium was born in Isin, a city south of Babylon and dozens of miles from Nippur, whose best days were behind it. It was the fifteenth century BCE, about 120 years after Evelit's death, and decades after the fall of Babylon to the Hittites and its conquest by the Kassites.

Savium was the third son of downtrodden parents – a father who lashed out violently, and a weak mother. The home was a quarrelsome, vicious place for the children, so they spent as much time as they could outside of it, obtaining their daily bread by any means possible.

He was no normal child – clever, quick and strong – and he stood out among his siblings and friends. When there was a need to "put things in order" at difficult moments, whether by violence or by sweet-talking, he would rise to the occasion. It was no wonder that he was the one who exhibited concern for others when they couldn't provide for themselves.

Savium had almost no relationship with his father, who was out of the house most days. When he did bother to show up, he would beat his wife, who supported the family through prostitution. More than once he came home to find other men with her, and this did not help his mood.

Savium didn't see anything wrong with this lifestyle. In his childhood, his life was "perfectly fine." Many of his friends and contemporaries had similar lives, and he accepted his role as a leader naturally. He wasn't sentimental or sensitive; he didn't display his emotions readily, but even so, there were times when he could not hide his emotions – for example, the time that he managed to arouse the anger of some grown-ups who had caught him stealing. The man who caught him beat him viciously, and two other adult men joined in; seeing him as the leader of a youth gang, they decided to eliminate him and "clean up the neighborhood." The children with him ran away pell-mell, while his older brother told their mother what was happening.

She didn't hesitate for a second, grabbing a wooden stick and running to rescue her son. Her anger and fury were unrestrained. She struck the three men and screamed at the top of her lungs, and the moment they released him, she grabbed him and dragged him after her, all the way back home. Savium, who was unconscious, only remembered waking up in his mother's lap as she caressed him and applied various ointments. He saw the tears in her eyes, but also her determined look, and then he smiled at her and buried his face in her bosom, feeling secure and loved.

The years passed, and the boy became a young man. Because the regions had debts to pay to the crown, he was drafted into the king's forces, which spent their time expanding the borders of the kingdom and suppressing local revolts. Savium acclimated easily. Military service fit him like a glove, and in short order he became a commander who was respected, admired, and even praised by his troops – even if his methods of persuasion were not always the most acceptable. Very quickly he discovered how useful his whip was for dealing with disobedient soldiers. The spear and dagger proved useful against internal enemies as well, and he soon discovered that the more he abused his soldiers, the more he was respected.

This worked even with his commanders. Savium found that the quicker he "delivered the goods," as it were, the more his stock rose among them; violence against the enemy, at times even accompanied by brutality, allowed him to do this. Vicious treatment of one village would intimidate the villagers as well as those in surrounding settlements; harshly guarding the roads and transit points kept people from moving freely and challenging the military. And if one could also partake, from time of time, of the local delicacies and womenfolk, all the better!

However, a number of events then occurred that undermined his confidence in this course of conduct. The most serious of them had taken place while he himself was involved in combat, as the blood was boiling in his veins, and as he was full of energy and vigor. He always acted with the deep knowledge that this was correct and necessary, without stopping to ponder the situation. However, on one occasion, he was invited to accompany a number of senior commanders touring a village close to Isin. Entering the village, he had an uneasy feeling, as if he were familiar with the place, although he had never been there before. When they walked among the burned-down buildings, seeing injured children and old people, women in shock, and men whose heads hung low, he felt a twinge in his heart. At first he thought it was momentary weakness, but the feeling kept recurring, and it slowly gained a foothold in his heart.

A year passed, and they were ordered to go down south, to the city of Ur. There were worrisome reports about growing unrest that had reached the army commanders; Savium, together with a number of units, had been ordered to report there for duty. The regional commander updated them about what was going on; indeed, they soon sensed the glances of hatred and anger directed toward them and, from their point of view, this was sufficient proof of the danger of revolution in the air. They were military men, accustomed to following orders, and it was not their business to stop for a moment and examine the claims or requests of the residents. The order was to thwart the unrest before it grew into a full-blow revolution, and they organized themselves accordingly.

The local commanders told them about Ursin, a town not far from Ur in which some of the main proponents of the unrest lived; there was the main source of the problem, they argued. Their recommendation – go there and take action – was clear.

After many hours of traveling, they arrived, but when they entered, Savium was overwhelmed by a feeling of *déjà vu*, as if he had already been there, accompanied by a strong sense of fear.

The operation went quickly. They located the wanted men, verified the claims about them, and dragged them to the city square. They then gathered the rest of the residents by shoving, clouts, and blows. Savium already knew the procedure. The accused were to be executed before the eyes of their neighbors; if unrest and resistance cropped up again, they would teach the village a lesson and give the residents an education – by way of murder, arson, and destruction. Beyond "educating" the village, this would be a message for the entire region, and he and his fellow soldiers could go back to their homes up north.

The execution was a ceremony, as Savium and his men read the indictment, and then quickly and efficiently began executing the "lawbreakers" by decapitation.

The audience was shocked, and it was as silent as a tomb, save for the weeping of children. But then, as the soldiers shoved one of the accused ahead of them – a young man who seemed to be no more than a boy – the crowd begged for mercy. When he was executed, they howled. From this point forward, the screaming only increased, and the soldiers' warnings could not suppress the sounds. Savium, whose nausea was only getting worse, wanted to get it all over with and get out of there. He gave his soldiers the order to start wrapping up the operation as quickly as possible, but then he caught sight of her.

He saw her and was dumbfounded: a short woman, cradling a crying child in her arms. She caressed his head and spoke to him quietly; the child buried his head in her bosom and smiled at her. The young mother raised her head and stared at Savium with blazing eyes; Savium felt that he was trapped in her gaze. She smiled at him, and he felt love. At that moment, a great tranquility, accompanied by images of his childhood, descended upon him, and he remembered the horrific day when he was a child, curled up in his mother's arms. An enormous wave of sadness washed over him. "What a waste of a life!" he thought to himself. Then he closed his eyes, and from his throat burst forth a dreadful scream that echoed through the mountains, and some say it made it all the way to Babylon: "Nooo!"

The years passed. Aged Savium released his soul, me; and here in the area of orientation and enlightenment, I thought about him... how he was kicked out of the army in disgrace after he was accused of treason for preventing his troops from carrying out their orders; how his father, disgusted, rejected him; how he had to abandon everything and drift to faraway places; and how he had found happiness when he married, had children, and raised them differently than he and his siblings had been raised. The process of healing was relatively short, and quite rapidly I "ascended" to a higher plane of existence, to places in which the physical sensations were very far away – places in which objects have no existence, but only in consciousness, in feelings that are not physical.

Conducting a life according to the script gives a soul the feeling of success, and such a life, in which conscious choice is integrated in a proper and good way, is even better. In light of these insights, with the lofty Guide at my aside, helping and directing, I could look inward, into my innermost being. I could also reflect on whether Savium had fulfilled the hope that I placed in him, whether he had learned the lesson, and whether I had learned the lesson. When we finished documenting the story of the life that had just concluded, it was our feeling that the answers to these questions were affirmative.

Then there was the answer to the most important question of all – had I cleansed myself of the trauma of Evelit's life, or were the awful experiences of that life still trapped inside me? Did my soul still have a scar that would influence my future choices and the life cycles in which I would be incarnated? I could get this answer only later, when I was in the plane of spiritual existence,[5] with and among my soul family. The lightness of my being was evidence of repair and cleansing. I had returned to my previous nature, which was a soul characterized by compassion, assistance, and healing.

The only question that remained was whether the script had been precisely executed. Now, as my prenatal memories as Savium returned to me, together with the details of his life, I couldn't help but realize the exceptional genius of the precious entities who arranged and planned it in such a wondrous way. All I had left to do was to thank my twin soul, manifesting in marvelous direction and timing in the form of the same woman with a child who stared at Savium with that look, a look that allowed him to choose differently, a look that allowed him to overcome and repair the severe trauma I experienced.

Now, as the Evelit chapter was closed and I had been cleansed of its influences, the question about evil itself arose in me.

Human life is conducted according to our plans, the souls' plans, and aside from those changes that emerge from a person's freedom of choice, life takes place in fairly tight coordination with them. In the spiritual worlds, evil does not exist, as evil cannot coexist with us; it belongs to the spectrum of human emotions that are foreign to our world, but are common and even widespread among people.

---

5 To continue the explanation from Footnote 3, the plane of "spiritual" existence is a lofty plane, upon which only the consciousness dimension exists. Energy here has no known pattern and its motion is in constant changing of its essence. Maybe "its motion is constantly changing its essence"? Objects do not exist here as things, and time and space are irrelevant. As a rule, one can meet others and merge with their pure thoughts, with their feelings and with their energy; there is no need for words or language here, and everyone knows everyone else. Thoughts, feelings, and energy in this dimension have a separate consciousness from us, yet they are part of us.

Therefore, a few questions arise; among them are what its source is, and where it comes from. It's true that the life plan often involves difficulties, but evil just for the sake of evil? Cruelty for its own sake? Killing takes place in nature, of course, and is part of the process of survival for predators, who must consume prey to survive. But killing on its own? Brutality for the sake of pleasure? Where do these even come from?

As soon as the question arose, the answer formed in my consciousness. That's just the way it is for us, but to explain it in human terms would take me more time.

The process of development and change that the soul must undergo from the beginning of its existence is undertaken in the physical world, as we have already discussed. This is thanks to the dynamic processes and activeness within it, as well as the constant transformation in human beings that allows the soul to experience, to try, to learn and to develop. The main engine behind this capacity to change is the duality that exists only in the physical world, which causes events in your world to move between the two poles of light and darkness, good and evil, and joy and despair. The "positive pole" in your world is the divine soul and spirit that reside in all elements of the physical world. But the negative pole – where does that come from?

Would it surprise you to learn that it, too, comes from the spiritual realm?

Within the depths of Creation, there is a constant, infinite bubbling that creates gigantic webs although you are not even aware of their existence. This is the engine from which the lofty entities of energy support the existence of the entire universe and all the compressed energy, the material that is in it. Angels as well – along with the other entities that allow the existence of life in all of its hues upon the Earth – emerge from there, and the same is true of those souls that reside in a human body and the entire system that supports their activity. However, it is not just them; a wide range of entities whose aim is not directly tied to the physical world, of which you are not even aware and whose essence you cannot grasp, are also created there. Everything takes places as if it emerges *ex nihilo*, like a spectacular chain of Big Bangs from those same depths of Creation.

And from that infinite bubbling something else emerges as well – what you call "darkness." Here, in the spirit world where everything is airy, loving, and enlightened, the unique essence of these energies does not exist; in the material world, in compressed energy, however, they play an important role in enabling dualism. There, in the human body, these energies enable the opposite of the divine good and sustain the extreme side of the duality. Human beings refer to them as "evil," likening them to "the forces of the netherworld," "Satan," and other words and nicknames thought up by humans in an attempt to contain this very frightening, incomprehensible thing.

"The entities of darkness" present evil along with all that it brings with it, but their presence allows the dynamism of your lives, which develops and expands the range of human experiences. I imagine that your first response would be "No favors!" However, you must understand that without evil, good does not exist, and without darkness, light has no significance.

And how is the darkness assimilated in yourselves? Darkness is multifaceted, and people identify it in many different formats. There are those who will see it as evil entities, as demons; there are those who will see it as parasites who attach themselves to people when they are weak and suck energy from them; others will see it as energy stirring in the atmosphere of a place. These differences in its perception are an outgrowth of culture and society.

There is an additional explanation. The soul, which descends and connects to the human being, brings with it good and purity, and therefore every person contains the divine spark. On the other hand, the darkness or evil that is on the Earth exists as well in every single human, by virtue of their being physical. The two of these together create an internal tension that influences the entire life plan of the soul that moves between the two sides. The more the soul develops, the greater its capacity to draw near to the pole of purity and good and to realize its plan; the more it is weakened, the more it is drawn to the side of evil, which frustrates the realization of the script.

Evelit went through two difficult experiences, one as a child and one as a teenager. These two created the severe trauma that had a deep impact on me, the soul within him, weakening my ability to resist, and that is how I found myself drawn to evil like a magnet. Only several reincarnations later could I overcome my evil, and only during Savium's lifetime did I recover.

I will take this opportunity to address my ambition at the beginning of my journey. When I had just been formed, I thought it best to start my path among humans at the nadir of belligerence and suffering. In fact, this was a pure idea based on "common sense," which dictates that from the lowest place, one can only go up. Now I understand that the many Guidances that surrounded me and vehemently opposed this proposal already knew what I could not have guessed. They understood what might develop when a soul is not strong enough, when it is inexperienced with regards to the pole of evil, when it is not aware of the deep significance of human freedom of choice. All that remained for me to do was rejoice in the position they had taken and be grateful that I had chosen to listen to their advice.

These events, from Evelit to Savium, became an incomparable lesson about humility towards the lofty entities, towards the Guidance.

The development of souls also has an aspect of the general plan, the plan of Creation; we will soon discuss this further. This plan's grand aim is to create unity, which will be accomplished when the gap between the poles is so minimized as to utterly disappear. When that happens, evil will no longer have a place or a function, and human beings will live in the perfect unity of good and love.

Parenthetically, I will add that human history has already proven this, and in the era in which you, dear readers, live, the level of evil and cruelty across the globe is immeasurably less than it was in the distant past, and even in the recent past.

CHAPTER SEVEN

Here with Us, Beyond the Veil

At times I am overwhelmed by the desire to stop for a moment and look back, to attempt to understand everything I have experienced – and this is one of those times. I am no longer a young, inexperienced soul, and in the various incarnations I have experienced throughout the millennia of my existence, I have developed and learned. Today I am no longer "just another soul," isolated and independent, existing according to its needs. My presence in the world beyond now had additional meaning, exceeding the very fact of my being.

My activity in the family of souls grew, and throughout our shared history, I was involved in the life cycles of many people - of course those in whose bodies I was incarnated, but also through advice and counsel for those in whose bodies my sibling souls were realized. The cumulative learning, experience, and knowledge allowed me to work with other souls and not just with new souls that joined my family from time to time, but also souls from outside the framework closest to me. It became clear that I was dealing with this more and more. I was often invited to be present as they struggled during their time of preparation for a new life, or to help them analyze the tale of an incarnation that had just concluded. This development had an additional significance, which was expressed in the changing nature of my connection to the Guide who accompanied me; now we were friends, more than trainer and trainee - although you must forgive me for using a term as human as "friends."

If I were describing my development in "our" language, I would say that my being as a soul grew to contain much more love. Pure love, nothing else, and nothing beyond it, because love is the only thing that does not have duality or separation. I understand that human beings may have difficulty understanding the connections between love and the ability to support, to comprehend, and to give advice or plan life paths, but this is yet another distinction between being in the spiritual world and being in the physical world.

I had reached a certain peak in my development during the life of Savium. To his ability to overcome, in the moment of truth, the norm for his lifetime, there was a significance that went beyond his life as a human being and even beyond healing my soul wound. His capacity to "think outside the box" and to diverge, at a dramatic point, from the standard response of people in his society, adopting an approach that embraced kindness and compassion, presented a very high level of development; by doing so, he abandoned his future in order to save the lives of people he didn't know, acting in a manner totally foreign to his troops and to the military as a whole. It appears that here, as well, they saw it as such, since once I had completed the processes of cleansing and acclimating after his death, my Guide quickly turned to me and told me – in celebration – that this was "it," that I had completed an important stage of my becoming, and he was no longer able to serve as my Guide. I had to move on to a more experienced Guide.

Were we human beings, we would have fallen into each other's arms, saying, "Thank you," or "I'll never forget you," or other sweet, sentimental words that you won't find here. Truth be told, we don't even have a hierarchy of trainer and trainee or senior and junior as you do. In fact, using the term "Guide," for example, as I do constantly, is only meant to be understood by way of illustration, in order to make it easier to explain.

When I say this, the thought arises that perhaps the time has come to explain to you how things appear – practically. It's a nice thought, but carrying it out is complicated. Nevertheless, I'll try my best.

Imagine that in some magical way a person manages to observe souls and wants to distinguish between them – for example, between a young soul and an older one, between an inexperienced being and a soul with a great accumulation of knowledge, between a "beginner" and a more developed soul. Presumably, one would look for signs, for something visual. If souls were to be distinguished by their coloring, for example, this would make things easier, right?

Indeed, many people who have experienced "astral travels" to our domain during meditation see souls as entities that differ in their coloration. For example, a new soul appears white; as it develops and acquires knowledge and experience, it becomes cream-colored; it then becomes yellow, indicating a moderate level of experience; then light blue, dark blue, and violet. The highest souls, the ones that humans refer to as "avatars" - although I would assume that most people never come in contact with such a soul - appear in a mixture of dark purple and dark blue, encircled by light. I have heard it said that avatars appear at first like a shining white light, and only afterwards their colors are discernible.

A human observer looking at me would notice that for a long time I had been yellow. Now, the first signs of bright blue were visible. Were we to continue with this visualization, then my new Guide would be bluer, and you might even see the beginning of some purple spots on him. However, don't forget that these colors are only the product of the brain of the human observer, and they don't exist in our reality.

Now let us take away from the observer this magic, and let us leave the observer to see our world as it really is. The first thing such a person will discern is absence- the absence of all known features among the surroundings.

The first sensation of absence is "There is no light." Dark, but not the darkness that is sometimes accompanied by fright. Light is one of the forms of energy that emerges from the sun, along with heat; these two forms allow your existence. For us, everything is different. We are, after all, not material, so we have no need for the sun as a source of energy. When we talk about light, we think about something internal, related to consciousness – not the light you measure in units of intensity or wavelength. We have no body, and we have no eyes. The absence of physical light means nothing to us.

Now, once the observer gets use to the lack of "light" in the human sense, he or she will notice the utter silence. And why should there be any noise or sound? Oscillations and vibrations in your physical environment generate the movement of soundwaves through the air. The air doesn't distinguish between different waves; from its perspective, a door's creak is the same as words of affection between lovers, and a cricket's chirp is exactly the same as the birdsong. Only when these soundwaves enter and cause the eardrum to vibrate in a similar way, so that the sounds can be converted into a message that the brain understands, do these soundwaves mean anything. It is only the human consciousness that knows how to receive the information from the vibration of soundwaves.

However, we don't have air, and we don't have ears. We transmit messages in a much more straightforward manner, known as telepathy. Thus, from the outside, there appears to be nothing but silence.

Now for the additional part, which is difficult to understand. I would like to address the words "Here with us." Where is "with us"? I won't even try to begin to explain. I will only say that this is a matter of different dimensions, that "with us" is not about the place, as we don't have measurements of length and width, and we don't have above or below, so material location has no meaning. So where are we? We are just here... nowhere and everywhere.

However, what is more important than anything else is that this fortunate human observer, who came to see and hear but found nothing, won't feel alone or feel like a stranger. Instead, the observer will feel the might that exists here (you call it "energies," so let's stick with that term). This feeling will not be necessarily felt by the five senses, as our energy is converted inat the human being's brain into consciousness, and every one of you feels this differently. Some of you will feel a chill, others will feel like someone is touching them and may even be frightened by it; there are also those who will imagine that they hear delicate, soothing, enjoyable tunes, while others will hear it as immeasurably joyful music. Still, some will be flooded by colorful lights, while others will receive only the understanding that they are not alone. In practice, it doesn't make a difference how a person feels in our presence, but most people feel elevated, as a wave of infinite unconditional love washes over them, accompanied by great joy.

Even the communication among us is different than what you are familiar with. When I say, "I was invited to consult," I simply know this. There is no courier service, there is no email, there are no messages conveyed by the internet, and there are no applets as there are in the physical world. *I simply know.* When I want to get there,

I don't call a taxi; I just "move on," and it happens immediately. Try and consider this as pictures. You're in a room, then suddenly, by your invitation, the picture changes and you're in a different place. Our world is so different from yours, and your language has no words to express it, or even to approximate it.

I already can hear what you're asking. "If this is all correct, what about the entities that some of us see? Who are the angels who appear before our eyes when they're closed?" Ah, the answer is very simple, and it may even be disappointing.

Everything you and others see is the product of your imagination, and I'm not saying this mockingly. In fact, your imagination is a very powerful tool; it is the platform by which we can transmit information to you. The figures you see? Everyone will see them a bit differently. And why? Because they are the product of each and every person's individual culture, understanding, and education. We don't have wings; after all, how could we use them when there is no air? You can't even make a breeze with them... So I will say it again, the figures of angels with wings, the lofty entities, glorious and splendid – all of the living things apparently present here - these are all the products of your imagination, your method for interpreting what happens here. Please forgive me if I have ruined a bit of your sense of the reality beyond.

However, I urge you to continue to see us as you are accustomed to, if only because we actually have a figure, but the form of our bodies is based on "materials" with which you are unfamiliar, the existence of which you are unaware – thus, this form differs from anything you recognize. The forms created in your imagination are good for demonstrating the variance, the uniqueness, and the vastness of this place in human terms. Just remember that it is far bigger, more magnificent, and more amazing than any superlative and anything else you may imagine.

And now, after speaking a bit about how things appear here, let us return to my tale...

So I met the new Guide, and indeed, he immediately impressed me as authoritative, high and exalted, a spirit of the type that serve as Guides for the Guides. But wait a minute! I am not a Guide! Then perhaps...? Do they really see that as my destiny, I asked, and the answer arrived immediately, "Yes, and let's talk about it."

The decision about this, it became clear to me, had been arrived at even before I was incarnated in Evelit's body. I remember that in the process of the preceding incarnations, as my character as a caregiver began to take root within me, I had the feeling that I was missing something, a different type of life. I already told you about this, and I said that I was very surprised when it was suggested to me that I accept the role of a military man. Now I finally learned the reasoning behind it. In order for me to function as a Guide, as they already saw at that point, I would have to experience life cycles different from my central character as a caregiver. In practice, I had to experience an extreme, opposing lifestyle, so that if I needed this information as a Guide, it would be available to me from personal experience, not second-hand. The process I went through in the framework of Evelit's body and the repair I affected in subsequent life cycles, prepared me very well for the role.

"Now," the new Guide said to me, "you must plan and realize life cycles in which a number of motifs will be relevant. You must experience different perspectives of spousal relationships; you must experience a person who leads, who advises and directs others, to be a person who is not afraid to be a trailblazer. Brashita," he reminded me, "did this, but she relied on personal characteristics that were unusual for her era and were part of the plan of Creation. Now you must do this with people who live their lives like everyone else."

My friends in the soul family were very happy for me and eager to help. Now I am once again resorting to anthropomorphization of the spiritual world using words from the physical world, but there is no other way. When I speak of their happiness, you understand that they did not offer a toast; and when I say they helped me, I don't mean that they held lengthy board meetings or used their pull to benefit me… In any case, in light of the direction I received from the Guide, they devised a plan that I realized – namely, a course spread over more than 500 Earth-years since Savium's death, in which I'd reincarnated seven times in order to complete the development process to become a Guide, even though the plan was for only four. I learned once again that not every reincarnation follows the script precisely; sometimes, as when life presents challenges and there are crises not connected to the general plan, one must return to parts of the script in additional reincarnations, and this is what happened to me throughout this epoch.

During this period, I experienced various types of spousal rela-tionships, sometimes as a man, and sometimes as a woman. There was love, there was indifference, there were kids, and there were also episodes of loss of life. I experienced moments of violence, but also periods of gentleness. I won't describe the entirety of this course, but I will say that every life cycle was somewhat influenced by one of the life cycles preceding it, even though I didn't know that while I was still in a body.

I always realized these reincarnations in the same region, the east-ern coast of the Mediterranean Sea, and witnessed the political and demographic changes that occurred in it, e.g., the power dynamics among the superpowers, such as those from Egypt in the west to the Hittite Empire in the east. I saw the Israelite tribes enter the area and settle in their land; I also saw the small and great covenants among cities and states that coalesced and then disintegrated in the fascinating process of the rise and fall of local and regional powers.

In the last life cycle of this course, I wanted to continue Brashita's path and live as a trailblazing woman with the innermost strength to overcome social conventions and act according to an innovative and different pattern of thinking. Savium's success encouraged me to "take a risk," and already at the beginning of the period I raised this with my Guide; he accepted this with great esteem. After consulting the group of entities that deals with the planning of scripts, he told me that we would experience this life cycle together. My Guide explained to me that he would be born as a woman, and when the time was right, I would be reincarnated and live as her daughter. This woman, by her conduct, and through the script of her life, would create the foundation upon which I could concretize my goals; during that time, and even more so afterwards, I would learn about the cooperation of a soul and its Guide.

The main topic of this reincarnation was to be that of a woman standing up for her right to live life her own way in an era in which this right was reserved exclusively for males – husbands, fathers, brothers. Therefore, and as preparation for this reincarnation, I experienced the last two life cycles as a woman suffering from the aggressive nature of a man who enjoyed the pain of others. I would plant these difficult memories in the subconscious of the fetus before birth, with the hope that the woman who would be born would develop distrust and antipathy towards men, and therefore she would need to search out an independent path.

Thus it happened that my Guide was born as a woman, who grew up to give birth to me. It was an interesting experiment, and I present to you the tale of these two women: Achsah, the mother, and Tirzah, the daughter.

CHAPTER EIGHT

The Caravanserai

Tirzah was eight years old when the king died in Jerusalem. Years later she would say, "I remember those days as if it were yesterday. The villagers, the whole tribe - some say the eleven other tribes as well - they all adored him. It was a sad occasion, and for the nation, we might say it was concerning as well. Mother was very worried, telling me that the throne was beckoning to two of the princes, even though the late king had already designated one of them as his heir apparent, even anointing him for the crown. Mother, like many across the kingdom, was concerned that the king's death would lead to a civil war. After all, the late king had not inherited the throne himself, but rather seized it after the death of his predecessor. Now they were worried that all the quiet and the good in our lives were about to vanish. Mother always said that a war that reaches home's threshold remains stored in the people's memory, even if it happened long before they were born.

"I was a little girl, so I didn't understand all of these discussions. As a matter of fact, they didn't interest me at all. I didn't love the late king; deep inside, I hated him, even vengefully rejoicing a bit at his death. My personal revenge. Perhaps he was admired and adored, perhaps he brought us honor and economic success, perhaps in his last years he even brought peace and tranquility - but he is the reason my father is dead.

"They all talked about the great honor of my father's death, doing his duty for king and country. From my perspective, however, it left us a fatherless home, and - worse than that - strangers came to fill his place, men I did not like. My mother had to support us, and found more than a few men who were willing to help. I understood that she had no choice; I knew that the men, even the strongest among them, needed a woman by their side, and they were ready to do a lot for her sake. However, all I wanted was Father at home. I never even got to meet him. He was killed when the king sent him to battle, and Mother was still pregnant with me.

"Ultimately, the civil war everyone feared did not break out, and our current king, Solomon, assumed the throne within a few days. He was the one King David had designated and anointed, and he quickly put to death those who had challenged him, including his brother. But I love him. He is the reason my husband is dead."

Achsah

Achsah was young, attractive, and intelligent, the daughter of one of the most distinguished families in the village; she was married to Othniel son of Baanah, a handsome, skilled man with a finger in every pie, who built their house on the outskirts of the village adjoining the king's highway, leading to Jerusalem the capital.

He established a small roadside inn, and the family lived happily, well-off due to the guests and the orchard planted behind the house. Othniel was known in the village and in the surrounding area, and it was said about him that he had no equal in kindness and courage. It would take until five years after they married, after many attempts, that their first son was born, and a year and a half later, Achsah would become pregnant for a second time.

In retrospect, it turned out that his reputation for decency and courage caused him a great deal of trouble. A group of soldiers who belonged to the units known as "David's warriors" stopped for a rest at Othniel's inn. The soldiers liked him, and it wasn't long before a courier arrived, summoning him to report to the army commander, Joab son of Zeruiah, David's own nephew.

Joab offered him a position in one of the elite units, even promising him proper recompense. The last thing Othniel wanted was to be involved with combat or the military, but Joab was not a man to be easily turned down. Othniel wanted at least to limit his tour of duty, and Joab agreed to this. The two men parted with a handshake, and Othniel was assigned to a unit whose main duties were supervision, assisting in tax collection, and quelling the small pockets of resistance that developed from time to time, mainly in cities with a concentration of Philistines. Othniel, who always did his best, distinguished himself in this role as well, and his name became known far and wide, reaching the upper echelon – even King David's table.

Othniel's years of service were a serious challenge to the young couple. With him away from the inn, a shadow was cast over the business's future, so the onus of keeping it going landed squarely on Achsah. In fact, Othniel's brother came to help, and Othniel himself was often able to return home, as he was frequently stationed close to the village. Even so, this was merely offering assistance; the burden was mainly upon Achsah. She did it with love, and she carried out the task magnificently. When her son was born, her mother and Othniel's mother helped her with the work. They suggested she hire a wet nurse, a proposal Achsah thanked them for but declined, as she wanted to suckle her son herself.

Finally, Othniel's three-year tour of duty was coming to an end, and Achsah, now pregnant for a second time, was eagerly anticipating his return. However, life had other plans, as it turned out that before his demobilization date, Othniel was surprised to have his name raised in internal political debates, as the "war of the generals" between King David and his army commander reached a tense climax. The king made certain demands of Joab son of Zeruiah - one of which, bizarrely, was reneging on the agreement with Othniel.

Joab understood the trap in this demand. He knew, just as the king knew it, that this interference had been beyond his authority – and improper. Acceding to the demand would undermine his reputation as a commander, and his word would no longer be his bond. On the other hand, he couldn't refuse to obey a royal command. After giving the subject much thought, Joab arrived at a solution that conformed to his character and conduct, whereby he decided to bring about Othniel's death in battle - much as he had done to Uriah the Hittite - before his demobilization date.

And so one night, shortly before Othniel's discharge, a runner came to the unit's barracks to report on a revolt that had erupted suddenly in the Philistine city of Ekron. The messenger brought a direct order from Joab son of Zeruiah, to send by midnight a smaller unit, under Othniel, to survey and evaluate the situation. Tragically, the soldiers of the unit fell into an ambush and were all killed.

The incident reverberated through the ranks. Strange ideas and theories were floated, including whether their supreme commander could have been behind this inexplicable rebellion, which had petered out as suddenly as it had arisen. Nevertheless, they were quite wary about enraging the officers, and this narrative would remain concealed in their tents, in their private conversations. Still, these thoughts did find their way to one other place – to the home of the very pregnant Achsah.

Now everything had changed. She was two months away from giving birth, and the future was not clear. She was furious to hear about Othniel's meaningless death, filled with an anger she had no outlet for. Her father understood that there was no reason to turn her wrath on such high-ranking individuals, and the risk of such a move far outweighed any potential benefit. He tried to console her, to help her as much as possible, but Achsah did not find his logic compelling. She took out her bitterness on the soldiers who arrived at the inn, whether alone or in groups, telling them loudly and angrily about the suspicions conveyed by her fallen husband's comrades. Her father's attempts to calm her down failed, and his requests to stop spreading the story fell on deaf ears.

In the meanwhile, her beautiful, smiling, good-natured daughter was born..She named her Tirzah, after the youngest daughter of Zelophehad who, together with her sisters, managed to convince Moses, master of all prophets, to promulgate a new Torah law that would let them inherit their father's portion even though they were women. Achsah hoped that baby Tirzah would take after her father; like her namesake, she would be a trailblazer, Achsah hoped. This was her hope, but she had no idea what awaited her. Trailblazer? Indeed! But hold your horses – or at least, don't put the cart before them.

Achsah and her family decided to continue managing the place. Officially, they all understood, an authoritative male figure was needed to run the business, and it was natural for Othniel's brother to take on this responsibility, but practically, it was Achsah who took charge - and quite successfully. The years with Othniel, as well as the years when he was in the army, had well prepared her for this role, and she managed the place aggressively.

Time passed. Achsah was busy most of the time, but she didn't stop missing her beloved husband. She continued to tell, at every opportunity, what she called "The Tale of Betrayal by the King and Joab;" frowning, she rejected her father's pleadings to lower the flames of her passion, to swallow her pain lest it swallow them all. Indeed, as her father had worried, late one night a few months after Tirzah's birth, when they were all in bed and the inn was silent and locked, loud knocking was heard at the gate.

One of the workers opened the door, and three men stood there. "Get Achsah out here at once!" they ordered, and the voice left no doubt as to the implicit degree of threat. Achsah put on warm clothing and came to the door. "Are you Achsah?" they asked.

"Yes, that's me; but pardon me, honored guests, this establishment is closed for the evening. The kitchen is dark, and all our rooms are occupied. So how may I help you?" A soft rustling could be heard behind them, and a tall, well-built man with a harsh, penetrating gaze made his way towards the front of the group.

"All I want is to speak with you," he said. "May I come in?" His height, authoritative voice and penetrating gaze gave her the oddest sensation - neither fear nor danger, but curiosity. He had a *je ne sais quoi* she could not ignore.

"Of course, my lord, come in. Will your companions join you as well?"

"No, they will stay outside to guard it."

"To guard it?" Her eyebrows shot up as "Guard from what?" was what she wondered to herself.

She invited him in and offered him a chair and a drink. "I won't beat around the bush, ma'am. You probably know my name, but from what I've heard, not in a positive way." He stared at her, and even before he opened his mouth again, she knew who he was. "My name is Joab, Joab son of Zeruiah."

What happened next took nothing more than a few seconds. She was overwhelmed by a sense of urgency, that she had a once-in-a-lifetime opportunity; she instinctively stretched out her hand to the heavy bowl on the table next to her. He did not move, fixing his gaze on her, and she felt that his eyes were boring into her and he could see her thoughts, as if he said, "Let it go, girl; do not let evil touch you, and don't pollute your hands with blood." She slid her hand to her side, her head hung low and she said quietly, "Please have a seat here, and I'll bring you a hot drink to warm you up from the cold of the journey."

Achsah fled from the entrance hall to the kitchen, and only there could she let her tears fall. "Be strong," she whispered to herself. "Be strong for your two children; be strong for the memory of Othniel, your love." She breathed deeply, put leaves in the cup, poured hot water over it and turned to go back to the entrance hall. Out of the corner of her eye, she saw her father approaching. She motioned to him to stay quiet, and she whispered a request that he conceal himself and listen to what was happening.

"I knew Othniel," Joab began. "He was one of the finest men I have ever known, and I've known many. He was a hero, and I am pained by his death, which proved what he was made of. Even when he was wounded, he continued to fight bravely, providing cover for his comrades. Unfortunately, there were too many Philistines, and he couldn't defeat them all.

"The day I first met him, I gave him my word, as you undoubtedly know. I promised him that at the end of his tour of duty, he could return home and conduct his life as he saw fit. But he fell in battle just a month short of his last day, and I was left with my promise, the vow I had made to him, which I could no longer fulfill.

"I came here tonight in order to compensate his family, so that the wife he loved so much and the children born to preserve and elevate his name may subsist in dignity and without worry. I don't know if this counteracts my vow, but this is the least I can do. I hereby swear to you now that this house will always be protected as long as I hold this position, and all the convoys of soldiers and supplies will stop here to rest and relax, to eat and drink, before they continue on their way. This is the small gesture I can offer to honor one of my best soldiers, Othniel."

Achsah, who in the meantime had calmed down and regained her composure, knew that she would be asked to give something in return, and she couldn't help but wonder how many other families had the "good fortune" to receive such a benefit under similar circumstances. She didn't believe one word of his nice speech, but she realized that the man would not have shown up personally unless something very important motivated him to do so. She also knew that he had the power to fulfill such a promise.

"My lord, I am humbled by your kindness towards the children of my beloved Othniel and to me. Were the matter in my hands alone, I would absolve you of the vow you made to my husband, so that our future might be secure. But I cannot do that unless you let me give you something in return. What do you desire, my lord? What do I need to do so that this vow will no longer be on your shoulders, the shoulders that bear the burden of providing security for our people and for our king?"

Joab looked at her, and he could not help appreciating the woman's intelligence and determination. He knew that she understood the truth; like him, she was playing the game of negotiation.

"I do not desire anything," he assured her. "Moreover, I seek nothing in return; more than that, I would even be pleased if this very visit is kept private. However, since you raise the issue, I will ask for one thing, which I am sure you will be able to do without much trouble, which I did not even come here to ask for. All I ask is that you address the fiction which is being spread that I had some role in your husband's death. There are those who whisper in my ear that the source of this rumor is right here. I simply ask, ma'am, that this myth be denied and that it disappear."

"My lord," she replied, "you know that there is only one thing that occupies my family and me, and that is our survival. Why would we spread gossip? And if I have no way of knowing the what, the who, and the how, what denial could I possibly offer? If they ask us on what basis I deny this, what can I say? Of course, I cannot say that my lord came to visit me in the middle of the night and told me all of this."

"You speak truly, my dear lady, and I would never question your high morals. Nevertheless, there are those who say that this rumor originated here, and I will therefore ask you to see to it that this malicious slander, if it indeed comes from here, be utterly erased."

"I can do that, my lord. It would be a great joy and honor for my lord to be present when we name this place after my fallen husband. We will even add that it happened while serving under the great warrior, Joab son of Zeruiah."

Thus, they reached an agreement. Joab vanished. Just as he arrived quietly, he departed; aside from her father, no one knew about the visit. Joab fulfilled his pledge, just as Achsah did. The story of the intrigue between the king and Joab that brought about the death of Othniel was replaced with the myth of his heroism, even though within the family, he remained the central reason for anger and for hatred of the regime and its symbols. The family maintained itself and its caravanserai, which grew and flourished.

Achsah acted as if she had overcome the loss, but this was only on the surface; in reality, she had lost interest in everything other than her work. Her appearance and unique comportment were renowned among the men who came to the inn, and many pursued her romantically. However, she, bucking conventions, rejected her father's suggestion that she remarry. The caravanserai was Othniel's House, a memorial to him, and she couldn't bring in another man. Achsah was fortunate that her father and brother-in-law, knowing her unique abilities, were able to accept this deviation from the norm, and even if for a fleeting moment they had a stray thought about finding an innkeeper as skilled as she, Joab's nighttime visit had cemented her status in their eyes. Her father, who of course had been eavesdropping on that fateful night, was convinced that Joab would make her fall to her knees to beg for her life; a mere hint from him about the available options for putting an end to this embarrassing episode would bring any man, all the more so a woman, to collapse. Despite this, Achsah had proudly stood before him and held her own in their conversation, making her a powerful figure in their eyes, and so they acceded to her unvoiced request.

However, time and body have their own plans. Slowly, as the years passed, Achsah yearned for a man's touch. Some of her guests had projected vital masculinity, while others had been witty and engaging conversationalists; both types contributed to a growing, burgeoning thirst. Many attempted to flirt, and Achsah discerned over time that this platonic intimacy bothered her less and less; she was quite surprised to discover that the touch of a hand or a friendly pat was quite pleasurable for her. Eventually, she did not object to such contact, and she started to await the man who would allow her to express the sexual needs that arose within her. The first time it happened, she enjoyed it quite a bit; nevertheless, she was glad that it was a man she was not familiar with, one who disappeared at daybreak.

Still, Achsah stuck to her decision not to remarry; nevertheless, a widow has needs, and so she could not remain celibate forever and saw no reason to avoid physical intimacy with the men who came to the inn. Othniel's House had a good reputation and brought in many young men, so she could have her pick of the guests.

The years passed. When Tirzah was eight years old, King David died, and his son by Bathsheba, Solomon, ascended to the throne. On his deathbed, old King David gave his last will and testament, which included instructions to his son. First and foremost was for Solomon to build a temple in Jerusalem; the second... was to take care of some troublesome figures, including Joab son of Zeruiah.

Solomon didn't hesitate to eliminate his cousin, the army commander, taking advantage of the very first opportunity. He did, however, struggle with what to do about his older brother Adonijah, who had threatened to seize the throne even before Solomon's coronation; however, when Adonijah sought to marry Abishag the Shunamite, the beautiful young woman who had lain in King David's bosom in his old age, Solomon saw this as a challenge to his authority. He had him executed in a humiliating and controversial way, as the fugitive Adonijah had grabbed hold of the horns of the altar in order to be granted refuge. Beyond fortifying his political status, Solomon also introduced innovations in the administrative and economic structure of the kingdom, rejuvenating the leadership, clearing obstacles, developing trade, and raising the standard of living – all of which led to a flourishing economy as well as a sense of security among his subjects.

Othniel's House also felt the impact of these changes. The increase in trade meant that more caravans headed to Jerusalem, leading to more travelers and more guests at the inn. However, since Joab's protection had been removed with his death, there was also a sharp and distressing increase in violent incidents, both in degree and in number. The inn thus became a less popular destination.

At the same time, Achsah's beloved father was showing his age, and his involvement in the management of the business declined. This meant that a permanent, official male presence became a pressing need, and Achsah felt that the time had come for a change. Relationships that had once seemed taboo now seemed to offer a solution to the situation, and the idea of perpetual widowhood was replaced with the possibility of embracing the institutions of her society once more. The thought of sharing her life with another man was bubbling and rising within her; finally, as King Solomon marked his fourth anniversary on the throne and her daughter Tirzah turned twelve, her father announced Achsah's betrothal to Elhanan the Ahohite, a man of Netophah, in the territory of the tribe of Benjamin.

Elhanan was a well-to-do man who had been pursuing her for quite a while. Now, after the death of his first wife, left with his two concubines, he turned his attention to Achsah, using the full force of his charms. He was impressed by the way she managed the business aggressively, yet maintained her inherent cheerfulness; he also liked the idea of adding Othniel's House to his assets, via the great dowry that would be required. Thus, he proposed to Achsah, even agreeing to most of the conditions she laid out – among them, that she would continue to live in the caravanserai; that she would not be a concubine, but a primary wife; and that after her death, her son and her daughter would be entitled to inherit the business. Achsah knew these conditions might endanger the betrothal announcement, but her father supported her. He well remembered her encounter with Joab. If Achsah, who had learned to measure her steps prudently, who was as sophisticated as she was opinionated, saw this position as a calculated risk, she must surely know what she was doing. And that was indeed how it happened.

Tirzah

Tirzah was born in a small village in 978 BCE, in a household that was lively and wealthy, but socially isolated. The fact that Othniel's House was managed by a woman didn't prevent it from being a success; however, Achsah's prominent independence upset the local villagers, who shunned her and her family. Thus, Tirzah grew up surrounded by family as well as by slaves, both men and women. She was exposed to the guests, different kinds of people from different cultures, but she had virtually no friends. She loved the inn and the excitement behind the scenes, such as the noisy kitchen, the courtyard, and the stables. She loved spending time with the donkeys, horses, and camels. These elements helped make her childhood a happy one.

From time to time, she would invite girls from the area, and when their parents were not supervising them, they would dare to join her and experience the boisterousness of the caravanserai. On these few occasions, she learned that the other girls lived different lives. They grew up in houses blessed with many children, each together with her mother and additional women, with siblings and half-siblings; one father, the master of the household, would support the entire family. This made her feel different, and there was a twinge of jealousy in her heart.

There was also another feeling: the dark shadow cast by the abusive treatment her mother endured at the hands of men.

The first time she noticed this, she was five years old, and she saw Achsah making love to one of the men, and Tirzah interpreted the loud groans and energetic thrusts as violence. She ran to help her mother, but Achsah saw her and waved her away. Tirzah thought that her mother wanted to protect her from the evil man.

The little girl burst into tears, then ran to one of the slavewomen in the kitchen. The thickset woman always hugged her, and Tirzah told her in a strangled voice what she had seen. The woman caressed her head, doing everything in her power to calm the weeping girl, but she couldn't hide from her the giggles of the other women. Tirzah would encounter Achsah in similar positions again and again, until the latter noticed it and began to send her to her bed whenever she was with a man. However, this exposure, which would recur throughout the next few years, didn't do any good for the girl. She grew up with the repressed knowledge, somewhere in the recesses of her mind that men were abusing her mother. Even when she matured and discovered that this was sex, she was still persuaded that evil was harming her mother.

Achsah's conduct with a number of the male guests of the inn found its way outside the house, which only fed into the consensus among the villagers about the caravanserai and the family living in it. It came back to Tirzah through the daughters of their neighbors; for her part, she was convinced that their parents were mistaken, that the truth had to be diametrically opposed to this view. More than once she would argue with the girls who accused Achsah of being a prostitute who brought dishonor on the place, instead of blaming the situation on male aggression.

The era in which she lived, and the country in which she dwelled, were ruled by conservatism. The people believed in the Torah of Moses, and everything that could be defined as fornication was a sin. However, the girl could not conceive of a distinction between fornication and necessity, between force and consent by choice. She was convinced that her mother was being forced into these sex acts because she could not conceive of Achsah choosing to do so of her own free will.

In addition to the "abuse" of her mother from time to time, there were also violent events in which soldiers and other guests were in-volved; in the young girl's mind, they all came together to form a general picture of the male sex in general, and soldiers in particular. At age seven, she was first exposed to the tale of the king from Jeru-salem who sent her soldier-father to his death, and her anger towards men took a prominent place in her life story. It was not merely that she was left an orphan because of them, not just that they got drunk and were violent towards each other – they also took advantage of the situation to abuse her mother. This was no reason to love or honor them, she thought to herself.

And what of Achsah? She was too busy to notice what her daugh-ter was experiencing. All she could see was her daughter's beauty, her joy, and her impressive intellectual development. She looked at her, pleased, thinking of the name Tirzah, which she had chosen. This is a girl who knows what she wants and desires and has the mental strength to reach it.

Now Tirzah was twelve years old. The young girl was growing up; her body had begun to change. Her budding breasts had begun to emerge beneath her dress, and before her family she was becoming a beautiful young woman. Her grandfather was gratified to hear from Achsah that as a gift for her betrothal, Tirzah had given her the joy of her first period. Indeed, he thought, the time had come to think about his granddaughter's betrothal as well. Achsah had just become betrothed, which meant that her nuptials would take place in a year's time; she should be given the option of dedicating herself to her husband and establishing her household without having to worry about taking care of her daughter. Tirzah had reached puberty; who knows, her grandfather smile to himself, I may get a grandchild and a great-grandchild on the same day! Thus, he began his search for an appropriate mate.

He told his family about his decision over dinner as the Sabbath began, and they all shouted for joy. However, he soon found what was already clear and obvious to all the residents of the area – that it would be difficult to find suitors for the daughter of Achsah, with her reputation as an independent and licentious woman, which had spread far and wide. A daughter raised in such a home was no hot commodity in the marriage market; neither her personal beauty nor her wealthy, privileged family background could help. Days and weeks passed after the grandfather's announcement, and no husband was on the horizon.

Tirzah saw the girls from the surrounding area getting betrothed, one after another; she was astounded that there were no suitors jumping at the chance, but it didn't truly bother her. In her innermost heart, she was actually glad about it. Her misandry became her lifestyle; the more distant the eventual wedding day with some man remained, the better.

In his search for a husband for Tirzah, the grandfather had to look for a compromise. In the end, it took half a year, but he found someone. The man in question was married, about thirty years old. A simple man, not particularly intelligent, the grandfather would not have positioned him among the first rank of candidates; indeed, he should perhaps not have been a candidate at all, but he was who was available – and at least he owned property.

When the betrothal was announced, the light in Tirzah's eyes went out. Achsah saw this, but there was nothing she could do. Her father allowed her to make decisions, but when it came to his granddaughter, he insisted that in the absence of a father, he was the one who had to see to her affairs.

The wedding day was celebrated with a tremendous banquet at Othniel's House, and it continued for seven days with the participation of many guests, including many wealthy people, customers, residents of the area, and, of course, family members. The groom arrived splendidly arrayed, escorted by a great entourage of those closest to him, and their rejoicing reached the heavens. Tirzah, who had just turned thirteen, was surrounded by female companions, but they did not manage to relieve the tension she found herself preoccupied with.

Achsah, who was dealing with all the guests, was sure that the handmaid Tirzah so loved would support her and watch over her. Naturally, she wasn't aware of Tirzah's misandry, so she wasn't aware of the deep depression that grew and grew as her mother taught her about sex and her wifely duties.

On the night of that first day, when she saw her betrothed, Tirzah's heart fell and despair overcame her. He was old and ugly, coarse and loud, and the terrified Tirzah ran out of the house, stifling her tears, and hid. The crowd clapped their hands at this display; they thought she was merely a modest, bashful young woman, and they sympathized with her.

Only the handmaid, who knew what was in the girl's heart, ran after her and found her in the stable, sitting and crying next to her favorite horse. She didn't say a word, just embraced Tirzah and sang her a song that she loved from her earliest childhood.

Soon enough, after Tirzah had calmed down a bit, she took her hand and told her, "Dear Tirzah, your old life is over. You are facing difficult days, during which you will be compelled to do things you won't like and are not accustomed to. But remember that your name is Tirzah, like the daughter of Zelophehad who never gave up, who stood up for herself and taught everyone that anything is possible."

The handmaid stopped for a moment, took a deep breath and then continued. "I am to be your wedding gift, to accompany you, to serve you in your new home. Your mother didn't say anything; she wanted to keep this a surprise until you were on your way, but I feel a need to say this to you right now - and to tell you how happy I am about it."

The handmaid raised the girl's head and looked into her sparkling eyes. "I know, even if it is not clear to me how, that this is not the final act. Your life story will take many turns in the future. So, beautiful girl, hold your head high, put a smile on your face, go back home, and welcome your husband!"

Tirzah would never forget the first night, with her husband as stinking drunk as Lot. The girl grew into a woman, as if a magic wand had been waved over her. Calmly, she welcomed him and offered him a seat next to her. Then she did as her mother had taught her - she stripped him slowly, driving him mad. With the motions of someone learning "on the job," she laid him down, nude, and then forced herself to strip silently and slowly, even though touching his body disgusted her, and his erect member scared her. Her husband looked at her, suspecting for a moment that he had been tricked, that she was not a virgin; only after her scream of pain and the sight of his blood-stained member did he relax and rejoice with his bride.

The next morning, when she knocked on the door and brought them breakfast, the handmaid looked at them and understood. She saw his satisfied look and the disgust reflected in Tirzah' eyes, knowing that the girl had been victorious.

A month passed. Tirzah adapted to her new home. In addition to her, her husband had three veteran wives; two of them were older, while the youngest, Ahinoam, had joined the family just a year and a half before Tirzah and was fifteen years old.

It took Tirzah a few days to realize that the women did not share the same status. The oldest was the "house mother," a woman with a son and two daughters who was deeply respected by everyone, even her husband. The second was a bit younger, although she looked older than the senior wife, almost elderly; she had three daughters, which detracted from her status and the respect she was entitled to. Young Ahinoam, meanwhile, had arrived there to rectify the situation by bearing male children to her husband, but her status was quite lowly. She was assigned the most menial duties in the house, like one of the slavewomen. Tirzah did not understand this; was this to be her fate as well?

But her fears proved to be unfounded. Her husband, she learned, was a famed stonemason in Jerusalem who directed unique construction projects and hired others to help him. He desperately wanted a son, an heir whom he could train and who could ultimately take his place. However, his firstborn did not fit the bill, as he was a spoiled, frail boy. His second wife had only borne daughters. His third, Ahinoam, who was attractive and congenial, was supposed to fill the gap, but unfortunately she turned out to be infertile. Now he had married Tirzah to provide him with his anticipated heir.

Ahinoam and Tirzah, who were quite close in age, found true friendship. Tirzah found Ahinoam to be joyful, to have a sense of humor and be quite sensitive to her surroundings, and it was Ahinoam who revealed that her infertility was why she was treated in such a humiliating manner. Tirzah felt Ahinoam's fear of rejection, that she might be sent back to her parents' home in shame to waste away, alone, for the rest of her days.

Ahinoam thanked the Creator that Tirzah had been sent to her to put an end to her loneliness. Tirzah might be young, but Ahinoam found her to be mature and capable of great insight, a sort of guide or teacher sent to her. To her surprise, she found that she could be happy even when the two older women did everything in their power to demean her. When they sent her to the kitchen, she sang; when she went out to the courtyard, to the storeroom, to the corral or to the coop, she danced. The two girls learned to lean on each other, sharing their most heartfelt emotions, as all of their thoughts and fears could finally be expressed aloud.

Ahinoam shared with Tirzah her concerns about returning to her parents' home and about the older wives; she shared her pain and distress. The closer they got, the more she shared with her, even how great her distaste was for their husband. Ahinoam believed with all her heart that if only she had harbored some affection towards him, she would have become pregnant. "There is no barrenness in my family," she told Tirzah. "My mother's sisters have all had many children, and my older sister has children too. How could it be that only I am barren? I hate him so! I hate him, and that's why I cannot get pregnant." Then, in a barely audible whisper, making sure no one else was around, "I just hate men. All of them."

Ahinoam's revelation did not fall on deaf ears. Tirzah loved hearing it, and she shared her own struggles and thoughts, i.e., her own distaste for men, and most of all, for their husband. In fact, the idea that she might also be infertile made her happy. Unlike Ahinoam, she would have been happy to be sent home. She was therefore very disappointed to find one day that her period was late. When she told Ahinoam, the two of them held each other and cried bitterly.

However, a girl like Tirzah would not throw up her hands, and she decided to share the information with her faithful handmaid. The handmaid listened, and as was her wont, hugged the girl and said, "Now don't tell anyone about the delay in your menses. Let me investigate something." It took her two days to find a healer who knew how to end pregnancies, but she returned with the news that there was an option, although it was neither pleasant nor inexpensive. Tirzah didn't hesitate, handing her some jewelry to do what had to be done. After waiting for two more weeks, when it was clear that this was a pregnancy and not merely a late period, Tirzah left the house, accompanied by Ahinoam and the handmaid, for an "outing." She returned exhausted, weak and pale - but with the pregnancy ended.

The old woman who had taken care of her had also given her materials to make it difficult for her body to get pregnant again, but she added the warning - that it was not an airtight solution.

Life at home continued normally. Every weekend, before the Sabbath, the husband would return, and he would come to Tirzah's bed once, and once to one of his two senior wives. Tirzah anticipated his arrival with fear and distaste. When he arose from her bed and went back to his room, she would quietly climb into Ahinoam's bed, where she would cry and curl up in her warm arms.

The days passed, and the months ticked by. Tirzah succeeded in her scheme to avoid pregnancy, but she was worried that she could not maintain the ruse. And her husband? He began to suspect that he had fallen into a trap twice - but that didn't stop him from trying, so that the times he spent in Tirzah's bed became longer and longer, sometimes even full nights. Tirzah longed for her friend, Ahinoam. Whenever the two would finally meet, they would enjoy their mutual contact. Without understanding how or when or by whose initiative, they found themselves engaging in intimate relations, which they enjoyed quite a lot.

Tirzah felt that she was trapped. The Torah spoke only of a prohibition of sex between men, not between women, but her society could not tolerate any such connection among females either. She was worried that perhaps she was committing a grave sin, both in the eyes of man and in the eyes of God. But one night, as the family sat down for its Sabbath dinner, it was their husband who gave them his permission, inadvertently. He told them about the topic of discussion among the men at his workplace in Jerusalem, going as far as to share the gossip about the palace. Although the prophet Moses had said of the king, "Neither shall he take too many women, lest his heart turn away," Solomon had taken many women, and not just Israelites. Then he uttered those fateful words, a balm for the wounds of the two girls. "Is it any wonder he acts like this? King David's great-grandmother was Ruth, a Moabite! Everyone knows that her connection to her mother-in-law Naomi was more than personal admiration. Two lonely women, each finding the other - the gossipmongers even say that they may have spent their time together not just in the kitchen, but in the bedroom as well!"

That night, after he had left Tirzah's bed, she went straight to Ahinoam's bed, and the two of them enjoyed each other with rapturous joy.

Now Tirzah's life consisted of enjoyable weekdays alongside onerous and painful weekends. But whatever man does not know, heaven knows; there they saw the girls' distress and delivered a speedy, sharp, painful solution.

One wintry day, with the wind gusting and rain pouring, a stranger knocked on the door of the house. He summoned all four of the wives, and with a gloomy face informed them of the death of their husband in a work accident. He described the new project in Jerusalem – that of building a House of God. King Solomon was fulfilling his father David's dying wish, to build the Temple and bring the Ark of the Covenant there. "This is a gigantic building requiring precise masonry, cutting enormous stones. Your husband was a master stonemason, and he was recruited for the job, along with others. They were in a quarry near the city when the mountainside collapsed, causing a massive rockslide. The huge stones rolled down and crushed a number of the workers, killing them on the spot. Your husband was one of them. His death was quite honorable, giving his life to build the House of God. You should rejoice in that fact."

This death struck the women like a bolt out of the blue. The older ones mourned his death, but the younger ones were greatly relieved. They felt that a new light was breaking through over their lives. Already the next day, Tirzah sent her faithful handmaid to Othniel's House to tell the family and to seek their advice. Achsah and her husband heard what had happened and decided to send a scribe, a person they relied upon, to be present while the estate was divided, in order to come to decisions about her next move. However, Achsah saw something in the eyes of her handmaid. She could see that the story was more complicated, that for some reason the handmaid was not telling the whole story.

That evening, when everyone else had gone to bed, she called the handmaid and together they went out to the courtyard. "Tell me," Achsah demanded, "what are you hiding?"

The handmaid cast her gaze to the ground. Achsah, in a totally uncharacteristic move, extended a hand to her and said, "I know, I was not the best mother. Tirzah was fortunate to have you around, and that's why I sent you together with her, to give her what she never received from me. But look, I'm going to have a child with my new husband, and I want to turn over a new leaf. I miss Tirzah terribly, and I feel her pain. I just want you to share it with me. You won't be betraying that dear girl –you'll be opening the door for a new life."

There was a moment of silence, and then the handmaid began to speak - a torrent of words, unstoppable, until she had told her everything... well, almost everything. She couldn't look into her mistress's eyes and tell her that Tirzah's attitude towards men was a product of Achsah's conduct, but she told Achsah how miserable Tirzah was with her husband, told her about the abortion, told her about Ahinoam and the powerful friendship between them. Then she fell silent.

"And?" Achsah prompted her.

"And what?"

"You started to tell me, so you have to tell me everything. What are you hiding from me about Ahinoam?"

So she told her.

It took Achsah a long moment to digest this, but afterwards she took a deep breath and told her, "Tirzah is my daughter. I will do anything I can to bring her back here. If she wants, Ahinoam will be welcome as well. We are sending the scribe to address the legal matter, but I will join him. It's time for me to be a mother."

Othniel

The two weeks that passed before the handmaid's anticipated return were quietly tense, characterized by inner seclusion, as Tirzah was full of qualms and uncertainties. What would it look like if she were able to return home? Would she even be allowed to do so?

When she saw Achsah sliding off the donkey and entering their house, her first thought was that her mother was there to make sure Tirzah received her rightful portion of the estate and would remain in her late husband's house; she was surprised when her mother embraced her firmly and she felt her tears. Achsah held Tirzah's face with both hands and whispered to her, "I know everything. If you want, you can come back home with me. If you want and she wants, Ahinoam is welcome as well."

Tirzah then burst into tears, liberating tears, joyous tears, tears that she had not been able to shed all those years. One moment a girl, the next moment a woman; one moment a mother, the next moment a friend. Tirzah took Achsah's hand and ran into the house joyously shouting, "Ahinoam, look who's here!"

It was not easy to reach understandings with the family members about the future, and the scribe had to use all of his abilities. The main difficulty was from an unexpected direction. The dead husband's brother, short and ugly, demanded Tirzah as a wife. "I am the levir. My brother had no children from her, so I will take her as a wife."

No one expected such a demand, and no one knew how to rise to the challenge. Achsah sent the scribe posthaste to find a priest or a Levite who could offer a learned opinion on the matter. When he found such an authority, he discovered that levirate marriage was limited to instances in which the dead brother had no one to carry on his name, which was not the case at the moment. Despite this, and since there was widespread ignorance, people would use this law in order to assert control over young brides. When he returned to the house and explained this to Achsah and Tirzah, his recommendation was to try and purchase Tirzah's freedom.

Achsah empowered him to conduct negotiations for a levirate release, but when this failed and the danger became palpable, it reminded her of the incident from her youth, her encounter with Joab son of Zeruiah, and she decided to use similar means.

She summoned one of the inn's regular customers on whom she could rely, making clear to him what she needed. The man did not waste much time; he met the extortionist brother and made him an offer: either a levirate release with a monetary bonus, or his life. Two weeks later, they were on their way back home.

Ahinoam's case was simpler. Her family was not overly interested in what she did, so her decision to join Tirzah was accepted unanimously.

Tirzah's return was a matter of great local interest. Othniel's House was one of the settlement's predominant institutions, a place that provided a lot of fodder for local gossipmongers. Everyone knew the beautiful Tirzah, so her return with her friend, which brough with it rumors that they shared a bed, made for a particularly juicy subject.

The days passed. Tirzah became more and more involved with the caravanserai, and the same was true of Ahinoam, whose singing and dancing abilities became well known. On warm summer nights, she sang and danced for the villagers.

A few months after her arrival, a girl came to Tirzah, embarrassed, and asked if she might seek her counsel. "I am attracted to women," she said, "and I detest men. What am I supposed to do? They all said that you would understand and you could give me advice."

This was how Tirzah discovered that she had earned a reputation among women undergoing similar crises. Some gathered their courage and came to her, and slowly a support group was formed around the two women at Othniel's House.

As time passed, Achsah understood that Tirzah was becoming a leader in her own right, a source of strength and encouragement to many women from the surrounding area, and even from more distant reaches. She thought to herself that Tirzah, daughter of Othniel, was truly the doppelganger and successor of Tirzah, daughter of Zelophehad.

However, life has its own rhythm and dynamic, and the connection between Ahinoam and Tirzah was close to being exhausted. Moreover, Tirzah noticed that one of the inn's customers had fallen for Ahinoam; she also saw how Ahinoam blushed when his name came up. To her surprise, she accepted this development favorably, rejoicing for her friend. Indeed, Ahinoam's father came, not long after, to inform her that he had decided to marry off Ahinoam to the man who had sought her hand.

Soon enough, Ahinoam married and left the caravanserai; not long afterward, she sent a special messenger to let Tirzah know about her pregnancy.

When the child was born, Tirzah went to visit. She watched as Ahinoam suckled her infant, held him, and felt the longing come over her. She yearned for a true family, for a child of her own.

And when there is a will, and one's faith is strong, the groom shows up soon enough – which was what happened for Tirzah as well. Her new beau's appearance, his sensitivity, and his *joie de vivre* eradicated the last remnants of her childish belief in the inherent evil of men, so when her suitor sought her hand from the grandfather, he was overjoyed to accept.

Agreements were signed, understandings were arrived at, and Tirzah moved into her beloved Naphtali's home. Ten months later, she invited her family to the circumcision ceremony of her first-born son, and his name was to be known in Israel as Othniel, son of Naphtali.

CHAPTER NINE

The Guide

Now, after Tirzah's life had ended at a ripe old age, as the mother of four and the grandmother of fourteen, the time had come to investigate this unique life cycle.

The story of these two unique women, Tirzah and her mother, Achsah, presented me with the meaning of human dependence - of one relying on the conduct of another's life - and therefore how much power soul contracts have, as well as the mutually written life plans. I learned an additional lesson when I discovered how much my Guide could help and direct me, even when his soul was reincarnated in Achsah. This was a special lesson, as Achsah and Tirzah lived at the same time. My Guide was incarnated in Achsah, while I was in Tirzah; still, he could realize his role and continue to serve as my Guide. I would adopt this lesson in later lives, and we will discuss this further.

The script of Achsah's life was devised to realize that soul's plan, but the measure of its success in learning and completing the lessons it sought is not our issue in this context; however, the soul plan it signed with me did have great significance in the success of this life path for me.

Achsah's choice to be a single mother was important because there was a need for Tirzah to see with her own eyes the model of a woman living without a man. Achsah could have gotten married a short time after Tirzah's birth, but she chose otherwise. This was her path, this was her part in the soul contract, and Tirzah could only observe and learn. Achsah's acquiescence and ability to change her relationship with Tirzah and become a real mother for her, even accepting Ahinoam into her house, were part of the contract, and her contribution to the success of Tirzah's plan was considerable.

There was an additional lesson, which was not new for me, but proved to be valuable once again – namely, understanding the great influence of the previous life. The events I implanted in Tirzah before her birth, which found their place in her subconscious, allowed her to interpret Achsah's love affairs as a source and reason for hating men.

This life cycle, the last in a series, presented most of the goals preceding the transition to being a Guide. In this life, Tirzah experienced marriage to a man she did not desire, and then to a man she sincerely loved. She experienced a different kind of love, love of women, and grew up to be a leader for women seeking "approval" or at least advice for their same-sex lifestyle; she was also a pioneer in setting up a support group- not just any support group, but one for a group of women whom society rejects and discards. Most important of all, she had the strength to eschew the easy path and pick the right way for her, even though it defied the conventions of the society she lived in.

For my dearest friend of all, my soul twin, I reserved in this life a small but incomparably significant role. She appeared for a brief time in the form of an infant, the son of Ahinoam who captivated Tirzah and aroused in her longing, love, and the desire to embrace her own child. I was loath to take any risks at this critical juncture. Since in the first few weeks of a human life, the soul maintains a certain awareness of the world from which it comes, I relied on it to remember its role and do everything babies know how to do to capture a person's heart.

Now, after I had examined and studied this just-concluded life, recording it in the book of life in the library, and after I went back and rejoined my soul family, to my great joy I was summoned to the Council of Elders. I had already encountered those whom I call the Council of Elders; essentially, it is a group of angels and higher entities, most of them avatars, veterans who have already completed their reincarnation periods. (Although some continue to be reincarnated, they do so sparingly, and only in those periods and places where they are needed and have the ability to influence their surroundings for the good.) The first time that I was in their company was while I was looking for the way to self-repair following the wounds I felt after Evelit's life; now, ten life cycles and reincarnations later, I returned to them- this time, at their request.

I cannot describe any excitement I felt about the meeting, nor any sense of fear and trembling; these sensations are foreign to us here. There was a powerful, clarifying feeling of transcendence, of respect, of a unique encounter. Meeting angels closer to higher levels, closer to the Source itself, is special and rare; the atmosphere in that place reflected all of these elements.

It was not a conversation about roles, nor a meeting with speeches congratulating me or emphasizing the responsibility inherent in the role; neither was it a ceremony with medals and awards, or the bestowal of noble titles by the king. Instead, it was an occasion in which I understood the significance of the transition to the Guide level, the responsibility accompanying this role, and what this level represents in our world. This was all in a kind of "initiation" in which I suddenly knew all this, and I felt them in every bit of my being. I was there as the feeling of glory suffusing the occasion hovered in that place, but without any lofty or impressive symbols of domination. This was the most sublime greatness of simplicity; this was the purest modesty; this was the cleanest conceivable iteration of giving not for the sake of receiving.

And when I left, I was something else.

Now I function on two levels. I continue to be reincarnated, because I still have a lot to learn, to gain experience, and to repair, but I also help other souls as their Guide. If you ask me how I can still do this while I'm in a body, I'll tell you that only part of the soul is inside a living human. The soul is bigger than what may be contained by the body, which does not need all of its resources. Practically, in most cases, I enter the body only by a third, and sometimes by half, of my might and size. Thus there is always a lot left for me to turn to other assignments. However, this is only part of the answer, because based on the physical character of the world beyond, we have the ability to do a number of things simultaneously- as they appear to the human eye, and we will soon discuss it further.

Before we talk about my role as Guide and Mentor, I want to describe for you additional life cycles tied to the region from which Tirzah came- the Kingdoms of Israel and Judea. Since this was the era in which I was trained for my new role as a spiritual Guide, I chose life cycles in which my aims as a soul coming to learn and to repair would be ostensibly "easy," even though, from the human point of view, they were likely to be difficult.

Tirzah, born in the last days of King David's reign, lived most of her life during that of King Solomon. She even managed to see his son Rehoboam ascend to the throne, after which the land was split into the kingdoms of Israel and Judea. Two states, one people.

My next life cycle after Tirzah was as Amariah, a man born in Jibleam, a Levite city in the area of the Tribe of Manasseh, part of the Kingdom of Israel. The king at the time was Omri, who ended a contentious half-century of rivalry between Israel and Judea, the two brother states. However, Amariah spent most of his adult life under King Ahab, who ushered in an era of economic prosperity, but also religious and moral upheavals. He was even witness to one of these, the story of his fellow winemaker, Naboth of Jezreel (northwest of his own town, just a half day ride from Jibleam). Naboth's vineyard was seized by the king, leading to the resentment of Ahab, who could not say no to Queen Jezebel, his non-Hebrew wife from Sidon.

In the next life cycle, about fifty years later, I was born in the Judean city of Eshtemoa, in the days of King Amaziah. I was killed near Beth Shemesh, in my late teens, in the battle waged by Amaziah against the Hebrew king of Israel, Jehoash.[6]

Following that, I lived in the days of King Zedekiah, last monarch of Judea; his fall would mark the end of Hebrew rule until the Hasmonean revolt four centuries later. The fall of the Davidic dynasty was something we knew was coming, and I thought it would be best to be there and be incarnated in Athaliah, a healer and caregiver at the time.

---

6   King Amaziah of Judea hired some 100,000 soldiers from Jehoash to fight against Edom. According to the Book of Chronicles, Amaziah decided not to use these troops and sent them home, which infuriated them. This led them to raid Judean cities, killing 3,000 villagers and looting their homes. As soon as the war with Edom ended, in 785 BCE, Amaziah declared war on Israel. King Jehoash of Israel tried to dissuade him; war broke out anyway, and the Judean army was defeated. The Israelite army breached the walls of Jerusalem, looting all the gold and silver in the Temple treasury and the palace.

I could not have imagined how difficult and painful war could be. Athaliah was a native-born resident of Jerusalem, but the siege was now starving the city and turning its inhabitants against each other violently, to the extent of losing their humaneness. The cruelty of the Babylonians only encouraged the Jerusalemites to imitate them, and Athaliah the caregiver was often called on to help, day and night. The harsh battles that breached the city walls took a heavy toll – the lives of her husband and two of her five sons. After the destruction and burning of the House of God,[7] Athaliah and her children were banished from the city, as were most of its inhabitants. Thus began a long, crushing journey eastward to Babylonia. After more than a year of wandering, they found refuge there in the city of Nippur, south of the city of Babylon, in a neighborhood close to the massive local water source, the Kebar River. There was already a stable Hebrew society there, which had arrived a few years earlier.[8] She even met a man there, a unique and precious individual, a great prophet, by the name of Ezekiel son of Buzi, whose sermons and speeches were greatly sought after by the members of the community, who drew tremendous comfort from them.

I could describe Athaliah's life story at length, how she rebuilt her life and remarried in Babylonia. I could tell you about the culture there, about the megalomania of King Nebuchadnezzar II, who expanded the city into a metropolis famed the world over, a man who constructed one of the Seven Wonders of the Ancient World,

---

7   The First Temple was destroyed in 586 BCE.

8   King Jeconiah had been exiled eleven years before the destruction of the First Temple, in 597 BCE, along with most of the aristocrats, the wealthy, and the powerful. The prophet Ezekiel joined them about five years later. In the previous note you write that the First Temple was destroyed in 586, so 11 years before that would be 575.

the Hanging Gardens, and who built the Ishtar Gate and the Ésagila Temple. However, Babylonia's other claim to fame far predated Nebuchadnezzar, the cruelty of whom I've already told you in the story of its native son Evelit, so I'll suffice with that.

During these life cycles, which lasted for centuries, I dealt with the role of Guide as well. I educated young souls, helping them to plan their upcoming lives; I accompanied them when they took form in a body; I waited for them at the gate when these lives ended; and then I accompanied them through the process of recuperation from and investigation of the just-concluded life.

The process was fascinating, and it allowed me to broaden and deepen my interest and knowledge in the soul/human process as I discovered new angles of soul plans that I had not previously been aware of. I also had access to senior entities, whose vast experience and stupendous knowledge afforded me a fresh perspective on the processes of soul development and the progress of humanity. I discovered paths to the plan of Creation itself that I had never known about before.

My sense of responsibility towards human society grew by leaps and bounds, so much so that I felt that I was a partner in the plan of the Creator- and so much closer to Him.

Now I could be reincarnated to a level I had never before experienced; and see a range of perspectives new to me. The first of these I would undergo in Hellas, the place now known as Greece.

Penelope

Penelope was a skilled musician who loved her lyre,[9] which was always by her side. Her friends would say that she would rather share her bed with it than with any man, except perhaps - here they smiled - Pythagoras, husband of her good friend Theano.

As a child, Penelope was a bit odd. She was born in Kroton, in Magna Graecia[10] in Italy, in 543 BCE. She was her parents' first daughter, but they eagerly awaited the birth of a male child. The gods smiled upon them, and after Penelope came two boys. Penelope's mother dedicated most of her time to her sons, leaving Penelope no choice but to find other pursuits, which often surprised her parents.

Her musical abilities were impressive. She would absorb tunes and melodies as if from the very air, and she had a beautiful singing voice as well. She quickly learned to accompany herself on an old lyre that she had "borrowed" from a wayfarer who had left it for a moment on the roadside next to their house. The girl had true virtuoso abilities, integrating the sounds of the instrument with those of her own voice. Her talent was so exceptional that when she grew up a bit, her father would take her to markets and festive occasions to play for pay.

Still, music was not Penelope's only remarkable talent. Her other exceptional skill was revealed when her father was herding his goats to the corral in their yard, and the girl idly noticed, as she leaned

---

9   The lyre is a stringed instrument that was very common in the classical era; in fact, some think that this is the biblical "David's harp" that he used as a young man in the court of King Saul.

10   Kroton is the city of Crotone in southern Italy. In this region, beginning in the seventh century BCE, Greek communities developed, descended from the Achaeans who lived along the coast. Because of their settlements, it was referred to in Latin as Magna Graecia (Great Greece).

on the fence, that one goat was missing. Her father looked at her with a smile and asked her how she knew that. She simply replied: "I watched you when you brought them in." No one would have remembered this occurrence, had it not been for the news that arrived the next day about a group of nomads passing through the region who "collected" goats from a number of different herds. Her parents took note, and they started to track this bizarre ability of their daughter's. They were amazed to realize that this talent of hers continued to grow and develop. She could effortlessly divine numbers in ways that defied logic; she could easily calculate amounts; she could even reckon the odds in games of chance in the marketplace. Her father knew how to take advantage of this skill and combine it with her exceptional ability to play music and sing, which increased the number of spectators and the family's income.

However, Penelope was not interested in any of this. She didn't enjoy performing in front of people. It was so noisy, the sounds of wagons and donkeys mixed with yelling male voices, along with curses, violence, and aggression. This was the daily state of the marketplace, which Penelope didn't relish, and she would have happily passed it all up. When she was at home, she preferred to be alone in nature, to hike and explore. She inspected petals and tried to understand the connections between various flowers based on how many petals they had and their structure; she also loved to gaze at the heavens at night and track the movement of the stars in their orbits, trying to predict future phenomena, so she was happy about every revelation.

The uniqueness of this girl, which in other eras and other locations might have earned her respect, was considered, in this setting, to be utterly inappropriate for a young woman; to say the least, her reputation did her no favors. Her musical ability, coupled with the benefit that her counsel and logical perceptiveness brought to her family, friends, and neighbors, annoyed many people. Even her brothers were jealous of her, and they did everything they could to hurt her and belittle her.

The girl's strange qualities only grew more powerful and intense as the years passed, worrying her parents in a way they had no idea how to deal with. She gained a far-flung reputation, and her parents were concerned that someone would harm her; they worried that these abilities would prevent the girl from getting married. They refused to even consider giving her to a man who would only want her for his own benefit and gain, but suitors from the area avoided connecting with a young woman who seemed to be an emissary of the gods. The result was that any marriage proposals they received were rejected out of hand by her father, and the others, which she anticipated, never came. Her parents began to worry more and more, as she was already twelve years old and they hadn't received one serious proposal for her hand in marriage. Moreover, the promise given to the family when Penelope had turned ten had now been broken, as the suitor had simply cut off contact.

Then something happened that changed everything. A poet and philosopher by the name of Brontinus, who lived in Metapontum, two days' ride away, had arrived to visit his two renowned teachers, Pythagoras, and Alcmaeon of Kroton; there he saw Penelope when she performed in the marketplace. He sought out her father and introduced himself, saying that he had just arrived in Kroton and needed a place to stay for his daughter and him. His noble appearance and the money he offered were enticing, and he was invited to be a guest in the family home.

Shortly before sunset, the guest was invited to supper into the andron, a room reserved exclusively for males. His daughter joined

Penelope, her mother, and the other women to eat in a small room off of the kitchen.

There something wondrous happened when Penelope discovered an interest in the girl who was their guest. Never before had she cared about a girl her own age. The two young women found a common language, and they simply disappeared into the courtyard, talking with an unfathomable seriousness that belied their ages. Brontinus watched from the window as the bond was formed between the two girls, but he was not surprised; he had, in fact, anticipated as much. He knew how capable his daughter was, and he had noticed the same characteristics in Penelope – which was why he had wanted to stay with her family.

He went out to the courtyard to listen to their conversation, and when he returned to the andron he addressed Penelope's father. "My daughter Theano is a very special girl. She has great wisdom and intelligence, and her scientific skills are quite impressive. As a scientist, I am very happy about that. Yesterday, when I saw your daughter in the marketplace, I knew that it was no coincidence that I found myself there; the gods themselves know that our daughters will grow up to occupy prominent positions in our world. I came to your city to meet the scientist Pythagoras, son of Mnesarchus of Samos, who recently moved here. I want Theano to study with him. I think it would be wonderful if your daughter were to join us."

Penelope's father was astounded by this. He didn't know who Pythagoras was, but Brontinus's stories about the man left no doubt about his importance. Besides, how could a person so famous and important degrade himself to the extent that he would accept girls into his institute?

A concern began to gnaw at him. Was this man recruiting

hetaerae,[11] the acclaimed courtesans of ancient Greece? The idea that his daughter would become a prostitute upset him. In fact, the whole matter displeased him, mainly because this man, Pythagoras, had just arrived in the city, and it was unclear where he had come from. Was he really a famous scientist? Penelope's father suspected that someone had seen her singing and playing in the market and concluded that she was a "victim" they could recruit.

However, his wife disagreed. She saw in this proposal a way to "get rid of" their worry about Penelope's remaining a permanent dependent. She suggested that her husband join Brontinus and meet "this man, this Pythago... Pythago what? You can form your own impression of him."

The guest did seem to be very trustworthy, radiating light and nobility around him, which raised the idea of the honor, glory, and pride that would come from forging a link to an important scientist; but this could not overpower his opposition or dissuade his refusal. The next morning, immediately after breakfast, Penelope's father rejected Brontinus's proposal, so the latter had to leave them with great disappointment, taking his daughter and setting out on his journey.

Only as the sun began to set did Penelope's family realize that she had disappeared. Her father, who made the discovery, summoned his sons and some of their neighbors, and they began to search for her. They went out looking for Brontinus, and they tried to discover who this man named Pythagoras was - and where he lived, if anywhere. The people they met on the street directed them towards the wealthiest quarter of the city, which only made them more concerned that

---

11   Hetaerae were the most highly-regarded prostitutes [among women meant to pleasure men] Is it necessary to say something so obvious?. They were well-educated, having studied poetry, music, and philosophy, and they even participated in symposia with men.

the girl had been seduced into a life of licentiousness.

They quickly arrived at Pythagoras's house, and when they entered the courtyard found many people there, all splendidly dressed, standing in small groups, having conversations that were low and measured. The atmosphere was one of tranquility and edification – certainly not a location for men to satisfy their lusts.

Penelope's father noticed Brontinus, who was standing off to the side and speaking with a few men. He approached Brontinus, who smiled delightedly and said, "Ah! I am so pleased that you've come. I hope you're here to retract your refusal. So now you will allow Penelope to join us and study at this venerable institution?"

While Penelope's father was still confused and contemplating how to reply, his youngest son came over and said, "I saw her in the courtyard with Theano." His gaze downcast, he added, "She asked me to leave her alone and not tell you where she is."

There was silence among the men, and Brontinus noticed the furrowed eyebrows and the fire of anger igniting as the fury of the girl's father raged. He extended his hand to him and said, "Please.wait a minute. Listen to me. When we left this morning, I saw Penelope run after us and walk next to our donkeys. I thought that she was escorting us on our way, mainly because she and Theano were chatting and laughing. When we were a distance from your house, I tried to send her home, but she refused. In fact, she looked me in the eye and said that she wanted to study. *To study*! I'd never in my life heard a young woman say that – not even my own daughter! I was deeply distressed that I could not grant her request, but I forbade her from coming with us. I told her to go back home. Then she left us and disappeared. When we arrived here, the honorable scientist was waiting for us in the courtyard. We've known each other for a long time, and we have met at many symposia. I introduced my daughter to him, after having told him about her previously, and when he began to speak to her, Penelope suddenly appeared and declared, 'I want to study, too.'

"The honorable scientist was shocked, and he looked at me questioningly. I told him about her, but when he heard that you had forbidden her to come here, he sent her home. The girl stepped back, her gaze downcast. I was sure that she left after that, and when I saw you, I was certain that you had changed your mind and brought her with you.

"Please, let me introduce you to Master Pythagoras, and allow me to call Theano and Penelope to participate in the conversation. Don't decide until after we've had our meeting, and then we'll respect your decision, whatever it may be."

Penelope's father was shocked. He had never heard such words, in such a tone. He had never thought that a woman, a girl, could have a life outside the home and outside the kitchen, a life on her own terms - unless she were accompanied by a husband or male family member. Now, to his surprise, he heard himself respond affirmatively and send his son to summon his daughter.

We need not speak of it at length, as it would be difficult to describe the father's amazement as he listened to the conversation between Pythagoras and the two girls. Their vocabulary was beyond him, and the subject matter was beyond his ken. The most astounding part of his was the look in his daughter's eyes; he had never in his life seen her like that. The enchantment in her eyes made him feel that he himself was undergoing a change. The struggle over his daughter receded, and all the barriers fell away. All he wanted to do was to play a part in this unique experience. The thoughts that had arisen in his mind that very morning began to dissipate as soon as he entered the courtyard to see and hear those present and the way they spoke. Now, the remnants of his resistance melted away; instead he felt pride and a desire to belong to such a group. This also meant that he granted their request, with a few provisos, especially that he would be able to visit Penelope whenever he wanted; that she could come home whenever she wanted, but at least once a week; and that if the issue of marriage were to arise, he would still have the last word. This was agreed to, and Penelope embarked on her new path in life.

The Pythagorean School

Pythagoras was pleased. The institute that he established became well known and acclaimed, achieving success in both science and society.[12]

He had reached Kroton two years earlier, after extensive travels in Greece and the surrounding area, hoping to establish himself there and dedicate himself to research and study - above all, to open the school he had tried to found on the island of his birth, Samos, but without great success.

During his first months in Kroton, he spent most of his time and energy meeting key members of the community and recruiting students. He was busy organizing the inaugural event of the Pythagorean School, as he called it. When he received Brontinus's letter asking to visit, he immediately approved enthusiastically, even inviting him for opening day.

The conclusion of Brontinus's letter caused him to rethink an

---

12   Pythagoras's academy operated differently than all other contemporary institutions. He espoused simplicity, observation, proper nutrition, vegetarianism, and physical fitness, all of which played an integral role in his lifestyle. The studies were in philosophy and mathematics, astronomy and music. The students came from the aristocratic class, and their ranks included women, defying the conventions of Greek culture.

issue – women in the institute – that had occupied him for quite a while. He knew that allowing women into the school might harm his prestige and might even distance students from him.

However, his good friend's request to accept Brontinus's daughter - whose wonderful abilities Pythagoras had already heard of - to the institute had made him think otherwise. Since she had already reached the right age, he might be able to place her among the men. If this proved to be successful, he could invite other women to attend.

This would be no easy task, he thought, realizing that a rare opportunity had presented itself to him. If her presence hurt the institute, he mused, he could simply marry her. After all, he reflected, he was getting older and had not yet produced any children.

He anxiously awaited Brontinus's arrival. When his slave told him that the guests had arrived, he emerged to greet them and receive them in the courtyard. Alongside Brontinus stood a beautiful girl, whose age he estimated to be twelve, who stared at him with big eyes - inquisitive, curious, challenging. "Theano, I presume," he said, extending his hand.

She responded as if she had known him forever. "Of course. And you are Pythagoras! I'm so happy to finally meet you. You know that I am going to live right here, that I will be your disciple?"

Brontinus, his gaze downcast in embarrassment, suddenly heard Pythagoras, the sober-minded, the serious, burst into peals of laughter, joyfully replying, "Certainly! So where are your writing implements? Why are you wasting your time listening to two old men instead of exploring the campus?" But when he looked up, he suddenly heard another voice, the voice of another young woman asking, "What about me? I'm also here to learn." As he turned his head, he saw, to his surprise, Penelope standing there, her penetrating glance directed at Pythagoras.

Things were soon sorted out, and when it became apparent that Penelope was there against her parents' wishes, Pythagoras rejected her. He called on the slaves to escort her out of the house. Neither her supplications, nor Theano's - who was holding on to Penelope's hand in a display of protection of her new friend - could help.

However, Penelope had other plans. She understood that they would send her back home, but she was determined to stay with Pythagoras, no matter what. As soon as the slave turned his back and walked away, she returned to the courtyard, which was now buzzing with activity. People teemed all over the place preparing for the event. Some were putting together a stage, others were distributing torches and oil lamps, many were setting up tables and chairs for refreshments - all contributing to the cacophony. No one noticed the girl carrying a lyre and looking for a place to hide. She walked around among the participants until she eventually found a good location: the hayloft beyond the stable.

She soon saw Theano wandering through the courtyard and called to her. They were overjoyed to see each other, and with unfathomable seriousness sat down to plan the future, e.g., where the girl would sleep, how Theano would steal food for her, how she would find clothing fit for disciples, and how she would join their lessons from the outside. They didn't consider the simplest outcome – that her father would come looking for her.

The first few months in the Pythagorean School flew by. The two girls found themselves overwhelmed just keeping up with their studies and helping organize the place. They also had uncomfortable moments of being compelled to adopt new habits, and the transition to vegetarianism was the hardest of all. The other daily habits, even the almost compulsive calisthenics, were easier. Still, everything would shrink as evening settled, when the two were invited to supper with

Pythagoras. Penelope would play for everyone, and she was overjoyed to discover that Pythagoras himself was an exceptional lyre-player; the two supported each other musically and helped each other develop. Theano, for her part, was found to be a genius philosopher, who could play with numbers in a way that was astonishing. Slowly, these evenings became the highlight of the day for the girls.

Penelope kept her word, and every seven days her father would come to pick her up for a home visit. There was something fascinating in these encounters. She discovered an ability to observe the development of her relatives – albeit without being involved – which allowed her to offer advice. On the one hand, the older she got, the more she felt distanced and detached from the family atmosphere; her interest in the domestic issues, the stories of economic success and failure on the household level, progressively shrank, and the same was true of her interest in her brothers' tales of the girls they landed or the sporting competitions they won, even though she had once blushed and enthused over them. On the other hand, her own image in the eyes of her family grew and grew, and every visit was a cause for celebration. Her unique wisdom and vision became their lodestone, and Penelope, who was already approaching her fifteen birthday, understood this and maintained her intimate bond with her family.

Her mother became a friend, knowing how to listen to her experiences and her crises as an adolescent. She was even the first to pay attention to the growing closeness between Pythagoras and Theano, an idea that Penelope initially dismissed, saying, "That's ridiculous. You don't even really know her," but then she began to note the small gestures between the two. Once again, it was her mother who raised the alarm, this time because of the jealousy that might develop; she warned her daughter that it could be powerfully destructive, and this phenomenon did not take long to manifest.

It was a lovely evening at the conclusion of a term, and the three were reclining in the orchard, empty food trays before them. Their plates were filled with figs and grapes, and they drank wine from Pythagoras's cup.[13] Then they drank a second, then a third. Pythagoras suggested to Theano to accompany him into the courtyard, and he told Penelope to go back to her room. She did this, and she suddenly felt the full force of the jealousy her mother had warned her about.

Theano came back to the room they shared only very late that night, a light shining in her eyes. Penelope, whose lyre had helped soothe her troubled soul all through the evening, could not help but be happy as her friend told her every detail and moment from her nighttime experience with their beloved teacher.

About a month later, Brontinus showed up suddenly at the school, and Theano grabbed her friend forcefully and whispered, "Just let him say yes, just let him say yes…" To the joy of both, the marriage was announced that week, and it was not long before the wedding took place, well-attended and well-appointed.

When Theano left their room, a new student took her place, so that Penelope's life changed once again.

Adulthood

Penelope led a successful life. Detaching herself from Theano allowed her to work independently, and the scope of her research grew progressively. The connection to music and her abilities to produce unique melodies and chords helped the bond between her

---

13   Pythagoras's cup can be filled to a certain level. When that level is exceeded, the cup empties itself. This is a 2,500-year-old idea attributed to Pythagoras, in accordance with his rules of "moderation," fighting the gluttony of the disciples who lived in his house.

and Pythagoras develop. Their research on the connection between mathematics and music, expressed in analysis of the chords, reinforced Pythagoras's thesis about numbers as the factor behind everything extant in the universe, bringing about a deep connection between them.

Theano's life changed as well. Her status as Pythagoras's wife gave her access to the most learned people of the era, and she accompanied her husband in his travels as well as in his work. Theano was occupied not just with family life, bearing a firstborn son and then three enchanting daughters, but also pure analytical research, even discovering the golden ratio.[14] Her scholarly writings were also renowned.

As time passed, the two found themselves having differences of opinion, mainly about what Penelope described as "my independence as a woman." The institute hosted many symposia, and Penelope would often find herself standing in front of a male audience and lecturing on music, astronomy, or numerology. The idea of a woman giving a lecture to men merely by right of her being a human being, by right of her status as a scientist and researcher - and not being from the elite prostitute class of the hetaerae - was not always understood. This led the participants to direct indecent proposals to her. Penelope opposed this manifestation of masculine culture, but Theano, perhaps because she was the wife of the dean of the institute, made her peace with this conduct. She even complained about Penelope's opposition to it.

Penelope's refusal to accept this situation erupted into great anger and offense when a group from the institute was hosted at a

---

14   The golden ratio is a mathematical element sought by scientists and artists for thousands of years. The way you've written it, it's not clear whether it is still sought or was sought for thousands of years.

symposium in Athens, with Penelope as a featured lecturer. During one of the breaks, one of the Greek notables approached and suggested that she join him in an adjoining bedroom, as he thought she was a hetaera. When she corrected him, he refused to accept this, and the conversation became tense and threatening, but then Pythagoras arrived and saved her from the Greek notable. Theano rebuked her for what she saw as illogical behavior, and Penelope responded coldly, turning her back on Theano.

On their way back to Kroton, this issue was on the agenda, and so Pythagoras, who believed in the existence of the soul, the immortality of the spirit, and reincarnation, argued that in this incarnation, Penelope ought to conduct herself as women were expected to; even if she disagreed, she had no escape from marriage. In her innermost heart, she agreed with this idea, which had been ripening within her for some time. However, Pythagoras then added that the event in Athens had coincided with his own consideration of the matter, along with Theano, and in fact, he had recently approached her father with a proposal to marry Penelope off to one of his relatives.

Penelope was dumbstruck. It was only her deep admiration and affection for Pythagoras that kept her from replying, but a storm was raging in her soul. How dare she? How dare Theano collaborate, without telling her, without saying a word? Only when they returned to Kroton could she find free time with Theano to express her bitterness and disappointment.

Then she discovered who her prospective suitor was, and her offense and anger flared up. "That's it? Really, Theano? That's what you think of me? An ugly man who's pushing fifty? Fine, he's wise, a philosopher and all; he may have some money; he may have tried to court me more than once - but do you really see me in his bed? Will his hugs and kisses make me happy? Should I bring his children into the world?"

Penelope felt a rebellious fire burning in her bones again. The last time she had succeeded. Could she possibly do it again? Still, she understood that she had to marry. She recognized that there was no way to change the status of women in Greek culture. She also knew that she could not bring into reality a love of her own, "because it's just not done." She could not approach a man and propose marriage to him. The very idea was comical, even to her.

Still, she was saddened, because for a while she had set her eye on one man in particular that she wanted to wrap up, take and plunge in a bath, to wash and to anoint his body, to pleasure him and to receive pleasure from him, but he wasn't even aware of her existence... so how could it ever happen?

In her distress, she turned to Theano a second time, who saw this as an opportunity to rebuild her bond with Penelope. "So listen," Penelope said. "Do you know Anaximenes?" She didn't wait for answer, as she told her, "He's handsome and tall; he came to study here two years ago. He's smart, he's funny, he loves music. And I want him. I need you to help me. I know that women arranging their own marriages is unheard of, but that's what I want. If I come up with the plan, will you help me?" The answer she received was a loving smile, a tearing eye, and a giggle at the prospect of adventure as her brain began to work feverishly, weaving webs to trap their target.

The idea was to trip up Anaximenes, forcing him to propose marriage in order to maintain his honor. It was not an easy plan to execute, but it appeared that enticement and sensory stimulation might make the decision easier for him.

This was no easy task, as Anaximenes had of late been totally absorbed in his work and his studies, and he did not waste his time on entertainment and recreation. Penelope would not give up, and she started "spying" on him and gathering information until she could weave her plans.

The role of laying the first traps was given to Theano, who had just finished her medical studies. In a meeting with some of the students, in which Anaximenes participated, Theano turned to them to ask for help. She told them about a medicinal herb that was difficult to acquire but that she needed quite urgently. She knew where it could be found, in a certain spot along the river close to the city, and it could be identified easily in the early morning hours because of the unique way in which it bloomed. But she knew that these morning hours were devoted to physical fitness, and Pythagoras was very exacting when it came to attendance and participation. She asked them for ideas, as it was clear to her that no woman could go out unescorted to the river.

Penelope had told Theano that Anaximenes had recently received temporary permission to miss morning calisthenics in order to observe the sky at sunrise, and his observation point was near the river - he just had to make up what he missed over the course of the day.

Theano built on this information, going on about this special herb, until one of the other students quietly suggested to Anaximenes that he pick up the gauntlet, adding in a whisper, "She's the boss's wife, right?"

The young man looked at him and then answered, "Of course. It's no problem for me. When do you need it?"

The very next morning, Penelope was already in the river, waiting in the water for her victim to arrive. When she saw him leaning over the ground, looking for the herb, she emerged from the water naked as the day of her birth, and she burst out screaming, while "forgetting" to put her clothes back on.

Poor Anaximenes was petrified, so terrified he had no idea what to do, as Penelope stood across from him, close enough to give him a full view, far enough away that he could not grab her. She challenged him. "What are you doing here?"

Anaximenes gazed at her and swallowed hard. Damn it, she was beautiful. He did not hear her cries, he only saw her curves. He could almost feel the heat of her body.

Just as he felt the tension rising in his loins, she stopped screaming. In a cool voice, she chilled him, "You are in trouble, Anaximenes. Pythagoras will not like this story."

Then she turned around and bent down, her back to him, to gather up her clothes and leave. It took him some time to recover, but she soon heard him yelling behind her, "Penelope! It was a mistake. I'm not like that. I only came here because Theano asked me!" She smiled to herself, running happily back to the institute, to her room.

When he told Theano about this, apologizing for not finding the herb, she seemed extremely serious. "You are in big trouble!" she declared. He felt his heart shrivel a second time.

"Please help me," he begged. "You know very well why I was there."

"That's right," she replied, "but you could have just turned around and explained it, isn't that true?"

He blushed, confused, saying: "Yes... but..."

She smiled to herself and thought, "You're mine."

Penelope took full advantage of the situation. When Anaximenes approached her and tried to speak with her, she dodged him. Her heart ached when she saw his distress, but she had to stick to the plan. She managed to put him off for two days during which he didn't know what to do with himself. Her nakedness invaded his dreams, but in his imagination he heard Pythagoras's harsh words expelling him from school.

When Penelope finally agreed to meet him, she got straight to the point. "What do you propose?" she asked.

He, without getting mixed up this time, stood up straight and said, "I've known you and admired you for two years. Now that I have seen you as the gods made you, I know that I want you. Do as you wish, but I will go to your father and ask for your hand in marriage."

Had women been allowed to act in the Greek theater, Penelope would have been a sought-after actress. She appeared very surprised, almost shocked by the idea that revealing her body was what had convinced him to tie his life to hers; she would have to think about it, and her father would do nothing without consulting her. She only stopped speaking once she saw how miserable Anaximenes was, how impotent.

Then she approached him and said, "Allow me to say something controversial. We are isolated in Hellas. You are a special man, I am a special woman, and if it seems like audacity to say what I am about to say, that means that we are not compatible. But I love you, Anaximenes, and not just these past few days, not just since our encounter at the river. I want to be your wife, and I want you to be my husband. Will you marry me, even if my father refuses? Will you marry me even if I don't complain to Pythagoras?"

The answer was yes, even though it was not expressed in words. Were it not for their concern about the passersby and what they might see, they would have transitioned from politely standing there to something absolutely wild.

The years passed, and the Pythagorean School went through many upheavals. Pythagoras, who had always been opinionated - and not just in the realms of science - tended to end up clashing with politicians (in his youth he'd had to flee the island of his birth, Samos, for example, due to a quarrel with the island's tyrant, Polycrates).

Now, in his advanced years, enmity developed between him and a few of his students. One of them made contact with a crime organization, and shortly thereafter the institute went up in flames. Although many were killed, Pythagoras and Theano were fortunate enough to escape together with some of their closest friends, including Penelope and Anaximenes.

Theano took the reins, leading the survivors to the city of her birth, Metapontum, where they would live for many years, even after Pythagoras's death. Theano became his successor, leading the Pythagorean School; and Penelope, mother of five, was at her right hand.

When Penelope lay on her deathbed, surrounded by children and grandchildren, they were joined by many prominent people from the scientific and philosophical community. All the mourners admired her strong personality - the personality of a woman who blazed her own trail and led the way.

I was very pleased by the process and the events of Penelope's life. The topics that I sought to study during this life were many and varied. There were some topics that I had to complete from previous lives. One of them, for example, had to do with parent-child relationships – such as how a child who doesn't toe the line could find a way to keep a good relationship with his or her parents? Penelope wasn't pleased by the way her life was in her early years, but she had no tools to deal with the situation. However, the moment she identified an opportunity, she pounced on it and never let go. When she succeeded in her way, she knew how to value the emotional importance of parent-child relationships, keeping a warm relationship with her parents and brothers, even though she wasn't required to do so. Thus, Penelope completed her course with flying colors.

Still, there was another topic in this life. Even while we were devising Penelope's life plan, I knew that if she could manage to successfully complete her tasks, there would be ramifications for the future - and not only her own. The long-term goal had to be undertaken by an opinionated woman in a time and place in which such behavior would not be a trivial matter, so that the memories of her life would be joined to the stories of Brashita, Tirzah, and even the elderly healer.

In the proper reincarnation, I could assimilate them in the subconscious of a woman who would be a great trailblazer, who would influence all her surroundings, and perhaps even all of humanity. (We will discuss this later.) This was a monumental task, and therefore it was important for Penelope to withstand the challenge and be able to stand up for herself, especially in a society in which a woman had no standing.

We planned Penelope's life with great care. The detailed life plan was arranged; we selected parents who would resist the temptation to "sell" her to a husband who would use her abilities for his own profit; we determined an appropriate time and setting for carrying out the plan; we prepared character traits that would give her the skills she needed to allow her opinionated perspective to develop; and I assimilated them all in her DNA while she was still in the womb. Her life proceeded as designed, and Penelope grew up to be exactly who we hoped she would be. I was very proud.

CHAPTER TEN

A New Stage for Humanity

And here I am, in my beloved home with my soul family, already a different entity than the one you knew. Today, as a veteran soul and a spiritual Guide, there have been fundamental changes to my existence. Working in partnership with the new Guide intensified my interest and deepened my understanding of the bond between soul and human, expanding my knowledge of the soul plan as well; my sense of responsibility towards man and human society grew by leaps and bounds. I found that I had access to senior entities, those from whom the glory of holiness emanated; from their vast knowledge, I gained a new perspective on the processes of the development of the soul and on the processes of the growth of humanity. This made me feel like I was a partner in the Creator's plan and very close to the Creator.

Nevertheless, I had not yet completed my studies or my soul repairs. I still needed experiences that would allow me to learn, and this, of course, could be accomplished only amid the physical, the emotional, and the frenetic Planet Earth. That is why I continue to be reincarnated in human form, and at the same time serve as a Guide for other souls, helping others realize their soul plans, even if they are not at all aware of it.

I am a Guide and escort for the soul through the process of building a plan, and more than once I have synchronized the life plans of different souls and people, partners in an expansive strategy that they are not even aware of. I do all of this in parallel – reincarnating in a human body, helping other souls build their life plans, and synchronizing the different designs.

You must be asking now "How is it possible to do everything simultaneously?" Let me answer that.

I have already told you that a soul is much bigger than what the body can contain. In fact, the body doesn't even need all of those great resources. This being the case, you must be wondering which part of the soul that returns from reincarnation goes to the area of rest, orientation, and enlightenment. Does it act as two separate entities?

Well, then, this is a very human question. The idea of division belongs to the human world, a world in which there is separation and dualism. Here, "beyond the veil," there is no division. Such an idea is only human interpretation, because in the nature of the material world, there is separation, and there is dualism- light and darkness, good and evil, male and female – but, as you surely already understand, this material nature has no connection to the way in which we exist in it, and thus it is very difficult to explain the situation. You – flesh-and-blood human beings – cannot see the full picture and understand it.

Still, since I don't want to "evade" answering, I will try to explain it anyway. How can I do that? Perhaps it is best to use an example, a metaphor to make it easier to understand. The example is not precise, of course, but even so, as is the way with metaphors, it can convey the message.

Think of the soul as a huge lake, with a deep bottom; near the lakebed is a cave filled with water. This cave represents the human body. In the cave, all manner of things occur that are quite different from the activity in the rest of the lake. (This is very clear, right?) The cave is very dark, the temperature in it is somewhat different, and the life that develops there is also a bit different. Perhaps the fish are from a different species, there are different plants, and all the activity in it differs from that in the rest of the lake. Still, the water is the same water.

There is movement in this lake, there is a flow, and the water occupies the entire volume of the lake and of the cave as well. What happens in the cave seems to happen only in it- but in fact the water is shared by everything. Within the cave, local knowledge is accumulated and there are feelings and sensations that arise; they are all apparently connected only to the cave, but in fact the lake water is also part of it.

The water is the platform upon which everything happens.

Now, imagine that there are two caves in this large lake, or perhaps there are other areas, each with its own characteristics- here, too, the water is the same water, and its nature encompasses everything and is shared by everyone- emotions, knowledge, all the energy.

The water in the metaphor is the soul. It is a partner in everything that happens – not the material (the fish and plants), but the knowledge; not the vessel, but the emotions and consciousness. The full soul is always the same soul, and everything that happens in the human body, happens throughout all of it. When life ends and the soul ascends and passes into the area of rest, it does this as one unit, i.e., one full, complete being.

This ability of the soul to function in different places simultaneously has great significance, and in the next chapter of life I will tell you about it. However, before I get to it, I want to share another perspective with you.

The development of man - individually and societally - is a wondrous thing. I appeared in this space of energy as an entity only 17,000 Earth-years ago, and because of this I could not accompany humanity in its earliest stages, however, even in that small period of time, I witnessed processes of profound human development. I was even a partner, from the days of Roo until the days of Penelope.

Partner? Indeed — by the very fact that I spend part of my time in a living body, but there is something more. In those epochs when knowledge and memory were not inscribed or engraved, when instead stories were passed on from father to son, the progress of human society would have necessarily been glacial - if at all - were it not for our activity. We, the souls, in various incarnations, brought with us memories and knowledge from previous life cycles, from other locations across the globe, allowing development based on vast knowledge. In fact, this is the main contribution of the soul that is reincarnated in man towards the development of humanity.

Do you want an example? Here's one: When human beings were sufficiently developed and ready for the stage of permanent settlement, we souls began a slow process of implanting knowledge and embedding ideas in people in different locations. "Suddenly" people began growing their food in a controlled manner. People in different locales, with no connection, discovered, at about the same time, grains that could be cultivated, leading to the development of agriculture in cycles of sowing and reaping; this, in turn, paved the way for permanent settlement and the end of nomadic life. So what did you think? That it was mere coincidence? That suddenly, after tens of thousands of years of thinking man's existence, people all around the world started to grow wheat? Then the same thing happened with the domestication of animals. For example, herds of sheep were domesticated in far-flung, unconnected locales- without any exchange of information between people.

Have you ever considered that this didn't all happen on its own? Two and a half millennia ago, for example, before there was any contact between Central Americans and Europeans, the inhabitants of Central and South America already had an independent, advanced culture, including a centralized municipal government based on knowing how to utilize water sources for agriculture and cultivating a large assortment of plants, as well as building a flourishing economy and cross-country roads connecting distant settlements. There was even writing discovered among them, although this appeared a bit later. All this was without any connection to other cultures.

And in East Asia? There, a rich culture developed, with agriculture, writing, medicine, and technology, all without any link to the cultural centers in the West such as Mesopotamia and Egypt.

As I said, this was not happenstance. We souls made this change take place, as part of the broader plan of Creation, of which we are a part. We took advantage of the process of reincarnation, and we transmitted to human beings the knowledge and memories of others from other places who had already left this world; this allowed them to develop and advance this knowledge. Human beings – wondrous creatures that they are – took full advantage of this, creating other cultures and developing the world in an impressive manner. We only sowed, but humanity knew how to reap.

Now, a bit after the age of Penelope, it was time to reach an additional stage of human development, that of a spiritual leap. From the perspective of Creation, human beings are supposed to develop to the level at which they can connect with their souls as well as higher echelons of the spiritual world, to develop communication with them without any intermediary. When this occurs, man can look into his innermost soul more efficiently and transform all those lower parts of consciousness into a broader and higher consciousness, thereby improving quality of life.

The spiritual journey of humanity began tens of thousands of years ago, when man was "only" a living being with the sole conscious goal of survival. The aim of Creation, as I have said, has always been, and still is, to bring man to another place, a higher place, to a conscious connection to their soul and to Creation. This is a long process that requires precise planning and careful execution, one step at a time. The process began with man's recognition that something unclear and unknown was "running the show," something that man could rely on, could ask for help for in difficult circumstances, and could bless in moments of joy.

At first, this could have been the ancient tree at the foot of the hill or the stream from which they drank and with which they irrigated. As man developed, faith moved on to something more distant and more powerful- the heavenly bodies, from the sun warming the day to the moon lighting up the night, as well as solid objects that could be perceived with the five senses.

Seventy thousand years ago, with precise timing according to the plan of Creation, human consciousness reached a more advanced stage, leaving the first regions of its development to journey across the globe. In every place, man found local gods to worship and sanctify; as man developed, these gods became more tangible, in the form of statues and images they could take with them on their travels. These figures had spiritual centers, temples, and ritual ceremonies, but the representation was always material.

This was a precise process, and it developed the understanding that divinity is an entity external to man, whom man needs. They turned to it in prayer and to offer sacrifices, but the essential characteristic of it, for thousands of years, was having a form, a figure coming from the tangible world.

About 1,000 years before Penelope, human development reached the level that allowed the next stage of Creation, a conceptualization of God in the abstract, and not as part of the material world.

Acting precisely and deliberately, we helped human society develop a process that you might call a pilot program, the essence of which was the recognition of one God, abstract, with no form or appearance - the concept you call "monotheism." This experiment began in the Middle East with a small nation, the Hebrew Israelites, who developed the faith in a hidden God to an extent that He directed them in all aspects of their lives – such as when and what they would eat, how they would dress and, moreover, what was prohibited and what was permitted in interpersonal relations.

Now, 1,500 years into the pilot program, the time had come for this understanding to influence and enlighten the entire world. The time had also come to lay the foundations for a new, broad, monotheistic faith that would have an effect on the lion's share of the world's population.

This process was punctiliously and precisely planned, as much as was feasible. The souls reincarnated in human bodies that were tied to this process were chosen specifically, and we Guides had to accompany them as closely as possible. We were well aware of the power that freedom of choice gives to people, and who like us remembered the times when it served as an obstacle to the realization of the soul plans?

When it comes to me, the story begins 350 years after Penelope's death in Greece, years throughout which I was reincarnated twice, and even served as a Guide to many souls in their reincarnations.

This time, I was born in Sepphoris in the Galilee as a Jewish boy named Penuel. According to the plan, I was to be the great-grand-father of John the Baptist, who had an essential role to play in the building of this new faith; I would pave the path for his being raised in the proper time and place. In John's father would reside the soul whose development I would Guide, which would allow me to assist in moments of crisis, should they arise. Did they in fact arise? Was there any call for me to intervene? I learned the details of this tale from the souls that were involved, as well as from the cosmic library after the conclusion of the process- after John's death.

You are invited to read the story I tell as follows

Penuel

Penuel was the son of Jonathan son of Asher, a resident of Seppho-ris in the Galilee. In his youth, Jonathan met the man who would grow up to be Alexander Jannaeus, King of Israel, although his name was then Jonathan Alexander[15] His father, John Hyrcanus I, was es-tranged from the young boy and sent him from Jerusalem to grow up in Sepphoris in the distant Galilee. There Jonathan and Alexander became best friends.

At first, Jonathan was concerned about associating with an aris-tocrat, but he became a close friend and confidant of the prince who was stuck far from home. "My name is Jonathan too," the prince would say, "and just as our names are the same, our hearts are as well." This was a years-long friendship, and when Jonathan married Shelomith, Alexander (now king) was invited to the occasion. He even brought a unique wedding gift – a ring with the king's name,

---

15   Alexander Jannaeus - Jonathan Alexander on some coins - was born in 127 BCE and died of malaria in 76 BCE at the age of 51.

designated for the firstborn son of the couple. "This ring," the king promised, "will open many doors for the boy in Jerusalem."

However, for many years Jonathan and Shelomith were not blessed with children. Jonathan lived his life lazily. He did not marry until he was almost thirty, and he did not have Penuel, his first son, until he was fifty. King Jannaeus, invited to the circumcision ceremony, smiled and promised that he would attend Penuel's wedding as well. He could not have known that he would not have the opportunity to do so, as his soul e would return to the Creator the next year.

Penuel grew up to be a unique, brilliant boy, a proud Hebrew who loved his family and his people. Jonathan his father, whose connection to King Jannaeus made him a royal confidant, raised his son as a prince, and the royal ring either hung on a necklace or sat on his finger throughout his life. When Penuel was set to marry Mary (Miriam), Jonathan invited Jannaeus's son and heir, King John Hyrcanus II, to the wedding. The new king, who respected the bonds forged by his father, brought Penuel, his contemporary, close to him. This led to a bond of friendship and trust, much like the one between Alexander Jannaeus and Jonathan, forming between their two sons. Penuel would even act as an advisor when the need arose.[16]

Penuel was quite clever in using his connections to royalty in order to expand his business all the way to Jerusalem. He would go to the capital from time to time, either for business interests or for consultations in the palace. He and his wife Mary built their house in Sepphoris, and they established a model family. The couple lived in mutual respect and joy, eventually having three sons and two daughters – the firstborn, Shomria, and her younger sister, Hannah.

---

16   John Hyrcanus II did not last long on the throne, as he was deposed by his younger brother Aristobulus. John served as high priest, but the bonds to Penuel were maintained with John and with his brother.

The daughters grew up and became famous in the city and the entire region - and not just for being Penuel's daughters. They were active, talented women, and there were many people who wanted to be close to them. Shomria was good-natured, with many friends in her orbit; her sister Hannah, who was more serious, dedicated herself to trying to make the world a better place, helping the downtrodden and oppressed. They were renowned through the entire Galilee, and even as far as Jerusalem, which they would often visit. Their father would always take his wife and many children on his journeys, wanting to maintain the social bonds with the aristocracy of the nation, but also in order to make a pilgrimage to the Temple.

The years passed, with Shomria loving Jerusalem and spending much time in the capital, while her sister Hannah remained in the Galilee and married Jehoiakim, a distinguished Jew from Sepphoris who was quite wealthy, with business interests all over the region. Hannah supported her husband in his work, and through him she became deeply familiar with the beautiful town of Nazareth, atop the nearest mountain. The young woman fell in love with the place and convinced her husband to build a small summer home there. That was where their children were born, their favorite being an unusual and special girl named Mary - in honor of Miriam, sister of Moses, master of all prophets, as well as her own mother, Penuel's wife.

Her older sister Shomria found her place in Jerusalemite society, especially among the Sadducees, the Israelite elite whose priests ran the Temple. Eventually she met a young man, Aaron, who was handsome, intelligent and well-liked; like her father, he was a businessman with many commercial enterprises in the capital. The two fell deeply and hopelessly in love, and Aaron asked Penuel for Shomria's hand in marriage. Their wedding was quite the affair, and they became a power couple in Jerusalem's high society. They quickly had children, the firstborn being a beautiful baby that they named Elizabeth, recalling Elisheba daughter of Amminadab,[17] the matriarch of priesthood.

Elizabeth

Elizabeth grew up in Jerusalem, and like her parents was an indispensable part of the Sadducee elite; still, she maintained her family connections to Sepphoris, particularly her younger cousin Mary.

When she grew up and matured, Elizabeth met Zechariah, a distinguished priest who was a member of the priestly guard in the Temple; the two soon married. Penuel, who loved his granddaughter deeply, came all the way from Sepphoris and helped the two build their home in Ein Kerem, a small village surrounded by olive and fig trees on a hill southwest of Jerusalem, overlooking the beautiful vistas of the Judean Hills.

Elizabeth loved her life there. She and her husband hosted numerous fetes and feasts to which many of Jerusalem's glitterati were invited. However, as time passed, they encountered difficulties. Zechariah and his friends would drink excessively, and this had a negative effect on his usually congenial temperament. His conduct was altered, and instead of being good-natured and well-liked, he became arrogant and hurtful, spending most of his free time under the influence of wine.

---

17   Elisheba was the most distinguished woman in all of Israel at the time of the Exodus from Egypt: her father was Amminadab and her brother Nahshon, who served as the prince of the Tribe of Judah during the Israelites' sojourn in the desert. Elisheba married Aaron, brother of Moses; Aaron was the first high priest and their sons the first deputy priests, giving Elisheba the title "matriarch of priesthood." Their two older sons died tragically at the inauguration of the Tabernacle. Her grandson Phineas was a warrior who led 12,000 into battle against Midian.

Sorrow made its way to the couple's home, and there was another potent source of grief, when they discovered that Elizabeth could not become pregnant. One month passed after another, one year after another, and the couple remained childless. The fetes and feasts disappeared from their lives, and little by little, the two disassociated from all of their friends - and even from each other.

Zechariah dedicated most of his time to his work in the Temple. He was often away from home, but he took the intoxicants with him; the more he indulged, the more cut off and introverted he became. When his work was negatively impacted, he blamed others for his failures. It all came to a head when a senior priest in the Temple, who remembered what Zechariah had once been, summoned him. "God does not let His servants act in this way. This is sacred ground, and your shameful behavior degrades Him. You must stop drinking. Go back to your wife, and do not let your grief control you. You are a good man, Zechariah. You must reclaim that!"

However, this talk had no impact; neither did his friends' pleas. As much as they wanted to help, they couldn't break through the wall of self-pity and victimization that Zechariah had built. Things got so bad that he was summoned to the high priest's chamber. This was no minor discussion; the high priest was none other than John Hyrcanus II, who had been king but was deposed by his brother Judah (Aristobulus), the same John who was a good friend of Penuel. The high priest summoned him, both as a family friend and by virtue of his office. He radiated authority, and when he demanded that Zechariah look him in the eye, the junior priest felt as if he were nothing. All he wanted was to flee.

The discussion shocked Zechariah to his very core, and he was trembling as he left the high priest's chamber since he no longer knew what to do. When his shift was over, he turned towards the Sanctum

Sanctorum[18] and entered a small room, falling to his knees in the antechamber. Like a man mourning for himself, like a man who felt his life was over, a great cry burst forth from him. Only there, feeling that he was at his nadir, sensing his impotence within the darkness that befell him, did he understand that he needed help. Crying and praying, he turned to his God for clemency and assistance.

All this time I was in Penuel's body, but at the same I also served as the Guide of the soul in Zechariah's body; in this capacity, I tracked the conduct of the young couple in terms of their soul-plans, mainly regarding everything tied to fulfilling their role in the plan of Creation. The fact that their son had not yet been born put the entire plan in great jeopardy.

According to the script, two important people needed to be born: John, Elizabeth's son; and Jesus, Mary's son. The former was supposed to be a Nazirite, a preacher and famous spiritual leader. John would be the one to baptize Jesus and implant in him the idea of being the messiah (*christos*), which would allow his cousin from Nazareth to be the founder of the Nazarene faith, Christianity. But at this point, Elizabeth and Zechariah were not producing children, which meant that action had to be taken immediately.

Up here, we knew full well that Elizabeth was not, in fact, infertile. We also knew that the reason for their childlessness was Zechariah's indulgence in wine, which reduced his sexual potency; however, the problem was reversible. The couple themselves, naturally, had no idea, but we sought a way to rectify it.

Zechariah was being crushed in a vise. Not only was his soul hurt

---

18   The Sanctum Sanctorum (Holy of Holies) was the innermost chamber of the Temple, the place designated for the Ark of the Covenant. Only the high priests could enter, and that took place only once a year, on Yom Kippur (the Day of Atonement).

and he shut down down within himself, but he was being drawn deeper and deeper into intoxication. He needed a big scare, an event that would shake him to the depths of his soul. The opportunity fell into our hands after the high priest spoke to him.

I say it "fell into our hands," but that's not the whole story. After all, I was there the whole time, and it was I who, as Penuel, the high priest's friend, turned to him and asked him to get involved. I also brought into the picture the very high Guidance of the high priest himself, proposing that the next time the priest would "connect" to the Guidance - a not uncommon occurrence - it would give him the message that Zechariah could not continue to serve God in his present state.

Indeed, the conversation with the high priest shook Zechariah, shattering him inside; he prayed, deeply and sincerely, for assistance. Good. This was the exact moment I had been waiting for – which is how I connected to his spirit, to his consciousness, and he experienced revelation.

Never before had Zechariah had such an experience, seeing an image of what he described as "angels." He knew that senior priests were fortunate enough to achieve this, and now, to his great astonishment and terror, he beheld the figure of a ministering angel as it turned towards him, and he was quite taken aback. The angel seemed tangible, and the figure addressed him.

First, he felt a glorious wave of love surrounding him, filling him with tranquility and calm. For a moment he felt weightless, hovering somewhere between the dimensions, feeling as if he were cradled in the hands of a loving mother. A pleasurable sensation flowed throughout his body, and a sense of holiness encircled him. Then he observed himself, but from the outside, seeing Zechariah the harsh, the offensive, the egotistical; he also saw how he caused so much pain to his best friends. He suddenly saw his wife, his beloved, crying through the night, and he even saw himself walking among all of them, a blind man wandering in the dark.

Then the music arrived, a balm for his spirit - tones, peals, chords such as he had never heard before - and the angel began to speak to him. There was no anger in the angel's voice, no rebuke, just love and longing. Zechariah felt great pain and deep regret, and tears flowed down his cheeks.

Finally, when he was ready, I showed him an image of his wife as she hugged their unborn child.

He heard a question. "Do you love Elizabeth?"

He nodded.

"No," the voice continued, "don't nod. You must shout your answer to the heavens!"

Then Zechariah screamed with all his might, "I love Elizabeth."

"Do you want to embrace the son you are destined to have?"

Zechariah's voice rose once more, and he cried, "Yes, I do!"

"If I tell you, 'Stop drinking immediately! Go back to your house and embrace your wife,' will you do it?"

Zechariah raised his fists and screamed to the heavens, "I will pour out all the wine in my house, I will scatter the wine barrels to the four winds, I will embrace my wife and love her, I will go back to being Zechariah son of Israel, I will go back to being God's faithful servant!" He fell to the floor, his body convulsing as he shed unstoppable tears.

Hearing the screams, many priests from the watches ran to the spot, and they saw an astonishing sight. At first, they saw Zechariah convulsing in tears on the floor; then he stood up straight, held his head high, and declared in a clear voice, "The angel spoke to me.[19] As for me, I will keep my promise, and I will add that from this day until my son is circumcised, I will shut my mouth. I will not say one word." He glared, looking from one priest to the other, and his colleagues saw the Zechariah they remembered, a man on whom the Divine Presence rested, a man of determination. All they could do was cast their gaze to the floor in his presence.

Indeed, a year passed, and Elizabeth announced to her husband that their love had been restored, stronger than ever - and that she was pregnant.

Elizabeth felt the first kick when she was sitting in her courtyard with her beloved cousin Mary, who had come to visit and congratulate her on the pregnancy. The two of them didn't know that soon Mary, too, would be in the family way; with his birth, their world would change forever. When Zechariah and Elizabeth became parents, the first great-grandchild for Penuel and Mary, they called him John at the request of Penuel, who was already elderly and wanted to memorialize the name of his good friend, the high priest-king.

The new John became a well-known and well-regarded preacher among the Jews. He was known as John the Baptist because he believed that immersion in the river could purify and refine the soul of the participant. He taught his ways among the many believers who followed him. Within him, he believed, was the soul of Elijah the Prophet, who was destined to announce the arrival of the Messiah.

When his cousin, Jesus son of Mary, came to his isolated and distant home in the Jordan Valley, John baptized him and declared

---

19   This tale of angelic revelation appears in the Gospel of Luke, Chapter 1. According to the narrative there, the Angel Gabriel appeared to Zechariah, predicting the birth of John; it tells of the terror that befell Zechariah, along with his losing his power of speech.

that he was the Messiah. This ceremony, carried out by John, a pure, celebrated, unique man, had quite the impact on Jesus. From that point on, he became a preacher in his own right and attracted many disciples from all over.

In terms of the plan of Creation, the goal had been fully achieved. From now on, the spreading of monotheism would be handed over to Jesus and his disciples. John himself had other lessons to learn in this life, but those were a part of his own soul lessons.

His status was so lofty and celebrated - not due to the function or office he held, but because of who he was. But the price proved to be very high. John enraged the ruler, Herod Antipas.[20] When John criticized the ruler's religious and moral conduct, Herod Antipas was terrified of John's strong character and the revolt that he might inspire. John was imprisoned in the castle at Machaerus on the eastern side of the Jordan, and at the first opportunity Herod Antipas had John decapitated.

Man plans, but fate laughs. The site of John the Baptist's execution was the same castle built a century before by King Alexander Jannaeus - who had first formed the bond between the royal family and John's family.

---

20   Herod Antipas, son of King Herod the Great, was the tetrarch of the Galilee and Perea (the eastern Jordan Valley).

CHAPTER ELEVEN

The First Millennium

Another thousand years passed, and humanity continued to develop; their abilities increased at a dizzying pace, and Planet Earth continued to be an intriguing place, with mostly unanticipated changes. The human spirit continues to yield surprises.

The Hebrew state in which John and Jesus had been born was destroyed by the Roman legions. The Jewish faith survived, although only by the skin of its teeth, while Christianity continued to gain momentum, spreading across large swaths of the globe in just a few centuries. Jesus's disciples, the Apostles, spread the new faith throughout the world, even though its adherents were initially persecuted. It expanded and developed as the decades passed, until it became, in 313 CE, the official religion of the Roman Empire.

The new monotheistic faith spread throughout the world at a particularly impressive pace. Twenty years after Rome adopted it, the Aksumite Empire of East Africa, for example, did the same. You may know it today as Ethiopia.

Three centuries passed, and an additional monotheistic faith appeared on the world stage: Islam.

So how did a new religion, based on the worship of one god,

suddenly pop up in a region populated by pagans? It began with revelation. When Muhammad was forty, alone in a cave near the city of Mecca, the Angel Gabriel (Jibril) appeared to him, gave him a silk scroll, and ordered him to read from it. This was the Al-Alaq Surah (a chapter in the Quran), which opened with "Read in the name of your Lord." This powerful encounter motivated Muhammad to spread the new message of Islam; he received many more *suras* afterwards, which constitute the Quran, Islam's holy book.

Does that sound familiar to you? Intervention, from outside the human race? Was this also the hand of the plan of Creation? Come on! Of course it was! Human society was surging along the channel that Creation had carved for it. Humanity developed in the proper direction, and its beneficent future was ready for it.

Lest you think there were only religious revolutions that took place during this millennium, let me assure you that in fact the world changed in consequential ways – from the emigration of peoples to the establishment of new empires. These trends would influence world culture greatly, over a vast time span.

And as for me, the soul? Throughout those years, I stuck to my "personal" track of existence, as I developed and repaired my being. Within my innermost self, I knew that I still lacked a great deal of knowledge. I knew my character traits were not sure enough, that I had a lot to add and to learn, in particular in light of the recognition that the many changes in the structure of human society required accommodations and a new aspect of my own essence.

Throughout those thousand years, I lived through eleven life cycles, in different regions of the world, each of which developed at its own pace. In most of the reincarnations, I dealt with caring for and healing people. I was a physician, a midwife, and a tribal healer; in the meantime, I of course dealt with many other topics, such as realizing one's self-worth, altruism versus egocentrism, love of one's self versus love of others, and many other lessons as well.

You already know the fact of my eternal existence, even if it is a hard-to-digest fact, and you are also aware of the multi-tasking activities we conduct in different places, through many events, and through various activities, all at the same time – for example, the ability to dwell inside of and outside the body, and to be active to the fullest of my abilities in all places, all without interruption, as I told you via the metaphor of the lake and its water. During this millennium, as in previous ones, I also engaged in many other tasks related to the plan of Creation and directing the development of society.

But the activity that I relish most exists precisely on the banal, daily level, in summoning opportunities and events that allow the soul to realize its plan in the body, and I do this with great love.

For example, while I existed in a physical body, I received, by virtue of my role as a Guide and through our telepathic information-exchange system, knowledge concerning two young people destined to build a family together; due to their life circumstances, however, and perhaps because of decisions made individually by them, they had diverged from the soul script. A situation had arisen in which, if the current trends were to continue, the two would not meet or establish the family that constituted such a central axis in the plan of both. Therefore, it became necessary to create a pathway allowing them to connect to each other.

And how was it done? Quite simply. I was the soul Guide of a man close to the parents of these two, and on one of the occasions when he sat with the two fathers, I brought him quite easily into a situation where he needed urgent help. He was in real danger, and the two fathers jumped in together to help. After they rescued him from his predicament (of course), the survivor invited the families to a big thanksgiving dinner. At the celebration, the eyes of the two intended youths met, and fortunately they did not need cupid to shoot the arrow of love into them, as the sparks flew on their own.

I've done this sort of thing countless times, and people are not even aware that behind what appears to be a chance encounter or unplanned coincidence, stands the high Guidance.

Sometimes the events in a person's life bring about activity even after their death, such as when the soul has undergone a trauma that requires fundamental cleansing. This was the case of Antonia of Rome.

Antonia

Halfway through the fifth century, in 455 CE, the Vandals invaded Rome. They came from Carthage in North Africa, and they spread Arianism, their stream of Christianity, but they did so while they cruelly looted, slaughtered, and ravaged the Roman Catholic community.

On the first Sunday of June that year, a beautiful young woman emerged from the church after the baptism of her infant son. Antonia was accompanied by her friends, sisters and mother; she hugged her firstborn boy, swaddled in white, to her bosom as she sang a lovely lullaby. Passersby who observed the lovely tableau smiled at the group and wished them well. She was so happy!

Five days earlier, the Vandals had entered Rome. Citizens of the Empire, and certainly inhabitants of the capital, were aware of the ongoing war; terrifying stories had spread like wildfire. However, on that beautiful late spring day, as Antonia danced down the street to her home, nothing could distract her from her baby and her happiness with her life; she didn't even hear the growing cacophony on the other side of the street, nor the sudden warning cries of her own friends.

Battle cries, screaming, and yelling filled the air as people began to flee, but Antonia, in another world, didn't notice anything. Her gaze was fixed on the baby she loved, and she continued happily walking down the street until she was suddenly stopped by a cavalryman. She couldn't understand a word that he said, but a wave of terror washed over her as she realized she had been separated from her mother and the other members of her party, some of whom had fled from the horses, while others had been trampled and crushed under their hooves. Frozen to her spot, she couldn't move.

The cavalryman was joined by other horsemen who surrounded her and jumped down, moved close to her, staring with a terrifying look. He spoke, but she didn't hear.

He reached out, but she held the infant tighter, firing a furious glare at the cavalryman. His comrades yelled, and they appeared to be egging him on; he, for his part, unfazed by her stare, just grabbed the infant forcefully and tossed him backward to the soldiers who caught the "package" in the air, and with one swipe of a sword sliced the baby's head off and cast it to the ground.

Antonia burst into sobs, trying to rush toward the body of her baby, but a soldier stopped her. He pulled at her dress, and with his dagger, tore her clothes off her. Antonia was beautiful, and the more she screamed, the more she struggled, the more attractive she seemed to the Vandal and his comrades who were sitting on their horses. In a matter of seconds, his trousers were down and she was lying on the ground, kicking, screaming, and spitting in his face. He didn't care about her pain or sorrow, so he penetrated her forcefully, slamming her body down onto the stones of the street.

Once he finished, as she was lying there shaking and bleeding, his companions approached, one by one, and acted out their perverted lust. Antonia's cries brought many citizens out of their homes and they attempted to stop the soldiers, but the horsemen, toying with the idea, decided to arrange the citizens in a circle around the poor woman. Some tried to intervene, but after the first two braves ones were slaughtered by the horsemen, there was utter silence, broken only by cries of anguish from the stunned spectators. When the soldiers had sated their desires and finished abusing Antonia, one of them released her from her pain by stabbing her in the neck. She died as she gurgled the death rattle.

The first cavalryman, apparently the commander, stood straight and announced to all the assembled people, in slurred Latin, "This is the fate of all Catholics who deny the nature of God!"

Healing and Enlightenment, Renewed

Antonia's soul was on its way to the transit gate. A soul that ends its life in such a way, suddenly, in shock and suffering, will arrive in great distress. It needs someone to rely on, someone it respects, someone who will be a supporter and direct it along the path from life in a body to its existence as a soul, from the life of an emotion-fueled human being to the life of a soul beyond such considerations. Its Guidance is uniquely suited to doing this.

I was that Guide.

This soul arrived at the gate in an acute state of desperation. A human soul, upon the conclusion of its life, moves from the physical plane to the higher planes of existence, the first of which is the "ethereal plane." (See Footnote 3 on page ##.) At this stage, the soul is a bit confused. It is in a totally different energetic state, but still connected to the physical plane, emotionally tied to the human beings it has just left, and is feeling various sensations and emotions. Antonia's soul was still in total shock.

Many of its friends from its soul family waited with me at the gate, as well as others who showered great love upon it. They did everything in their power to give it the feeling of tranquility and security that it needed so badly. But Antonia's soul was still "there," on Planet Earth, and despite the enveloping and encompassing environment that received it, its abilities to undergo the change were impaired; it needed something else.

I connected to the soul, and it was possible to feel the immediate relief. I isolated it from the environment, and we transitioned to a state in which only the two of us were present; all the others understood that this was a special moment for the being of the soul, and that I, the Guide, was the entity that had to be with it. With mutual agreement, we passed from the gate to the area of healing, the sphere of orientation and enlightenment, where the soul could rest, be calmed, and be cleansed.

This is not an area of "pampering"; indeed, as we are energetic entities, there is not much activity going on. So what exactly takes place there? The energy is cleansed, and there is no better way to do this than flood the soul with pure love – unconditional love, freely given. This is our way here, and this is how we cleanse ourselves. When it reaches the moment in which it can remember its true essence, the moment in which it again feels the essence of pure love, it returns to itself, to its soul family, and the desire to return and continue self-repair and study on Planet Earth once again washes over it, setting it on the right path again.

Most of the time, we return from a life journey that has concluded in a way quite close to the soul plan (even if the life seemingly ends suddenly, at least from the human perspective), and we move on to a process of rest and detachment in the area of orientation and enlightenment. This is not such a simple process when the life ends in an unplanned way, or even with intense suffering; the soul arrives disoriented and the transition between the physical and spiritual planes is much more complicated.

Antonia's soul finished its life in a way that did not follow the original script with which it had descended to the world; it experienced this in a particularly cruel manner. When it ascended and returned, it was disabled. It was difficult to remember its original essence, and the planned script of its life seemed to be unreal or irrelevant. The area of orientation and enlightenment was the best place for it, as there it could once again absorb love.

When Antonia's soul felt that it needed advice, or a feeling of joy or connection, it would know whom to turn to, and everyone would respond to it. If it were still to feel unprepared, they would leave it alone and give it all the time that it needed. Now this isn't really time *per se*. Remember, we have different dimensions here, but it is the only way for you human beings to comprehend. As the Guide, I was in constant contact with Antonia's soul, without interfering or interrupting; it didn't even know I was there, except for the knowledge of being surrounded by loving entities that would respond to its every need, always.

So what have we learned?

In earthly terms, Antonia's soul stayed in the orientation and enlightenment center for a year and a half, and when it called me and said, "That's it. I've recovered," I could sense it. Was it cleansed of all the trauma it had gone through? My experience told me otherwise, but the soul felt that it was ready to advance to the next stage, and this was the most important factor.

Antonia's soul... You know what? Why don't we just say Antonia?

Souls have no names, and we don't need for them to have names. With a telepathic connection, all we need is to think of an entity, and it is immediately with us. But in your world, a name is the most important way of identifying someone, so I will call this soul Antonia, the name that her parents gave her when she was born in her last incarnation.

Antonia was a relatively young soul. She had "only" gone through a few dozen reincarnations, and the last life cycle had been a unique trial from which there was much to learn. In the next period, as she already knew, we would go over all of the details of her life to see how they measured up to the script.

When Antonia told me the story of her life, from birth to death, we spent most of our time on the moments that did not accommodate the plan; we tried to decipher the factors behind this divergence. We wanted to learn and understand the mechanisms of her thinking as a human being, the mechanism that led her to arrive at a decision that differed from the plan. This was an important analysis, the kind we always undertake at the end of a human life. Whenever we find a decision that contradicts the plan, it is our obligation, Guidance and soul, to understand what happened, particularly in light of the fact that the soul guardian and the directing Guidance escort the human being throughout life, and they generate opportunities to direct the life journey to the proper track and impede its progress when a human decision arises that diverges from it.

Bit by bit, we traced Antonia's life story – child, girl, woman; every detail was written in the book of her life and kept in the cosmic library.[21]

---

21   In many spiritual traditions, this cosmic library is called the Akashic library. Akasha is a Sanskrit word adopted in the West in the nineteenth century.

Antonia was a young woman when she was murdered. Many of the tasks from her life plan remained unfulfilled, and many lessons that the soul within her wanted to experience were never reached, so that this stage of research was relatively short. We quickly arrived at an analysis of that ruthless day in Rome.

Antonia's soul remembered the sensations, the pain, and the impotence in the face of such cruelty, but this time without experiencing the emotional difficultly. She understood the depth of the pain and its impact, and apparently she could, and indeed had to, dissect the event in a cold, detached manner – but this wasn't what happened. Antonia understood that the event had an influence upon her, upon the soul, and she couldn't relate to it in an external, indifferent manner; she understood that the event could influence her future decisions. The resolution of this crisis, she knew, could be achieved with the help of the other souls, especially the Guides (me among them, of course), whom she could consult.

But there's a time for everything, and it was time for studying. Antonia received a powerful lesson on the meaning of the emotional connection of mother to child from her experience, but also from the somewhat remote observation of Antonia's mother, who was present and forced to watch what happened to her daughter and grandson.

An equally important lesson was about the cruelty and fanaticism that tend to accompany faith. From our position in the higher worlds, we cannot sense the tide that overwhelms the human spirit. We can observe it, and we can recall it, but when we encounter it anew, it surprises us greatly each time, and we know that this inability is an obstacle when we build the life plan for a soul before it is born.

As for the substantial influence of this experience on Antonia, it was merely a potentiality, and only when we built her future soul plan could we know its scope and meaning, as well as the influence it would have when she would be reincarnated in a human body. This issue preoccupied me, and I hoped that now, immediately after finishing the process of investigating Antonia's life, when she would join her soul family, this encounter would have a positive impact that would allow her to understand her position and, in the next reincarnation, undergo a full process of repair.

We had finished the stage of investigating the previous life. We had defined and transcribed, in a precise and exact manner, the events in Antonia's life from birth to death, highlighting the issues from the original plan to which she wanted to return and complete in the next life. However, she was atypically quiet when she talked about them, and it appeared that the thought of another reincarnation generated some reluctance that she may not have even been aware of. I made a note of this for myself, regarding the continuation of Antonia's journey, and a little while after that I told her that she had finished the work of her previous life and it was now time to join her family. I told her this in a place in which there was a feeling of calmness, maintained by what I can best describe as music that was both playful and joyful; her relief was powerful, obvious, and overwhelming. All she had to do was express her wish- and transfer.

Rebirth

As things go, just with the very desire and expression of her wish, Antonia found herself within the bosom of her soul family, which of course knew about her arrival and eagerly anticipated it.

At this stage, Antonia ascended to the level of unity on the plane of spiritual existence, the level of pure consciousness, devoid of any ego, without body or corporeal semblance, upon which the souls maintain pure spiritual awareness. Here she met the members of the soul family and merged with their pure thoughts, with their sensations and their energy. There was no need for vocabulary or language, as each knows all the others.

The first to contact her was her soul twin - unsurprisingly, it's always that way. The feeling of love that swept over Antonia was powerful, and if she'd had eyes, they would have been full of tears. The thought that came from her twin was warm, intimate, and engaging. "I may not have been down there with you in a body," said the twin, "but I followed you and I was by your side from the moment that event began. I couldn't do anything, because the choice of the human beings was very strong and their path was so clear and decisive, and you know that we cannot, and in fact must not, tamper with their free will, as wrong as it may be; even if it is directed by entities from the darkness, it is still their choice, and we cannot do anything. All I can do is flood you with love and memories of existence here, the existence that is detached from the physical world, in order to lessen your pain. From the moment you came up here, I confirmed with your Guide that you were undergoing the process in the easiest possible way, and I am so glad that you made it through that period and are okay now. We will continue down the path together and, if you want, I will accompany you on your journey, with your Guidance, as you face your future tasks."

Antonia seemed to accept this warm welcome happily, as well as the love that her family showered upon her, but I, her accompanying Guidance, knew in my innermost self that the effects of this life-ending experience were not completely wiped away.

Indeed, as time passed, everything I had been worried about began to float to the surface. It soon became apparent that Antonia was reluctant to begin planning her future life. This precious entity began to engage in every intensive activity connected to the upper worlds, helping a great deal with souls that returned from an additional life cycle in crisis, and mainly worked with young children who had died before their time. She also participated in the activity of other souls who needed assistance in planning their lives, whether it was giving advice or helping them find information in the cosmic library; generally, she showed up wherever she felt she had the capacity to contribute and enlighten. No doubt, Antonia lit up her surroundings and she even evolved while doing so. Her activity made me quite happy, and apparently there was no need to worry, but whenever she needed to address her next life, she evaded the topic as much as possible – which was more than a hint about what would come next.

I could understand her reasons for avoiding an additional life. People are familiar with this when a person experiences trauma, that it is very difficult to return to the scene of the event and try again. What then do friends and healers do? They bring the person back there as soon as possible. Ostensibly, we do the same. The difference is that the soul that has gone through the ordeal no longer feels the fear and it does not manage it. It remembers the event, but without feeling the sensations anew, and since the memory cannot be erased, there is essentially nothing to repair.

Antonia's reluctance emanated from her empathy towards people. She didn't want to be in a body that would suffer as the young mother had suffered. If it had happened once, it could happen again. What she couldn't internalize was the fact that such reluctance could become second nature, and if nothing was done, she would not be incarnated again, her evolution could come to a halt and, at the end of the day, she would be harmed, she would be weakened, and it would be impossible to know what her ultimate fate might be.

It was essential for Antonia to understand and digest her situation. Practically, she already knew this, so the proper way was simply to allow her to experience the significance of her continuing to exist, if she were to be reincarnated in a human body, despite it all.

First of all, I summoned her to training sessions that young souls held with the lofty Guidances, and I chose for her the lessons in which the topic of discussion was the importance of cooperation among souls in the process of reincarnation. It was very important for her to internalize that her life in a body was not just the fulfillment of her private soul plan; she was always involved, through soul contracts, with the lives of other people. She had to digest how much she was hurting her friends in her soul family, who needed her in their life processes, by not participating in the cycle of reincarnations and by not signing contracts before they found form in a body. The trauma she went through at the end of her previous life had dimmed her gaze, and she needed to clarify anew on the meaning of love between souls.

Then I moved on to the process that would strengthen the important connection that exists between us and human beings. I invited her to join me for a number of cases where I served as a counselor when the need arose to help a person maintain the planned path.

We did this in the small details of life – for example, while following the story of a man and woman whose life scripts were directing them towards getting married, even if they themselves knew nothing about it, but various choices they made in their lives prevented the long-awaited encounter, and especially the reluctance of the man, who was already married, and preferred to stay with one woman.

The soul plan, written even before the man's birth, anticipated his opposition and prepared a solution through a soul contract entered into with a neighbor to his field plot, who mocked his cowardice at the prospect of dealing with two wives. "Your wife is really cracking the whip," he would tease him in public, "and you cannot handle her. It's no wonder that you cannot marry a second wife like the rest of us!"

Then one day, while the men were sitting in the town square, a foreign merchant arrived, "coincidentally" accompanied by his beautiful daughter. It was she who was destined to marry that man. The irksome neighbor, who was on the spot, opened his mouth to loudly mock and push him, in front of many other men, to muster up the courage to ask the stranger for the young woman's hand. The annoying neighbor did his job faithfully, and indeed, in the end, the stranger and his daughter were invited to dinner, over which the daughter and marriage were discussed.

Antonia watched how I got the daughter to join her father's journey and how I created the circumstances for the neighbor to be present at that meeting. She was amazed, as she didn't believe that the plan could come down to such precise details. It even surprised her that the man hated the neighbor for his abusive behavior without knowing that it was the soul contract that motivated the harassment - the soul contract neither of them was aware of.

Antonia accompanied me through many moments, completely banal in human terms, but precise in terms of the soul plan, allowing people to evolve and grow. There were many examples, and here is another one.

There was an intelligent man who could have succeeded in anything, and chose to become a trader. Unfortunately, he lived most of his life being suspicious of those around him, which prevented him from developing; the more he failed, the more he blamed those around him and those closest to him. The cause of his distrust was the education his father had given him. He didn't know that this was the lesson his soul wanted to learn, nor did he know that his father, who of course was also unaware of it, had signed a soul contract that dictated how he would raise the boy.

My role was to create opportunities that would turn his life around. He was met with several instances in which people of whom he had been suspicious turned out to be generous and helpful in times of crisis. These instances and moments caused him to be introspective and made him reconsider his own approach, and once he discovered that the truth of life differed from what he had learned as a child, he could change and evolve. It also became clear to him that his life as a suspicious person had taught him the same thing or two about human beings that helped him now, because he could take risks, engage in bolder business ventures, and succeed.

Antonia loved what she saw. Gradually, her sense of security increased, as the Guidance was a constant presence assisting each soul. We also observed difficult circumstances, such as souls who chose to live in the bodies of cruel people, and souls who chose to live lives of suffering. Antonia discovered and internalized that in most cases in which a person got into trouble, it was part of the soul plan, of the soul's desire to learn more and more, and knowingly share such events.

She understood that humanity was evolving, that violence and power were an integral part of this development, and that there were souls who chose to participate in these difficult moments because experience and learning are the platform for change. If not for the experienced soul, who could assimilate the memory in the next reincarnation, thus contributing to the subsequent generation, in order for humanity to change and correct itself?

Antonia shared her experiences with her soul family and received much encouragement from them, but one of the moments that influenced her the most was when it became clear that her soul twin was not being reincarnated, despite her strong desire and longing for human beings, simply because she needed Antonia to sign a soul contract so she could succeed in learning the lessons that were necessary for her own development. She was just waiting for Antonia to overcome her fears and decide to be reincarnated.

It is important for me to stop for a moment and explain something else to you, dear readers. Humans may understand the decision of the soul twin in different ways. Some will feel a certain element of anger towards Antonia here. Others may see in it the greatness of the soul twin waiting for her, and perhaps even an indirect attempt to exert pressure on her "to get back on the highway." None of these is true, and among us, none is feasible. We don't compete with each other, and we will never make a decision that is tainted by irrelevant emotion. Antonia would also never have concluded that her twin was trying to exert pressure, or that she was being harmed by her conduct.

She received this information, and it served as additional material for her to understand the mutual influence prevailing between us; it also showed her how every decision we make ripples out far beyond ourselves. This is the way it was when I took on the role of Guide as well. There was no rush of success or sense of "I deserve it," nor was it accompanied by a sense of condescension toward others who were not Guides. We are simply who we are and operate in a non-hierarchical system. While it is true that I have great appreciation for the lofty Guides, I don't feel that I have to do as they advise just because they say so.

My soul twin could have become a Guide and fulfilled the role no better than I did. But for reasons of structure, of experience, of belonging to different groups – and many other reasons, including her own choice – she was not a Guide, and I, although according to human understanding would be her "superior," did not feel condescending towards her; in fact, I would not be capable of feeling that way.

Now back to Antonia. Once I understood how far she had already come, I turned to her and raised the issue of the next reincarnation. She was a bit hesitant, but immediately afterwards I felt that she was filled with the determination and willpower that allowed her- and me, helping her- to start the process of planning a new life.

I won't weary you with the details of Antonia's soul plan; I'll just say that she had all the elements she had not been able to learn in her previous life, and to them were added the same lessons she wanted to learn from the events that ended her previous life. Once we had finished defining the various topics and goals she wanted to achieve in the next life, Antonia moved on to meetings with the training groups whose goal was to allow the plan to take shape. I have already told you about unique groups of lofty Guides who specialize in creating as accurate scripts as possible, in raising the possibilities of souls that will be supported in the process within the framework of a soul contract, in choosing the time period, place, parentage, and more. At this stage of her journey, Antonia worked with such a group in order to create the most suitable script for her.

At the end of the process, she was presented with three possible routes for realization. From a human approach, I would say that she was invited to a movie theater where the various tracks were presented as "films," and she was asked to choose the one that seemed best for her. Antonia "watched" and chose one, but asked to make some changes in the script, greatly complicating the process. Since it would be unthinkable to force on a soul the character of her future life, the team that worked with her went through the process of rearranging the puzzle, and in the end Antonia was ready and willing to return to the path of life.

It was a very happy day when I accompanied Antonia back to the gate, all in eager anticipation; unfortunately, I cannot say that she was emotional, because this is a human experience that we are missing here. Along with me came her siblings from the soul family. There was also her soul twin, who by now was already incarnated in a body and looking forward to the moment when the two would meet on earth as people unaware of the soul plan. Many other souls accompanied her over the course of this period.

We felt the energetic change that took place as Antonia materialized in the body of the fetus, and a huge wave of love erupted from all of us towards the unborn infant.

CHAPTER TWELVE

The Second Millennium: The World Changes

Only two decades had passed since the Sack of Rome by the Vandals, and the world was in chaos. The Roman Empire had split in two, Attila's Huns were overrunning Europe, and kingdoms were rising and falling across the globe. Bit by bit, however, the world that you recognize, dear readers, was coming into being.

The insight of abstract divinity was sweeping across the globe, as Christianity and Islam spread at a dizzying pace, while Buddhism was spreading through East Asia, even reaching Japan by the fifth century; along with it, the Dark Ages were beginning in Europe, the medieval era that would last until about the midpoint of the second millennium. The first centuries of this millennium would see Crusades to the Holy Land, while almost all of Asia would be conquered by the cruel, shocking advance of Genghis Khan, whose combat methods would form the basis of modern warfare; he also developed the trade routes between East and West, changing the world forever.

Now, time does not exist for us as it does for you, but in order to elucidate the situation, I will say that this epoch was a very busy one in terms of my activities. On the one hand, I was occupied by the ongoing activity among the energetic entities in the spiritual world; on the other hand, I was working hard at my role as spiritual Guide with a number of souls, assisting the human beings in which they were incarnated. For example, I helped a priest with an open mind, to receive messages for himself and his flock; in other cases, I helped souls in times of crisis, as the person in whose body they resided veered far off the course their soul had hoped to complete, according to its soul plan. In parallel, I myself was reincarnated many, many times, but I won't trouble you with all the details. Some of them were quite brief, but I would like to mention those in which I lived in a way that conformed to my essential plan- as a caregiver.

In 575, I was born in an area of South America that you know as Peru, as the Wari culture flourished; there, I was a famous healer in my city.

About a century later, in 690, I was born in the newly founded First Bulgarian Empire, where I was a healer and caregiver in a small town on the slopes of the Balkan Mountains.

Two centuries later, I was a physician who joined the first settlers of Iceland in 875.

At the end of the first century of the second millennium, in 1099, I was a caregiver in Jerusalem, and I treated many citizens who were injured in the brutal war to capture the city that was waged by the Crusaders.

As a Mongol, I joined the medical corps established in 1201 by Temüjin, who five years later would be named Genghis Khan, Universal Ruler. This was a unique experience, because this was the first army to have a medical corps; women were even afforded the right to live with equal rights.

But more than any of these lives, I want to tell you about Alfonso.

Alfonso

Pablo was a Spanish artist from Toledo who was famous for the stained-glass windows that he made for both churches and synagogues. His *pièce de résistance* was his work on the Cathedral of Toledo, which became known throughout Spain. In 1462, his second son, Alfonso, was born; for many years, he would accompany his father at work, and even if he was not blessed with his father's great talent, he learned his skill and served as his apprentice.

Alfonso was a different sort of child; Pablo, graced with great sensitivity, felt this when the boy was a newborn. He seemed to have a halo over him, as if the Divine Presence itself dwelled within him and radiated through the light in his eyes.

Indeed, already at a very young age, Alfonso was shown to have bizarre abilities. For example, he claimed that there were figures who visited their house and the surrounding streets, day and night. At first, his parents attributed this to a well-developed imagination, but as these events continued to recur, they began to worry. What really alarmed them was his ability to receive messages from people who weren't even in the area, even from those who had passed from the world, whom the child could not have known. Alfonso himself, who didn't understand his unique nature, assumed that everyone saw this; he couldn't comprehend the great hullabaloo over his talent.

The family, as well as a number of friends, believed that there was a saint growing up in their midst, that God Himself had made the boy His emissary, but they were in the minority. Neighbors and other residents of the city differed on this, believing that the boy had in fact been sent by Satan, that he was his arms-bearer, and that this was why the dead came to him. This belief spread throughout the neighborhood, and Alfonso's parents began to worry that his life might be in danger.

In his distress, Pablo turned to the archbishop at the Cathedral of Toledo for help. Archbishop Alfonso Carrillo de Acuña was a man of great stature, and so Pablo believed that only a figure of such religious authority – who could see the truth – could help. To Pablo's joy, the archbishop was interested in the tale and even asked to bring the boy for a full day with him. Pablo didn't hesitate; the very next day, he came to the cathedral with Alfonso, and he entrusted the boy to the archbishop's aides.

Young Alfonso was no stranger to churches, as he had visited many with his father, even the cathedral, but he was anxious in the presence of such an august personage, especially when it became clear that he was expected to escort the archbishop throughout the day, whatever he did, from administrative activities to his priestly duties, even his meals.

Alfonso accompanied the archbishop from dawn to dusk, but he heard not a word from him. The archbishop did not decided this lightly; he wanted to "get a sense of the boy," and so throughout that first day he simply observed him, noting his movements and responses, looking at what he looked at, what attracted his attention, what piqued his curiosity and indeed, he noticed the "halo" the boy's father had referred to.

As the day was ending, after supper and shortly before bedtime, the archbishop took the boy's hand and they genuflected before the altar and crossed themselves, with the archbishop praying to the Holy Trinity for assistance and guidance towards the proper path.

Then, as he felt unity with God, the archbishop knew that Alfonso was open to the upper worlds, in a way that no other human was fortunate to be. He perceived that it was not the worlds of darkness that controlled the boy's soul, rather that his ability was tied to his destiny in life. But he also understood the great danger the boy faced from the ignorance of those around him.

Once he understood all this, he decided to initiate a rare, unique ceremony that would "seal" the boy's soul and prevent him from receiving additional messages from the World to Come. This was a complex ritual that required him to lay hands on the boy's head, anoint him with holy oil, and complete the process of confirmation[22] anew. When the ceremony was over, he escorted the boy to his bed. Lovingly, the archbishop told him that he ought to ignore the visions if they returned; in any case, he must not share them with others, not even his own father. When he finished, he asked Alfonso to look him straight in the eye, and he saw there peace and security. He smiled, and the boy smiled back at him; it was a conspiratorial smile, as they shared this secret.

Indeed, from that night forward, the vision no longer appeared before Alfonso's eyes, and as time passed he became just like one of the boys, as the "threat" was removed and everything calmed down.

Years passed, the boy grew up, and he joined his father in his profession. He would go from one institution to another and repair the stained-glass windows created by his father; among them were various churches, synagogues, municipal buildings, etc., all of which needed Pablo's expertise, and Alfonso would go from place to place, installing and repairing. He became a well-liked young man, agreeable to everyone.

The change began when he was sixteen. There was a warmth in his nature that drew people to him, but a stray thought – that he was missing out, that he was failing to do something – entered his heart.

The most surprising thing was that he started to have flashes of memories and thoughts about the archbishop. Now elderly and in the

---

22   Confirmation is the Christian rite of initiation.

twilight of his days, the archbishop was involved in political intrigue, but a memory came to the surface in Alfonso's mind. Whenever the archbishop's name came up, the young man's memory would come back in dribs and drabs. At first, it would happen at small gatherings when the archbishop was mentioned, or when someone would tell a story about him. Gradually, these thoughts overwhelmed him; young Alfonso knew, without understanding why, that he had to seek an audience with the archbishop. Within a short time, the thought turned into action, and he was making his way to the cathedral.

However, to his disappointment, he was rebuffed over and over again. The archbishop's secretary knew and liked young Alfonso, but he had to reject his requests for an audience for various reasons, such as the archbishop was busy, he was occupied with matters of state, he was exhausted and his rest could not be disturbed - any and every excuse to avoid meeting with him.

Nevertheless, the thought kept rattling around in Alfonso's head and he kept looking for some way to get to the archbishop. The idea of how to do it simply popped into his head once, when he saw that the secretary had received a scroll designated for the archbishop's eyes only, which was passed on without any questions. Fortunately, as he had flitted around various churches in his youth, he had acquired the art of writing; thus, he decided to pass a missive to the archbishop. He wrote it down, rolled up the scroll, tied it up with a red string, handed it to the secretary and said to him, "If you want His Excellency's favor as I believe you do, you will give him this message."

There was urgency in his voice, and the secretary noticed this. He decided to go above and beyond the call of duty and grant the young man's request, so he took the scroll and handed it to the archbishop. "I neither know nor understand it," the secretary said, "but something about that boy convinced me to do what he asked."

The archbishop opened the letter, and once he saw who his correspondent was, his eyes lit up and he read, "I know that I must have an audience and serve Your Excellency. I do not know how this idea came to me, but it gives me no rest. If Your Excellency will accede to my request, I will come and dedicate all my days, my very life, to Your Excellency's service."

A short time later, Alfonso was summoned to the archbishop's chamber. This was an area of the church new to him, which he had never seen. Unlike the glorious appointments of the public areas of the cathedral, this room was simple and modest. He approved of the way it looked, and it matched the image of the archbishop he'd had in his mind throughout the years.

He approached the doorway, and one of the archbishop's aides in the hallway opened the door for him. Alfonso tiptoed into the room silently, afraid to disturb the priest. The archbishop was sitting in an armchair, with a nice, warm blanket over his knees and warm woolen miter. "Come in, young man. Why are you just standing by the door?" Alfonso approached and knelt, keeping his gaze downcast as he kissed the archbishop's hand, who reached out to touch the young man's chin. He raised his head and said, "The last time we saw each other, we looked each other straight in the eye. Your name, after all, is Alfonso, as is mine. Why should you be bashful now?"

Alfonso's eyes lit up when he saw that the archbishop remembered him, and he said, "Your Excellency, I was summoned here. I don't know why or for what, but I had to come."

"Slow down, young man. First of all, tell me how your father is doing. And what has happened to you all these years?"

"There is not much to tell, Your Excellency. My father is in good health and at the height of his powers, and only a few days ago he completed a new stained-glass window for the cathedral; if everything goes according to plan, I will install it next week. As for me, I am well. My parents have begun to talk about my marriage prospects, but I don't think that the time is right yet."

The elderly archbishop closed his eyes and asked, "But what of this summons you mentioned? What does it mean? Speak to me, my son. You know the truth."

Alfonso was quiet. He was not sure what he knew or what it meant to know something; he only felt, with all his heart and soul, that he needed to be with this person.

"My son, close your eyes. Look deeply into yourself, into your very essence; turn to your God and seek knowledge from Him. Have you come to serve me? Or have you come so I may serve you?" Alfonso was astounded, but the archbishop pressed on. "I am nothing; truly, I am not anything. I am a mortal, born to a woman; I am dust and to dust I will return. Everything that I have done has been for the sake of heaven, for the glory of our Lord Jesus and His Holy Mother Mary. This is the proper way to live one's life, the right path. You, in whom all these forces beyond your ken are incarnate, know the truth of the matter. Look into your heart and ask, my son; open your mouth and the words will flow through you."

Then there was silence. Alfonso felt his body going limp, thoughts disappearing from his mind, new images arriving and arising. "I am afraid to say what comes to my mind."

"Why is that?"

"It's not fitting to tell an archbishop that what he has done, and done for one's own good, is crumbling and disappearing. I am discovering that the promise I made with a smile and a look I cannot fulfill, and I am afraid, Your Excellency. I have no power to set aside what is left there, and I cannot avoid reaching out and touching the forbidden fruit. The knowledge will come back to me. I will see the angels again, I will again be a heretic who violates the strict prohibition of gazing upon God and His holy messengers."

He finished speaking, his gaze downcast, waiting for the archbishop's fury. When this failed to arrive, he looked up and opened his eyes. What he saw was not only an elderly man in the twilight of his years, he also saw a resolute man, determined to face the challenges before him without looking away, and he knew that he had to keep speaking. "May I say something else?"

"Of course," the archbishop replied. "You came here for two reasons, beloved child. You came here to ask for permission for your new-old way, and you came to make a pronouncement. You already expressed your request, so what do you still have to say to me?"

"It is about the war, Your Excellency." His voice changed, he closed his eyes, and a deep, authoritative voice rumbled forth from his throat. "The war[23] will end in a year's time. The Catholic Monarchs will sign a treaty with the Portuguese king, and Princess Joanna of Castille will leave Spain together with him." He fell silent for a moment and then continued, "Your Excellency, I know not what I say; the voice just comes from within me, and I cannot control it."

The archbishop, as if he had not heard the last sentence, furrowed his brow and asked: "And what about me? What shall my fate be?"

"You will have to surrender huge tracts of land," declared the authoritative voice which rumbled from the youth's throat. "You have aged and grown old, and your last years will be spent here. The

---

23   The War of the Castilian Succession was opposed by the archbishop, who had been a personal adviser to Queen Isabella; instead, he supported Princess Joanna *la Beltraneja* and the French-Portuguese alliance against Ferdinand II of Aragon and Isabella I of Castile, "the Catholic Monarchs." The war lasted from 1475 until 1479, when Ferdinand and Isabella won and forced Portugal to sign a treaty.

Archdiocese of Toledo will be saved for you." Alfonso opened his eyes and looked at the old archbishop in fear.

"But when?" the old man asked. "When will my day come?"

"Four years from now, to the day," the voice responded. "Then you will join your family up above. They await you with love and joy." Diametrically opposed to the tableau of a boy standing before an eminent dignitary and giving him bad news, young Alfonso instead seemed to attain a higher stature by this pronouncement.

The archbishop replied, "The message you have transmitted to me is meant for me. It does not emanate from you; you are merely the conduit. All that remains is for me to ask you to forget what has transpired here and not mention it to any man." Then the archbishop nodded off. After a few minutes of silence, he raised his head again and fixed his gaze on young Alfonso.

"Now, as for the first part of our conversation," he said, "your own request. I have heard it, and it was transmitted through you, but not by you. What we did when you were a child, we did for your own good. You were too young then, but now you have grown up and matured, and you have the power to fulfill the role placed upon your shoulders. All that is left is for me to wish you success and thank you for the privilege I have had to assist you in your important role. Now, please call my aides who are on the other side of the door." When they came in, he straightened up and said, "This has been a great day. An important day for Toledo and for Spain. Please escort this honorable man on his way; he is a holy man."

Alfonso felt a wave of gratitude and love washing over him, and the assistants who looked at him saw a man standing straight, his face beaming, as his eyes expressed both love and determination.

Alfonso returned to his house a new man. He gave his old-new abilities free rein. Suddenly, he began to see almost transparent entities accompanying people, and these visions interfered with his life, especially when he knew things about people whether he wanted it or not. He knew beforehand about the danger lurking for certain people; he discovered people acting in a manner opposed to their true needs; he saw human beings who had illnesses even if they themselves did not know about their conditions – but when he felt an obligation to help and began to tell people what he saw, he found that some of them did not even want to hear about it. Some saw him as a sorcerer, but others began to follow in his footsteps. Wherever he went, they followed him. Wherever he was, they were.

These events reminded Pablo of the threatening circumstances that had brought him and Alfonso to the archbishop initially, and in his worry that it was all coming back now, he advised his son to find a way to annul this ability. He was then surprised to hear from Alfonso the story of his renewed contact with the archbishop. Pablo, who knew nothing about this, wanted to know everything, e.g., the background, the motivation, the impetus, and what had happened during the meeting. Alfonso left nothing out, omitting only the part about the war. He concluded his words about his renewed path by saying, "The archbishop's directive still echoes in my head, and even if I wanted to stop, I couldn't." His flabbergasted father, as stated, had no idea about the whole matter, and so he was in disbelief; he worried that perhaps this power had driven his son mad.

"But the archbishop is preoccupied with the war; it is illogical that he would find time amid all that for a boy," he thought. Only when he spoke to the archbishop's secretary and heard directly from him what had happened did he understand that some kind of saint was growing up in his house, whose life was consecrated to a higher purpose than being an apprentice to a stained-glass artisan. So Pablo decided to help.

"First of all," he said to him, "you must practice achieving control of what you are seeing. God, in His grace, gave you this gift, expects you to use it appropriately, and for this reason you must learn how to utilize it. You must know how to control your thoughts, your imagination, whatever it is that you are experiencing. You must know how to block that which is unnecessary, to filter out everything else, and to ask for whatever you need."

Alfonso smiled at his father. "God, in His love, has given me two great gifts, the first of which is having a father like you."

After this, Alfonso began his course of study. He had no mentor, and he had no clear, known path. He simply relied on God, because if He had given him such a gift, He would give him the guidance to use it properly.

This was exactly what happened. The process was long and arduous, but Alfonso learned how to control his ability. Within a year's time, he already knew how to summon the information he needed. The further he progressed in his study, the greater he discovered the burden to be. He realized that what he received was not mere information; it contained within it knowledge that was just as important. For example, he discovered that he could diagnose disease, crises and problems – and most importantly, he had the ability to heal.

Within a short time, Alfonso was widely known as a healer who had supernatural powers. People believed he could heal almost anything - any injury or physical defect, from serious diseases to mental conditions, even financial difficulties - and the lines wending their way to his door grew longer and longer. Wherever he went, people followed him. He was so deeply respected that he was considered to be God's own emissary; however, Alfonso himself, who was very humble, did not let his success and honor go to his head. He remembered who he had always been, Alfonso the amiable and agreeable.

He knew that everything came from the heavens, that he was merely a conduit, and thus he didn't seek anything from these people that they couldn't give. There were those who didn't pay at all; others brought a modest gift or small present, but from Alfonso's point of view, he was simply fulfilling the Lord's ministry.

Everything was fine until he reached the age of twenty-two. The year was 1484, six years after the Catholic Monarchs, Ferdinand II of Aragon and Isabella I of Castile, had instituted the Spanish Inquisition, which was "intended to maintain Catholic orthodoxy in their kingdoms... primarily to identify heretics among those who converted from Judaism and Islam to Catholicism."[24] It was a year after Tomás de Torquemada had been appointed Grand Inquisitor.

The Inquisition, headquartered in Seville, in the south of the country, was intolerant of any divergence from the path dictated by the Catholic Church; although Alfonso was from Toledo, his reputation reached Seville, and people such as he piqued the interest of the Inquisition.

Alfonso was considered by many to be divine, although he had no formal education in medicine or religion and held no office in the Church. Moreover, his healing processes made no use of religious symbols or objects; they weren't even Christian ceremonies. In the eyes of the Inquisition, this in itself was more than enough to prove that he was a heretic.

However, Torquemada, who had known the archbishop, preferred to wait rather than directly interfere in the archdiocese, certainly not regarding someone who had been considered the archbishop's protégé; therefore, the first actions taken by the Inquisition against Alfonso were minor. Priests in Toledo who were connected to the Inquisition approached Alfonso, asking that his healing ceremonies

---

24   "Spanish Inquisition," Wikipedia.

be only religious. At first, these were mere discussions; later on, they became requests; finally, they turned into threats against him and his family.

At a certain stage, the priests tried to gather incriminating evidence against Alfonso, but they discovered that this was a nearly impossible mission. The priests and their agents were well known, and every time they tried to sneak into his courtyard to gather incriminating evidence, those who were waiting outside would notice them and disappear, leaving Alfonso alone in his courtyard with his family members. Their attempts to collect incriminating testimony from individuals also failed, as the locals refused, despite their threats, to show up and volunteer information that could be used against him. It was often said in the city that the spirits guarded Alfonso, and woe to anyone who would testify against him.

Two years after the death of the archbishop, after Torquemada had been Grand Inquisitor for a year, he began to take more aggressive action, and one weekend at midnight he had Alfonso arrested.

Alfonso was transported far from Toledo to the Inquisition's dungeons, which were hardly a rest home. After two days in the dark with no food, he was brought, feeble and famished, to an interrogator, who tried to extract a confession from him. Alfonso was accused of using methods in defiance of the Church, of embarking on a path of heresy and apostasy; they demanded that he confess and declare that he would discontinue his evil ways. However, Alfonso felt that he could not do this. In his eyes, the ability to receive information and to heal people was his destiny in life; the Creator had imbued him with certain abilities, and he was neither able nor allowed to deny them or denounce them as heresy or apostasy.

His interrogation went on for days, and he was not spared torture. However, Alfonso almost didn't feel it. He could direct his mind and his consciousness to other places, and he disassociated from his surroundings while being tortured. His body suffered, but his spirit remained steadfast. The more he minimized the torture, the more his torturers grew angry. The situation could have lasted forever, or at least until his body could bear no more, were it not for Alfonso's sudden realization that his interrogator, too, had been suffering for quite a while – from a urinary disorder. Alfonso looked the interrogator straight in the eye and told him this; without waiting for a reply, he offered to heal the condition.

The interrogator and his assistant were astounded. This was a secret that the interrogator did not share, and as the two looked at each other with trepidation, Alfonso stood up and came as close as his shackled feet allowed. He put his bloody hands on the shoulders of the dumbstruck interrogator, and in a soft, pleasing voice – very different from the hoarse whisper he had spoken in up until this point – told him to relax and go limp. The assistant stood there, terrified, yet determined to defend the interrogator from this sorcerer. Alfonso closed his eyes, and within two minutes, the interrogator felt the burning sensation subside and disappear. An insuppressible smile graced his lips.

When Alfonso finished his treatment and went back to his seat, the interrogator ordered his assistant to take Alfonso back to his cell and give him food and drink.

The next day, the cell door was unlocked and opened, and Alfonso was released. The interrogator himself came to the cell, supporting Alfonso and his wounded body; as they walked to the exit, he spoke of his conversation with the Grand Inquisitor and how difficult it had been to convince him to free Alfonso.

"Be careful," cautioned the interrogator. "I don't know who you are, and I don't know what forces guide you. They are categorically not Christian, despite the fact that the kindness and compassion within them are in the spirit of our Savior Jesus Christ and the Virgin Mary, but the Church will not always show compassion to you. The next time you are arrested, you will not be so lucky, and I will not be there to help you. May God be with you, Alfonso. Go in peace." He escorted him out to the street and went back inside. Once the door had been shut, Alfonso looked to the street and saw, to his great surprise, his father, wife, and young son. "The heavens are toying with me," he thought, and then it all went dark as he fainted.

When he opened his eyes again, he was in a comfortable bed, covered and bandaged. From the corner of his eye, he saw his wife, and a sigh of relief burst forth from him. His wife turned to him, her voice choked by tears, and said, "Praised be the Lord for returning you to us. We had already lost hope."

Gradually, the story became clear to him. When Alfonso's wife had woken up on that dreadful day, she immediately noticed his absence – a very uncommon occurrence. She called her father-in-law, who immediately set out to look for him.

As soon as he did so, Pablo ran into a stranger at his door, who informed him that he had passed by late the previous night and seen a carriage that had stopped next to their house, surrounded by churchmen. The passerby had thought of running away, but as soon as it occurred to him that it was Alfonso's house, he resolved to hide and watch. A few minutes later, he saw Alfonso leaving, more dragged than supported by a priest. He was shoved into the carriage, and it set out on its way. A few minutes later, the street was as quiet as it had been before. "I didn't say anything to you then, because I was drunk and couldn't be sure of what I had seen. I waited by your house all night until I was sober. Now I know it was the truth."

Pablo immediately understood what had happened. He sought out his friends in the Church, begging them to look for his son. It took a number of days for them to get the answer that the Inquisition had arrested him, and that he was in the center of Seville. One of Pablo's priest friends took him aside and whispered in his ear, suggesting that Pablo take his daughter-in-law and grandson to beg for Alfonso's life.

They wasted not one more moment, gathered food and blankets, and set out. Reaching the headquarters of the Inquisition in Seville, and looking right and left trying to decide what to do next, the door opened. To their great surprise, at that very moment Alfonso emerged, stared at them in astonishment, and collapsed.

Pablo's connections got them a room at a comfortable inn, and they found a dedicated physician to care for Alfonso. Even in distant Seville, Alfonso had a reputation, and people were praying for his recovery.

A few weeks later, when Alfonso had recovered his strength and could get out of bed, they prepared for the trip home.

Now what? At home, there were many discussions. Many people rejoiced at Alfonso's return and came to knock on the door and welcome him; however, he was still haunted by the experience of interrogation and torture. The members of Alfonso's household were waiting for him to decide when to return to treating people, and this was what they told the throngs who lined up at their door daily.

Alfonso struggled mightily. He was greatly worried about causing harm to his family. He worried about his parents, his wife, and his young child. The Inquisition had a widespread reputation, and the public knew about the excessive cruelty of Grand Inquisitor Torquemada. Only recently, for the first time in Toledo, an *auto-da-fé* had taken place, with the heretic being burned alive. At the same time, alongside his fears, Alfonso realized how special he was, chosen by God Himself.

He would never forget his meeting with the late archbishop.

Then, one night Alfonso found that he could not sleep. He got out of bed and went to the treatment room. As he sat and ran through various and sundry scripts in his head, he suddenly felt that a grand being had entered the room, and an unmistakable understanding was burned into his mind. "Good cannot come down into the world via a person who will be harmed by it. The Creator does not desire your suffering, Alfonso; He does not want to endanger your family. Therefore, we hereby release you from your destiny and from your abilities." The being faded away, and Alfonso, who felt as if he had just awoken from a dream, was left with endless unanswered questions.

He fell asleep, and when he awoke many hours later, he felt very different. Suddenly, he knew that his abilities were gone. His father and his wife heard this and rejoiced. The sick people outside did not share the feeling; they were familiar with him and knew that he would not simply abandon them, and those who didn't believe the tale accepted it with the understanding that even Alfonso could not stand up to the Inquisition.

The years passed. Alfonso went back to work with his father, and he found skills within himself that he had never known before. He had artistic talents heretofore unrealized, which had previously been the domain of Pablo alone. Deep in his heart, he thanked God that his healing abilities had been taken away, and he had received a fitting compensation.

More years passed. Alfonso and his wife lived a good life, surrounded by children and grandchildren. In their sixties, they returned their souls to their Creator, gratefully and thankfully.

So what did I think of this story?

The soul plan, established even before I found form in Alfonso's body, was to be reincarnated within a person who would grow up to be a unique caregiver, a caregiver whose knowledge would come from connecting to the Guidances and the cosmic library. This was an unusual life path, because so far the connection to higher Guidance had mostly been made through clergy and spiritual teachers only, whereas "ordinary" people needed a mediator. It was another attempt to have a person who could connect to the Guidance directly and receive information whose purpose was doing good.

Alfonso's life began according to plan. The parents chosen acted correctly, and his father functioned properly. However, the plan began to falter when Torquemada came into the picture. I won't go into the story of the plan of his life here, but he made decisions that go far beyond the plan of his own soul, and one of the victims of this deviation was Alfonso. My soul guardian, who felt the danger to Alfonso's life, contrary to the soul plan, shared this with the high Guide, which convened a council to discuss the matter.

Of course I, too, from that high, free part of myself, participated in the discussions and raised the fear that if Alfonso did lose his life because of his activity as a healer, it would constitute a karmic action against the people in whom I would be reincarnated, and my character as a caring soul would conflict with reality.

The decision made in the end was clear. The Guide would be revealed to Alfonso, and in a complicated operation that I cannot explain here, Alfonso's body would undergo a change that would "close" his channeling ability, at the same time releasing the artistic traits that existed in his body genetically but were suppressed before birth.

The Guides who worked with us also thought it would be appropriate for the next incarnation to take place very close to the end of the current incarnation. This way, the desire and longing to be a caregiver would pass to the next person born, lest it sink into many other incarnations, being assimilated in me and hurting my ability as a healer. Therefore, we had to start planning the next life while Alfonso was still alive. And so we did.

The completion of the planning took place close to Alfonso's death, and I, who was released from the body, was ready and prepared for the next story.

I had but a short "recuperation" time in the domain of reorientation and enlightenment. Immediately afterwards, I was presented with a number of alternatives as to how the next life would be realized; this time, I chose a track in which there would be an integration between the old, tribal world, and the new, cruel, strong world. I decided to be born as a Native American shaman in Peru in the sixteenth century. It was interesting to look at the lives of these Native Americans in light of the life cycle I had gone through in these regions exactly 1,000 years earlier.

The next life story, that of Maurier, taught me once again that I could never anticipate the power of previous lives' influence on a person's activity and life.

I invite you to witness this yourselves.

The Shaman

Maurier stood tensely, his chin raised proudly, as if to say, "Look at me!" Only he was aware of the weakness in his knees and the trembling he felt..Behind him were his parents, who stood tensely as well, staring at the shaman who was dancing toward them, following the beat of the drums pounding in the background.

The members of the tribe were crowded into a circle around the three of them, and they encouraged the shaman with calls and clapping as they stared at the tense six-year-old with a feather stuck in his braided hair, and his face and chest painted with the ceremonial colors his father had applied before the beginning of the event.

The shaman, as if unable to hear the hum of the crowd, continued the dance steps at an increasing pace, advancing slowly towards the boy and his parents. When there were only a few steps between them, the parents retreated, and the shaman began to circle around the child with frenetic movements, bounding up and to the sides, bending down and running around him bowed, all the while holding the sacred shaman rattle in one hand and a long spear in the other; a large mask was stuck to the top of the spear and he was rapidly waving it in all directions, very close to the boy who was standing there frozen and afraid to move.

Then, all of a sudden, he halted in front of the boy's face. The drums, as though at a prearranged signal, stopped playing, and silence descended on the camp. The shaman was painted in bright hues all over, his neck proudly carrying strings of brilliant crystals of various colors, one short and tight to the neck, others descending to his chest, and a long necklace dangling down to his loins. His painted body was shiny and radiant, and the scents of the various oils anointing his body carried far and wide. The boy stared into the shaman's eyes, and for some reason he found calm. A feeling of peace and security descended on him, and a feeling of love whose meaning he did not understand enveloped him; all he wanted to do was embrace this frightening man, to be with him, in his arms.

The shaman got down on his knees, and kneeling in front of the boy, began to speak words no one understood, a kind of prayer to the spirits of the tribe, to the spirits of the shamans wherever they were, to the spirits of all nature - the rainforest trees and animals, the spirit protecting and preserving the earth. His prayer was carried into the air while he lightly touched the child's head and body, initiating him and conveying to him, via this unique ceremony, the knowledge of shamanism and its connection to the highest spirits. Finally he pulled out a salver from somewhere and turned it over the child in a ceremonial motion, allowing the warm oil to wash over his head as the shaman's steady hands smeared his face and entire body in light, gentle movements. The boy, who had been standing there trembling and in awe, felt an amazement whose power washed over him and carried him to new realms of peace, security, and knowledge.

At the end of the prayer and initiation ceremony, the shaman stood up, took Maurier's hand in his large palm, and lifted it heavenwards. Slowly they began to turn a full 360°, showing themselves to the whole tribe. Their circuit ended facing the proud parents and the shaman declaring aloud, "Behold, everyone! Look at the new shaman, the messenger of the tribal spirits, the messenger of the spirits of the ancestors and the ancients; see my heir apparent! Young Maurier will grow up to be the next shaman of this proud, talented tribe!"

The drums began to pound again, and the whole crowd burst into acclaim and song that soon evolved into a great celebration for all the members of the tribe.

Without realizing how he got there, Maurier was suddenly with his mother, making their way to their tent as she pushed away and distanced the curious and even the close friends who had come to greet and hug him.

Maurier, who knew nothing of what was about to happen, was still completely stunned, and all he wanted was silence and a maternal embrace. His mother felt this, and they slipped away from the crowd.

There, in the tent, she tried to explain to the child what had just happened. She reminded him of the good relationship he had always had with his father's brother, his uncle, such as the times he went out with him on nature walks, collecting various herbs and bugs. She told him that these hikes had now become something more important for the whole tribe, which was very happy about this choice.

Maurier looked at her and asked, "But where was Uncle? I didn't see him."

She looked back at him in astonishment and burst out laughing. "Really? By my life," she said, "Don't you know? Your uncle is the shaman, and you have seen him many times in various ceremonies. It never occurred to me that you would not recognize him."

"Uncle is the shaman?" he asked incredulously. "But..." Then he remembered the shaman's eyes during the ceremony and understood why he had calmed down so much when his eyes met them.

Thus began the next period of Maurier's life − as the shaman's apprentice. In the years that followed, he accompanied his uncle constantly, hiking with him in the woods, learning the rituals of healing, and how to drive out evil spirits and disease. He connected to the spirits deeply ingrained in all nature, in trees and plants - even to the great earth spirit. He learned to brew potions and often surprised the shaman with new ideas and techniques that he developed while they were collaborating.

Six years passed, and it was time for the next significant stage in the boy's life − the ceremony of initiation into adulthood. His father, and even more so his uncle the shaman, prepared him as best they could for all the adult roles, inculcating within him the importance of responsibility for the entire tribe, the significance of the spousal bond, and reproduction to further its legacy. Although the uncle was no expert in the art of combat, he knew how to instill enough information in his nephew in this area as well.

When the day came for the boys to go out into the woods, the shaman summoned Maurier for a conversation and said to him,

"Do not forget who you are! You are connected to the spirits, you are their representative, and you are the one who will ask them to protect your friends. At the same time, you must be courageous; you must learn how to utilize all the tools you learn about there. And I have a warning for you: I have heard rumors about strangers who have come to our country. They are foreigners who are not familiar with the rainforest and do not know us. It is said that they are wont to harm us, steal our property, and kidnap our wives and children. They are dangerous people who bear massive swords and wield great power. Rumor even has it that they have blowguns that spit fire and strike with lightning speed and great power from a great distance. Be careful!"

Equipped with these instructions, the boy went out and joined his friends. Due to his role in the tribe, Maurier had not spent time with his peers in recent years; their games and mischief-making were not part of his routine. His shamanic pursuits filled all his time; when he finished his "hikes" with his uncle, he was exhausted, and all he wanted was to return home. Children's games did not appeal to him. When the shaman had informed him that he would be going out for a "training session" with the boys, a session that would take place outside the tribal borders and without the presence of their parents, Maurier had been startled. The boys' games, the noise they made in their activities, were all foreign to him; now, when he had to join them, he did so with a heavy heart. But the boys of the tribe treated him with great respect, and even though he was not often with them and did not play or spend time with them, his status alongside the shaman and his own intelligence gave him a senior status.

They stayed in the woods for about two weeks, and the adults who were with them did not let them be idle. It was not an afternoon stroll with their mothers; here the boys were thrown into the woods with all the dangers lurking in it, without provisions. They had to prove to the instructors that they were indeed adults, that they knew how to integrate into rainforest life with all its dangers, light a fire, find water, and hunt for and gather food and prepare it. They had to demonstrate proficiency in using bows and arrows, knives, spears, and blow-guns loaded with poisoned darts - poison they themselves extracted from wood resin.

They learned to do all this when they were alone, in pairs or in a group. Endurance and physical strength were of great importance when climbing trees or avoiding obstacles. The mutual responsibility was expressed, and they learned to know each other, e.g., who was a leader, who was an advisor, who was brave, who was agile, who could imitate bird calls, who knew how to listen to the sounds of the rainforest day and night and interpret them, and who was the best tracker among them.

Maurier participated in all of it, even though he did not excel in any of these fields. This was fine from his perspective; he was simply happy that the shaman, like his father, had not kept him from studying the fundamentals, so that he knew how to do most of things he was expected to do.

All this was true until the day when cries of pain were heard from deep within the rainforest. There was no mistaking the matter; one of the boys was injured. Everyone ran towards the sounds and soon saw one of the boys from their group lying on the floor, groaning in excruciating pain and shouting while pointing to his leg, which was very red and swollen. The leg swelled to frightening proportions, and the boy began to twitch as he screamed. The boys lined up in a circle around him and tried to help, but he couldn't stand the touch of their hands and responded with more screaming and shoving as they tried to touch him.

Maurier, who was with another boy in a more remote place, soon arrived at the scene, and within seconds ceased to be a boy in initiation; without realizing how or why, he saw himself as a shaman, as a healer. He walked over to the injured boy; in a quiet, confident voice, he ordered everyone to move away. He radiated authority, power, and knowledge, and the boys obeyed him. His healing belt was on him, and he thanked his uncle for instructing him never to take it off, even if it annoyed him and impaired his movements and agility.

He walked over to the boy and put his hand on his forehead. He called on the spirits to help him heal the injured boy and alleviate his distress. Slowly the boy calmed down, until he stopped his involuntary shuddering and seemed to have fallen asleep. Maurier looked at his leg and searched for the wound caused by the blow-gun fired by the foreigners. He was convinced that this was what had happened, and he was no less sure that he could overcome these foreigners and heal the boy. The point of injury seemed small, and strangely seemed to be nothing more than the kind of animal bite that he was familiar with from his hikes with his uncle, but he didn't let the bewilderment stop him.

Very skillfully, he applied a tourniquet (even if in his mind he used another word) near the boy's crotch, dripped a few drops down his throat that he knew would calm him, pulled out his dagger, cut deep near the wound site, and began to suck the blood and spit it aside.

When he finished, the boy was quiet, unconscious. His leg was still very swollen, and his body temperature was beginning to rise. Maurier asked the boys to guard him and ran to the trees. He knew what he needed. He looked for the right bush and the herbs he needed, and when he found what he was looking for went back to the boy, lit a fire, and brewed a special oil from it, then smeared it on his leg and bandaged it.

The boy was unconscious, and Maurier feared a malicious take-over of his soul by demons. He knew they were looking for such opportunities, and that if they could gain the upper hand, it would be very difficult to heal the boy. He stood up and painted himself in the proper colors for the purpose of eliminating the illness, then opened with a dance, accompanied by the healing rattle. At his request, the boys began to drum on everything they could find; through his rhythm, his singing and his rapid dancing, he was able to get into the correct position, into a trance where he could release his body to the spirits that would do everything necessary through him.

The rainforest was very quiet. None of the boys or guides were allowed to move or talk, and except for the sound of the drums and Maurier's singing, no sound was heard. Maurier continued to recite various chants in an incomprehensible language, singing and danc-ing for hours. He dripped sweat but felt nothing, just the fierce war raging between the spirits within him and the demons in the boy's body. Sometimes the forces of darkness would wax stronger, and Maurier would intensify his efforts, and sometimes it would be the spirits who gained the upper hand. Slowly he felt the demons retreat, as they were shrinking and fleeing, and how the power of the pro-tecting and preserving spirits eradicated them until they crumbled and disappeared.

And when he knew it was all over, he opened his eyes. What a surprise it was to find that night had already come and gone, and a new sun was already shining and warming the forest. He looked at the boy and saw that the swelling had gone down and that he rested more soundly. Only then did Maurier allow himself to rest; he sat down next to the boy and fell into a slumber, so exhausted he was, as if all his strength had left him.

Towards noon he awoke and looked at the boy. His complexion

was good, and his breathing was quiet. Maurier examined the boy's leg and changed the bandage, then anointed it with fresh oil and saw to his delight that the swelling was going down even more. The leg was slightly bluish, and he released the tourniquet from the boy's crotch so that blood could begin to flow back into the leg.

When he finished, he got up, turned around, and saw his companions. They stood in front of him, their heads bowed to the ground, and it was impossible not to feel the waves of respect and gratitude that emanated from them. Over the next few days, the injured boy slowly recovered his strength. The pain did not go away immediately, but it was clear that he was recovering.

It was not long before the process of initiation into adulthood ended, and the boys returned to the tribe and were welcomed back with drums and dancing. The news of the boy who was saved spread far and wide, and Maurier's parents and uncle were beside themselves with joy. When he arrived and they looked at him, they saw the change that had taken place. His uncle stared at him and said, "You've grown up, Maurier. I can rest at ease now, knowing that I have a successor. I have a great heir, and I thank the spirits for the privilege I have been given to train and educate you."

And so the years passed, and Maurier grew older. During his life he forged links with other tribes, studied with other shamans, and expanded his knowledge. His reputation as shaman, healer, and caregiver preceded him, and everyone foresaw a bright future for him.

When he turned eighteen, it was time to start a family. He'd had his eye on Rumiata, whom he'd known since they were both children. She was congenial and diligent, and listened to him when he faced crises in his youth, when he was living with his uncle under harsh, demanding conditions; she had provided a sympathetic ear for him, without even realizing it. He couldn't imagine how much everyone was already aware of their bond, how clear it was to everyone that these two were meant to start a family, so that even her parents didn't pressure her to marry anyone else, and she didn't ask for another man for herself. Her friends, and many members of the tribe, were also clear about the matter; in fact, everyone, except for Maurier himself, had no doubt about the pairing.

Thus, as soon as he understood this and asked his father to talk to her parents, the matter came to fruition very quickly and to the satisfaction of the whole tribe. The marriage of the two was blessed by the chieftain and elders of the tribe, the shaman, and even representatives of the neighboring tribes.

Now, with Maurier fully engaged as shaman, his uncle, who had grown old, could pass the role on to him. He did this willingly, knowing that Maurier's steady hand would hold the baton he bequeathed to him; as the tribal shaman, he would now be central to the culture and health of his people. He presided over all the ceremonies, and he was the one to whom they turned in times of trouble. Tribal life in the South American rainforest was not easy. Many were injured or killed while hunting or fighting over territory or food sources. The tribal healer had his hands full with his work. The young couple soon had three sons and, some years later had a daughter as well.

Everything was good in the tent of Maurier and Rumiata, and life was running smoothly. Maurier was greatly appreciated by his tribe and was recognized for his powers by the neighboring tribes as well; in time, he even began to recruit students. He was looking for "the one" to replace him when the day came, but couldn't find a suitable candidate. The candidates, although decent and sincere, lacked important skills, had difficulty connecting to the spirits, couldn't identify the herbs, and so on. Deep in his heart, he was happy about this, as he hoped his eldest son, Toriro, who showed signs of being a suitable candidate, would indeed be his successor. But to his disappointment, Toriro showed no special interest in the position.

However, everything changed when the father of Toriro's close friend was seriously injured, and the danger of death hovered over him. Toriro was exposed to the great fear and feeling of helplessness that descended on his friend's family, and he suddenly grasped the significance of the role of shaman. As he watched, his father tackled the situation with determination and complete devotion to care and succeeded in saving his friend's father; as a result, a passion for the vocation erupted in his heart. Like his father, he turned to his studies with the fullness of his energy, and Toriro began to accompany Maurier in whatever he did.

Maurier's joy knew no bounds. He jumped at the opportunity and devoted most of his time to teaching the boy and training him for the job. And when Toriro was about ten years old, about two years before the ceremony marking adulthood along with his peers, Maurier held the traditional shamanic initiation ceremony and presented Toriro to the entire tribe as his successor.

The years passed, and the sight of Maurier and Toriro as they worked together became familiar within the tribe and throughout the region. Father and son were comfortable with each other, and the quiet routine that descended on the rainforest and its surroundings allowed Toriro to delve into his studies fully and deeply.

No one imagined that these good days were about to end, and that a powerful catastrophe was about to engulf them and change their lives completely.

It all began when uninvited guests came to the forest and to the tribe. There was a small group of white-faced strangers who were dressed in strange clothes. To be precise, news of the presence of foreigners in their land had long been circulating among the tribes, but they had never met anyone who could testify that he had seen them, and in fact they didn't know for sure whether it was a rumor or just imagination - until they showed up in the tribe's territory.

They were received by the chieftain of the tribe, his elders, and the shaman. The guests arrived accompanied by a local native, who translated for them what was being said. They brought with them unique gifts, such as shiny, colorful necklaces, unusual clothing made of foreign materials, and fascinating cooking utensils. The foreigners presented the tribesmen with their famous "blow-guns" - which, to the tribesmen's amazement, turned out to be massively destructive, noisy weapons that could take down animals and people from shockingly far away.

The guests captured the hearts of the tribe's leaders and dignitaries. They called themselves "Spaniards" and said they came from afar, overseas, in huge boats. During the hours of meeting and conversation, one of the guests felt unwell, and Maurier, who examined him, saw that the man was flushed and very hot, his head aching and his eyes watery. He asked Toriro to bring some ingredients and brewed a potion for him and indeed, within a short time, the guest's fever dropped, he felt much better, and could not stop thanking the shaman. The foreigners stayed with them for two days and were guests of honor at the celebrations and meals the tribe arranged in their honor, serving them the best of their game.

But then something terrible happened to Maurier's family. A few days after their foreigners departed, Toriro showed symptoms that matched those of the Spaniard who had been ill, but the same potion couldn't cure him. Instead, his condition worsened from day to day, his fever spiked, his nose ran, his throat ached, his strength ebbed, and his entire body was wracked by pain.

To Maurier's dismay and anguish, he couldn't find a remedy. He did everything he knew, even summoning his aged uncle to help, but it was all in vain. The boy's condition deteriorated and grew more and more serious.

The moon was full that night, and Maurier turned to a ritual of advice. He went out into the rainforest to be alone, summoned the spirits, and asked them what he should do. This wasn't the first time he had asked for such help, and he usually received it; but this time, no answer came and no information was revealed. Perhaps he was preoccupied because it was his son?

He decided to bring an offering to the spirits in order to please them. After finishing the ceremony, he turned again and asked for answers, but again it was to no avail – as though they were ignoring him. Even when he sought their favor again and again, and asked and begged, he couldn't get an answer.

Suddenly a combative mood took hold of him. He rose to his feet and cried out, "Hear me holy spirits, hear me spirit of the earth, hear me the spirits of the ancients - everything I have done, throughout my life, has been for your glory. By your will, I labored and I healed. According to your instructions, I took care of people and saved them, and you never stopped presenting me with opportunities. Even as a teenager, many years ago, before I was even a shaman, under your guidance I rescued that wounded boy who was harmed by the foreigners, and here today I turn to you, imploring you to save my son harmed by the same foreigners. Do it for my own good, for the good of the tribe, and for his own good!"

Maurier recited all the formulas he knew, singing all the prayers, performing all the dances that might banish the demons. Then, and only then – totally exhausted, screaming, weeping – he received the message, the communication he had not sought. "Death has been decreed for the boy. It is neither your role, nor within your capabilities, to annul this decree. Go home and prepare for his death. Toriro's day has come."

Maurier was dumbfounded and refused to accept it. He dug his feet into the ground determinedly and proclaimed, "This shall not pass! This shall not be! You will not kill him! I request of all the spirits, from all of you together and from each and every one of you: Heal my son! It is not within my power to annul the decree, but it is within yours. I shall not move from this place until you reconsider and reverse your decision."

His voice was powerful as he summoned all the personal authority remaining in him to challenge them. "My son will recover and inherit my position. My son will be the shaman of our tribe! Do you hear me?"

When there was no response, he cried out to the heavens with all his strength. "By god, my child will live!"

Maurier then collapsed on the ground, sobbing uncontrollably and remaining there until he felt a soft human touch on his shoulder. It was his aged uncle. He knelt next to him and wept with him. "Maurier," the old man said, "you must stop. Cease such talk. Once fate has decreed it, we cannot challenge the spirits. Who knows that better than you? How many times have you witnessed it yourself? My child, get up, come with me to your tent. See your son one last time before he departs this life."

Maurier looked at him in astonishment, and something happened inside him. Suddenly he was exhausted, disinterested, as if he were not the same person. He got up and followed his uncle, dragging himself behind the old man until they reached the tent. Without saying a word, Maurier sat down next to Toriro, held his hand, and waited for his death. It was not long in coming.

After the burial ceremony, Maurier appeared before the chieftain of the tribe and informed him that he was no longer a shaman. He had lost faith in the gods and returned to them all his healing powers. He did not want it, could no longer handle it. The delegations that came to him didn't help, his family members who appealed to him didn't help, and it definitely didn't help when representatives of other tribes tried to dissuade him from his decision.

Maurier told all of them that he was finished as a healer. He had no interest in it anymore, and if the spirits refused to grant his totally legitimate request, he had no desire to maintain these abilities; thus they were taken from him and from his point of view, his time on earth was at its end. Indeed, it was not long before Maurier, who had lost interest in life, simply faded away. He soon joined his son, and his last request, to be buried alongside him, was carried out.

CHAPTER THIRTEEN

Reincarnations in Influential People

To his good fortune, Maurier did not live to see when the disease that took his son reappeared in other people in the tribe, and only when I returned here among my sibling souls did I learn that it was an influenza brought by the Spaniard, a plague that affected many Native Americans whose immune systems did not recognize European viruses, striking them down one after another. After that, I also learned that Maurier was spared the atrocities of the sixteenth century Spanish General Francisco Pizarro, those brutal conquests that destroyed the Incan Empire and almost brought the area's glorious indigenous culture to extinction.

I was quite unsettled when I got home. Initially, it was because of the continuity and connection to the material that characterizes the etheric plane of existence, as well the memory of life that is still burned into one's being - and then when we, my Guides and I, realized the magnitude of the failure.

Remember, I wanted to be reincarnated as a caregiver in order to minimize the impairment in my healing ability. While Maurier's life plan was designed to do just that, it also addressed other issues, most notably those dealing with loss. The lesson I wanted to learn was how to overcome a sense of loss combined with personal fail-ure and a crisis of faith. According to the plan, and according to his character traits, Maurier was supposed to put the good of the tribe above his private mourning, to continue the mission of his life and try to save people in the tribe, but this did not happen.

When the abilities of knowledge and healing were taken from Alfonso, he felt sorrow at the end of that chapter in his life and the loss of his ability to help and heal, but the process was also accom-panied by great relief with the removal of threats hanging over him and over his family. This deficiency also burned in me, in his soul. But for Maurier, the memory of the events from Alfonso's life hidden in his subconscious became a fear that steered him in the opposite direction from what we expected here.

Once again I discovered how far I, as well as my soul friends and the Guidances, are from understanding human behavior and foreseeing it. This was more than the failure of the plan and of the prediction of his life's path. The combination of events in the two consecutive incarnations – that of Alfonso and that of Maurier – and especially of Maurier's scream and his decision to give up caregiving and his connection the Guidances, had a real impact on me. What I had wanted, more than anything, to avoid in his life I had collided with head-on, compounding the damage.

When we are here in spirit and not in body, we don't need a physical experience to recognize the changes that have taken place in us. I knew about the magnitude of the damage and I was quite upset about it. The encounter with my family of souls, in which there are a number of higher souls from whom I receive the most love, alleviated my fears a little, mainly thanks to the conversations and discussions we had on the matter.

The common understanding for all of us was that I should abandon the subject for several incarnations, find form in the "normative" life of a person who loves company and finds joy in their lot, and seek to experience seemingly routine issues such as relationships and self-criticism, and maybe also the ability to deal with social pressure. Simultaneously, I could still serve as a Guide for people and for souls. Indeed, a new plan was drawn up, and after a period of several Earth-decades, I was reincarnated into the body of Johann, a kind-hearted woodworker and furniture-maker in Mulhouse, Alsace.

Accepting the Other

Johann was born in 1618 in Mulhouse,[25] a small town in the Alsace region, in a house that had been built by his grandfather on the northern outskirts of the city. The front of the beautiful house led to the main road that cut across the entire region, and in the large yard behind the house his grandfather had built a carpentry workshop and storage areas for logs, and even left a nice area for a lovely plot adjacent to the Ill river. Johann liked to join his father and grandfather in the workshop and follow their movements, which were quiet and professional. He spent hours watching them, and especially loved those moments when his grandfather held aloft a large log and examined it from all sides. At those moments, Johann could actually hear the ideas running through the old man's head about how to use a particular piece of wood and for what.

When he grew up a bit, Johann went out to the forests with his grandfather and father to look for raw materials and he was given

---

25   From the sixteenth century on, Mulhouse (Milhüsa in Alsatian) was part of the Swiss Confederation. It retained that status even after the Thirty Years' War, observing its Christian faith in keeping with Calvinist Protestantism. In 1798 its inhabitants voted to join France.

an important lesson about Creation. "The trees may not be animals," his father would say, "but they have life. They were here long before us and will survive long after us. The forest can teach us humans a thing or two about survival, about confronting the forces of nature, and about the way the climate changes." He learned there that the forest was a barrier to the fierce winds, as well as a dwelling place and source of food for animals, and he developed a respect for all the components of Creation.

However, Johann was not satisfied with the knowledge he received from his father and his grandfather, and as a curious teenager and adult he was always looking for ways to improve his skills and become a master carpenter. He was one of the first to adopt more advanced technologies and develop new methods for searching for and locating – with strikingly accurate and aesthetic techniques – trees to fell that would be the most suitable for the furniture he created and manufactured.

When Johann was sixteen he met Elsa, who became his wife and joined them in their magnificent home. Elsa quickly acclimated to the house on the Ill, and Johann's parents had great affection for her; the two maintained a spectacular home and were loved by all around them.

In stark contrast to the pastoral scenes of their city and their home, it was a tumultuous time in most of the countries in the region. The bloody Thirty Years' War was in full swing, affecting all of Europe. Because Mulhouse was a Swiss city that maintained neutrality, the locals were spared the worst of the war, but they knew about the extent of the ruination and great destruction all across the continent. Johann was born in the year the war broke out, and was thirty years old when it ended in 1648 with the signing of peace agreements between all the various states and principalities.[26] These agreements bore hope for an end to war on the tormented continent, for security on its roads, for soldiers to be demobilized, and for peace to descend on Europe.

However, Mulhouse was now threatened by a crisis that no one had expected. The end of the war left many refugees cut off from their destroyed homes and villages, and people set out on nomadic journeys in search of new homes. The reputation of tranquil, neutral Mulhouse in Alsace had spread far and wide, and many refugees sought their future there. The city was flooded with individuals and families who came from all over, and their numbers even exceeded those of the local population. The arrival of the homeless and jobless foreigners raised grave concerns among the natives. The municipal authorities were ill prepared for such a large influx of people, and the place, which had always been quiet and relaxed, became saturated with tension, incessant friction, and increasing violence.

In their house on the outskirts of the city, along the main road, Johann and Elsa were among the first to encounter these refugees. They saw the families and the people just as they were approaching the city – starving children, people in rags - and the carpenter and his wife were overwhelmed by compassion. They easily grasped the dimensions of the problem.

Johann understood the fears about the newcomers. He and his wife had three young children in their home, and just like their fellow townspeople, they were worried about the fate of their family. Crime in the quiet town began to skyrocket as homes were burglarized, food was stolen, and violent confrontations were breaking out on every

---

26   This was the Peace of Westphalia, which ended the Thirty Years' War and the Eighty Years' War (War of Dutch Independence). It would create the fundamentals of the politics and economics of modern Europe.

street corner. It seemed that the refugees were there to stay and that no one could deal with them, including the municipal authorities.

Violent opposition to their presence spreadthroughout the city and engendered evil and hostility from the residents of the formerly peaceful town. Johann, realizing these were only the first steps on a new, inauspicious path, decided that this was not the time for indifference, and these circumstances could hardly be dismissed as routine. He joined a rally calling on people to prepare to repel the "invasion," as the refugees' arrival was described. The rally's organizers fanned the flames, and soon the participants were goading each other on with cries of "We'll show them!" The atmosphere turned violent as the organizers divided the men into squads, examining which weapons they might be able to get their hands on.

Johann returned home with an ache in the pit of his stomach. He identified with the concerns of the residents, but deep down he knew that this was not the way and he felt an inner calling – whose source he did not know – to do something. He was of course not aware of Alfonso and Maurier, nor of many caregivers in previous incarnations whose memories were deeply engrained in his subconscious, thanks to which the way of violence stood opposed to the deep essence manifested within him. To his great joy, Elsa also opposed violence, and after a few days of profound deliberation that also required coping with the peer pressure that demanded he join the movement, Johann and Elsa, with much apprehension, but wholehearted commitment, decided that not only would they decline to join the campaign of violence, but that they would proactively pursue peace. In the depths of their hearts they knew that if they just persevered, they would have the strength to attract many others to their path.

The couple embarked on the path of receiving refugees and assisting in their rehabilitation. They set up tents for children in their yard, collected food donations, and helped refugees find housing and work. At the same time they set up a series of political meetings for the locals to encourage reluctant townspeople to understand the situation, to understand that violence was unnecessary and to welcome the refugees.

This activity received the full support of the heads of the city's Calvinist church, which provided financial, spiritual, and moral assistance. Johann's special personality and dedication to the mission led others to join him. At first it was just a trickle, as one or two joined, but soon this intensified and became a torrent that swept up most of the townspeople. Although the situation did not change overnight - privation and poverty were a constant challenge, and it was clear that the surge in crime would not subside quickly - but the belief in the "rightness" of their way sustained their determination. Indeed, within a few years, the town not only doubled its population but also established economic and social stability.

Johann's activities had gained widespread recognition in the Alsace region and beyond. He and his wife were invited to prestigious events, from meetings with Swiss leaders to a meal at the table of France's First Minister of State, Cardinal Jules Mazarin. Still, when Johann was offered the mayorship, he declined with a smile and said he would rather remain a good woodworker and a friend to all.

When he died at age sixty-eight, he was eulogized by many. I, who had just left his body, observed his burial ceremony from above, reveling in the pleasure of it. I thought to myself that this life could be a classic example of a soul plan dovetailing with a person's free choice to achieve resounding success.

When I returned home to the higher worlds and began preparations for the next chapter of life, I thought I would still prefer to skip the phase of repairing "damage" caused to my calling as a caregiver due to the events in Alfonso and Maurier's life; however, to my great surprise, I felt that somehow Johann's life had helped this effort. I felt lighter, which made it easier to continue with another reincarnation without addressing my essence as a healer.

Regardless, I felt it was time to address an issue I had been putting off for dozens of reincarnations - if not more – to find form in the body of a strong woman, acting with inner determinations against convention to bring about real change. I had already prepared myself for this in various incarnations, and have even told you about it, dear reader. I felt it was time to realize this and be reincarnated in the body of a woman whose actions would affect not only her and her immediate environment, but the status of women in general, via actions that would have a long-term impact.

It was the right move, because the broad plan of Creation speaks to the need to rectify the status of women, and the time had come to lay the foundations for it. Only one question remained: Was I capable of it? The answer was important because it illuminated an important side of our world. The more developed the soul, the greater and more stable a vessel of light and love it becomes, the more it is willing to be reincarnated in human beings whose influence on their environment is great.

Often, it is an ancient and well-developed soul that resides in people who are leaders, trendsetters who bring about great social changes or effect changes in thinking, as well as artistic or scientific breakthroughs; at this stage of my existence, I was already such, i.e., an old soul encompassing much light, love, and compassion.

It was clear that the process of changing the status of women would have a profound effect on the structure of human society, and because of this, I had to prepare for it with great care and extreme caution. Indeed, the various Guidances relevant to this matter were mobilized, and other soul plans that are also involved in this transformation of the face of human society were already in the planning and even execution stages. In other words, the process of change was in "full force."

According to the plan that was formulated, the segment of change that I would be involved in would come from the direction of the "weaker sex," and therefore we pinpointed the place, the period, and the person whose actions would contribute to the move, even if it would not fully materialize in her lifetime. We worked on this life cycle meticulously; the High Councils were in the thick of things as well, and finally, in 1759, I was ready to be born in England as Mary Wollstonecraft.

The Feminist

In 1756, Edward Wollstonecraft received a windfall in the form of an old building at 21 Hanbury Street in Spitalfields, in the East End of London. Edward didn't hesitate and eagerly renovated the house, and in April 1759, his daughter Mary was born there, the second of his seven children.

The first few years of her life were pleasant enough, but then her father's financial situation deteriorated and her home life underwent a major upheaval. When she was four, the family left the house on Hanbury Street, and they moved about every two years afterwards, just at the pace at which her next five brothers and sisters were born. Their precarious financial situation left its mark on her father; when he was drunk, which was quite often, he would exhibit paroxysms of rage and violence. By the time Mary was about six years old, she had heard her mother many times as she cried and begged the drunken Edward to stop beating her. "Please! Enough!" was a pair of words that accompanied her, and in her naïveté she thought that was simply how it was, that that was how everyone lived.

It was only when she was nine that she discovered that it was possible to live otherwise, when the family had to move once more, this time to Beverley, Yorkshire, where she met Jane Arden, her first true friend. Jane's father, a philosopher and scientist, instilled an intellectual, quiet, relaxed atmosphere in his home. The girls enjoyed reading at home, and there were plenty of books; they even attended Dr. Arden's lectures and listened to them attentively.

And so the next time Mary heard her own father's shouting and her mother's weeping, she burst into her mother's room and shouted, "Enough!" Her astonished father physically threw her out of the room; nevertheless, there was silence afterwards. From that day on, whenever her father was late returning home and there was a chance he'd be coming back drunk, the girl would lie down to sleep on the threshold of the mother's room door to forestall the next furious attack. She even found herself protecting her two sisters from her father's violence. Eventually she would realize that the seeds of opposition to male power and to discrimination against women were already sown within her at this time.

Mary and Jane were good friends, but her closest friend, and the one who influenced her the most, was Fanny Blood. Mary, who was still not content at home, made the acquaintance of the Blood family and their daughter Fanny. A close friendship developed between the two, and Mary felt that her new friend opened her mind to perceive the world correctly.

Meanwhile, the situation at the Wollstonecraft family home had only worsened, and when Mary reached age nineteen, she realized that she had to find a job. She left her parents' home and moved into the Widow Dawson's home, where she served as her companion.

However, she soon discovered that she was working for an angry, impatient, abusive woman who treated her cruelly.

Two years passed. Mary's mother was seriously ill, and Mary returned home to care for her in her last days. When she passed away, everyone thought Mary would return to Mrs. Dawson, but the young lady saw the period of her stay there as an important lesson.

Fanny tried to appeal to her heart: "And after all, Mrs. Dawson is waiting for you to come back," she told her. "You should be there for her, and you will not easily find another satisfactory position." Mary listened to her, but deep down she knew it was not her destiny.

She had to study and to teach, to evolve and develop, "to bring a message to the world," and she couldn't do that if she went back to the Widow Dawson. Fanny felt the power bursting from her best friend, and she understood that she could not dissuade her. As a result, she suggested that Mary move in with the Blood family, and Mary was happy to accept the offer.

The seeds of independent thinking that had sprouted in Mary continued to bloom, and after a while she realized that the Blood household was not her place, either. In Fanny, she found a faithful partner in her desire to do something different and exciting. The two energetic young women dreamed of another life, an independent one - despite their being women. Their dream was to establish a girls' school in a downtrodden community. Thus, with the help of Mary's sisters, the school under Mary's management was opened in 1783, and Fanny and the sisters took part in teaching independent thinking while instilling innovative values regarding the meaning of being women.

Two more years passed, and the fortunes of the young women abruptly changed. Fanny fell in love and married, but then became ill and had to travel to Lisbon for treatment. When she became pregnant, her illness worsened, and Mary left the management of the school in the hands of her sisters and went to help her. Fanny's condition only worsened, and she passed away immediately after giving birth. Brokenhearted, Mary returned to the school, but it didn't last much longer and had to close its doors.

Mary soon found out what it meant to be a woman in eighteenth-century England. It wasn't easy for her to find a job, and only after several friends enlisted to help her that she found a job as a nanny for the Anglo-Irish Kingsborough family. The girls she taught loved her and listened to her unconventional views, and one of them, Margaret, even said, "Mary freed me from all the superstitions that clung to me."

Still, it was a little excessive for the girls' parents, and Mary was fired after only a year, but not before she had time to write two books and publish them at Joseph Johnson Publishing House in London. Her first book was *Thoughts on the Education of Daughters*; it was based it on her experiences with Widow Dawson, her years of running a school, and her recent experience at the Kingsborough family home. Her rebellious and stubborn take on the status of women is well represented in the book, as she observes that limited career options are open to respectable, yet poor women, in a chapter entitled "Unfortunate Situation of Females, Fashionably Educated, and Left without a Fortune."

Mary believed that there was another way. She wasn't willing to accept the situation in which a woman, simply by virtue of being a woman, would not be able to make a living according to her abilities and inclinations. Even when she was a nanny, she wrote to her sister, "If I exert my talents in writing, I may support myself in a comfortable way. I am then going to be the first of a new genus - I tremble at the attempt." Indeed, when she returned to London and went to meet the publisher Joseph Johnson, she sat down in his office and stared him down.

The respectable man saw in front of him a young, determined woman, talking to him without fear - "almost like a man," he thought to himself - about the status of women, their rights, and the injustice done to girls in the area of education, issues that were taboo to mention in those days. Johnson, famous for his liberal approach and publishing the writings of radical writers - some were even said to be anarchists - was fascinated.

"And where would you live?" he asked.

Smiling, she told him, "But *you* know, for you will help me find a place in which I can reside and write, and I would be quite gratified of course if you could find me a position as a writer."

"Naturally," he replied.

And so Mary moved to London and began working as a deputy editor and literary critic. She soon learned more languages and began translating books from German and French, as well as having her own books published. Mary, a beautiful, intelligent young woman of twenty-eight, became popular at the famous, sought-after dinners hosted by Johnson, where she met many celebrities from the London intellectual society, including writers - mostly radical - and artists, and even Thomas Paine, a famous reformist politician who advocated "simple logic."

In 1789, at the age of thirty, Mary met the handsome, married painter Henry Fuseli at one of the dinners, and a forbidden relationship developed between the two. Mary did not favor the institution of marriage in the first place; and her liberal attitude – promiscuous and irresponsible in the eyes of others – allowed her to relish the relationship with the attractive young man. In her great openness, she even proposed a revolutionary triad arrangement to him and his wife – neither an orgy, nor a life of hedonism, but a platonic system in which the three of them would share a common home. However, Henry's wife was shocked by the idea, vetoed it, and forced her husband to immediately sever ties with Mary.

The French Revolution broke out, and Mary published *A Vindication of the Rights of Men* the following year, expressing her support for the ideals of The Enlightenment. The book earned a reputation throughout England, and she was compared to leading writers on social theory; she even had her portrait painted by one of the best-known artists of the day.

Two years later, her most influential book, *A Vindication of the Rights of Woman*, was published. It claimed that women deserve education as befits their status in society; since they are integral for the nation, they should be regarded not solely as spouses, but also as companions. Most important of all, the book argued that men and women should share the same fundamental rights.

In the book, Mary writes, "I have gained a profound conviction that women in particular, are rendered weak and wretched by a variety of causes" – primarily the nature of the education that male society provides for them. Therefore, she presents a demand for a different education for women, an education to allow them to develop intellectually, as far as possible, to the same level as men.

What a stir Mary raised with this book! In it, she dares to challenge even the philosopher Jean-Jacques Rousseau in his book *Émile*, who argues that the education of women has only one purpose, i.e., the pleasure of men. In the book, Mary takes aim not only at education, but also at the institution of marriage. What connects and will connect couples even at the stage when their ardor fades, she argues, is the affection between the two, and therefore the institution of marriage itself is superfluous. A formal framework will not be able to hold people together; only affection between the two can last.

Wow, what bravery! Whenever she encountered someone who delivered an established, thought-provoking critique that was based on logical data and appropriate to the period and setting, Mary remembered her friend Fanny and her attempts to persuade her to give up.

Fanny reinforced her time and again, even from heaven, and in the face of all the hesitations and twists and turns of the mind, Mary only grew stronger and more resolved to fulfill her destiny.

At the end of 1792, Mary traveled to Paris to take part in the "Celebration of the Revolution" and to promote her ideas there. She looked for a way to enlist the authorities to help her pass a law, or at least establish a school to educate girls according to the principles and values she believed in and wrote about, but she soon discovered that some statements and principles look good on paper only. The Jacobin regime in France rejected her beautiful assertions, including everything related to women's civil rights, and Mary faced a dire failure.

The British government in those days also underwent a change, losing its tolerance for liberal views, and Mary, who failed to put her ideas into practice, found herself between a rock and a hard place. She not only failed to bring her plans to fruition in France, she was also prevented from returning home to England. To her delight, she met a group of exiled English intellectuals in Paris and joined them. There she also met the man who would change her life.

Gilbert Imlay, an American merchant and adventurer living in France, caught her eye one evening. He was impressive, handsome, intelligent, and well-spoken; he enjoyed group discussions, whether the subject was something light or heavy. In the heat of these debates, he turned to her, challenging her that while she was a fine writer, it was all theory, not practice - as she was not prepared to undergo a true emotional test herself.

"I? You exaggerate, sir!" she responded.

"Is that so? Then what would your opinion be about dinner and a glass of wine at my home?"

Indeed, after an enjoyable, romantic meal, which was peppered with many compliments for both her intellectual and physical attractiveness, and thanks to a great deal of wine, they moved on to the bedroom.

The young American taught the English philosopher the practical aspects of life – in the permissive French atmosphere. He gave her an "education" in sexuality, teaching her the nature of sensuality and driving her mad during passionate nights unlike anything she had ever experienced, and she fell head over heels in love with him.

Soon she became pregnant, and when she was thirty-three gave birth to a daughter and named her Fanny, after her best friend. The arrangement was convenient for Mary. She, who preached against the institution of marriage, was now raising an "illegitimate" daughter and she liked the situation, especially in light of Gilbert's cooperation.

Then things started to get worse. France declared war on Britain, and the latter responded with a blockade. The Jacobin regime of terror in France began to arrest and execute English expatriates on the guillotine, including some of Mary's friends. The couple, unable to return to England, fled to the north of France, and Gilbert, who as an American was allowed to import food to France despite the British blockade, gained local trust and could move around the country freely. He traveled to the U.S. Embassy in Paris and declared that Mary was his wife – which was how Mary acquired American citizenship and was able to save her own life.

Mary continued her hard work, and in the wake of the rampant terror in France even published another important book in England,

An Historical and Moral View of the French Revolution and the Effect It Has Produced in Europe; nevertheless, the troubles kept coming, and this time – from home.

Living with Mary, who was constantly busy writing and caring for the baby, became tedious for Gilbert. He was tired of the routine of the house, and life in the periphery did not improve along with his moods. He began to venture out for long periods, and it wasn't long before Mary realized that Gilbert had a new lover.

She had never expected to experience a clash between her views on love and intimacy, on the one hand, and her personal life, on the other. The affection between the two was not strong enough to maintain the framework as she believed and preached, and jealousy was driving her mad. The simple realization that "He is betraying me!" echoed in her head, and images of him with another woman constantly popped up in her mind. She wrote him letters every time he left - harsh, emotional, desperate letters - and begged him to come back, but Gilbert did not answer her pleas.

The story of her life from then on was a difficult one. Gilbert left for London, but Mary was afraid to return there and so remained in the north of France until the fall of the Jacobin regime. She then returned to Paris during the most difficult winter in France in centuries. The city experienced hunger and disease, the relationship with Gilbert grew weaker, and her situation worsened. Mary decided to return to England, under the name of Mrs. Imlay, still hoping that the man of her dreams, living in London, would agree to renew their relationship.

But Gilbert was already somewhere else. Although he appreciated Mary and her abilities, and they did meet from time to time, he couldn't bear the thought of her being his wife from then on, and he couldn't understand the magnitude of the crisis she was going through. As far as he was concerned, she was supposed to behave just like a man. Wasn't that what she preached in her books and articles?

He did not know that Mary was deeply mired in depression, and that her condition was getting worse, nor did he appreciate how serious the situation was until the day he found her unconscious in her home. Mary, it turned out, had decided to put an end to the matter by committing suicide. She obtained laudanum[27] and she drank a large amount of the drug dissolved in a glass of water, but by chance Gilbert arrived home just in time and managed to save her life.

Mary saw her miraculous rescue as another chance to reconnect and tried to conquer his heart in various ways, including a business trip to Scandinavia in order to raise funds to help her partner out of his financial predicament and the heavy losses that he had suffered. The trip was successful, and she even produced a new book, but none of this brought Gilbert home. Realizing that her options had run out, she tried to commit suicide once again and left him a letter.

Let my wrongs sleep with me! Soon, very soon, shall I be at peace. When you receive this, my burning head will be cold... I shall plunge into the Thames where there is the least chance of my being snatched from the death I seek. God bless you! May you never know by experience what you have made me endure. Should your sensibility ever awake, remorse will find its way to your heart; and, in the midst of business and sensual pleasure, I shall appear before you, the victim of your deviation from rectitude.[28]

She folded the paper, signed it and sent it off. That very evening, she headed for the bridge to throw herself off. Greatly determined to succeed this time, she started to climb the fence.

---

27   A common painkiller invented in the sixteenth century and based on 20% pure opium.

28   "Mary Wollstonecraft," Wikipedia.

However, the whole universe seemed to conspire against her. During the climb, the hem of her dress was caught in the fence and prevented her from continuing. She cursed loudly and pulled at the dress desperately until it tore and came loose, and she was able to put a foot on the top of the railing. Her sharp movements and the noise she made caught the attention of a carter passing by; he braked his horses with great noise, and leaped and grabbed her before she could fall.

Apparently Mary's time to die had not yet come, and she began to internalize this. Now, after her second failed attempt, she seemed to be waking up from a nightmare and slowly returning to herself, completely cleansed of her love for Gilbert and ready to come back to life.

Two years passed, and Mary returned to her work with full vigor, writing and publishing prolifically; then, when she was thirty-seven, she met William Godwin again. They had met ten years earlier at one of Joseph Johnson's dinners. He was a philosopher who criticized Thomas Paine, and the two had engaged in heated debate, with Mary attacking and challenging him throughout the evening. That encounter had ended poorly, and they had been happy to go their separate ways and never meet again.[29]

However, the years had their effect, and one day Godwin came upon the book Mary had written on her journey to Scandinavia. In response, Godwin wrote, "If ever there was a book calculated to make a man fall in love with its author, this appears to me to be the book. She speaks of her sorrows in a way that fills us with melancholy, and dissolves us in tenderness, at the same time displaying a genius that

---

29   Thomas Paine was seized in France during the Jacobin Reign of Terror, the same series of events that motivated Mary and Gilbert to flee to the north of the country.

commands our admiration." The two ran into each other, and the events of that long-ago evening now became a humorous episode. They began to spend a great deal of time together, and it wasn't long before Mary discovered that she was pregnant again.

Despite their principled misgivings about the institution, the two of them decided to marry.

It was William who suggested it, "for the benefit of the child" who was to be born; life experience also led Mary to come to terms with reality. She understood that in the society in which they lived, especially in conservative England, there was logic in William's request.

And so it happened that the two got married. But when they went to register, it became clear to everyone that Mary was not "Mrs. Imlay" at all and that she had in fact been "living in sin." Mary was amused by this and Godwin didn't care at all. In fact, he had even published a philosophical political essay called *Enquiry Concerning Political Justice and Its Influence on Morals and Happiness,* in which he argued against the institution of marriage and called for its abolition, but still, many friends abandoned the two. This couple was too extreme for conservative English society.

Mary had her second daughter soon afterwards, but she soon showed signs of puerperal fever (also known as childbed fever), a terminal illness that was very common in those days. Ten days later, on September 10, 1797, at the age of only thirty-eight, Mary passed away.

The Journey Continues

I could feel the satisfaction with my life as Mary as soon as I passed through the gate. Afterwards, once I left the sphere of orientation and enlightenment and reviewed, together with the Guides, the details of the life that had just ended, I understood that Mary's free will had further emphasized the goals I sought to accomplish in a "strong woman."

In her daring war against the most sacred institution of society in those days, that of marriage, Mary also reduced the distress created in me as a result of the previous life, which I postponed dealing with until later incarnations. Alfonso didn't dare endanger himself and his family, so he accepted the sentence and gave up his path as a healer; however, Mary's war against society as a whole remained in full force until her last day, without her backing down or expressing regret. Maurier's defiance of the Guidance also lost its power. Mary proved that with help, like the intervention of the Guidance in foiling her suicide attempts, she could stop, look inward, and accept an important change in her life – to the point of falling in love again and bringing another child into the world. Maurier did not have that power.

My feeling of success as an individual being was better than usual. You must be asking yourselves, "Good, but what's the difference between this life cycle and previous reincarnations?"

Throughout these discussions, I have mentioned more than once "the plan of Creation" versus "the soul plan." Here, it is worth expanding on the subject.

The term "soul plan" is clear, isn't it? We've talked about it extensively, but perhaps I should focus on the topic once more just for the sake of edification. When the soul descends to earth and finds form in a body, it has several purposes. It is important for it to repair the "soul wounds" created when it parts from the divine source; it also wants to learn many lessons in the material world, because this allows it to examine, learn and experience everything in the most comfortable and beneficial way. It is also able to repair the traumas created by life in the material world, including man's free will. And how does the soul do all this? By preparation ahead of birth, a strategy we call the "soul plan." For the soul, the success of this plan has great significance in its development and growth; for the living person, this success is expressed by developing and transforming one's consciousness into a higher human consciousness, by improving the quality of life within the society in which one lives, and by increasing one's contribution to their surroundings.

And the Creation plan? Remember Brashita from Jericho? Her soul plan dictated that she was to be born different from other people of her time. And why? In order to fix something? To learn something? Definitely not. It was part of the Creation plan, the plan that sees humanity as a whole and knows that it achieves its goal through individual change. This was also the reason for the birth of John the Baptist, who in his life allowed a great transformation for all mankind, and so it was with Mary Wollstonecraft.

Wait a minute! You must be thinking that if the plan of all of the Creation is realized through individual plans, how can we understand the plan and its goals simply by connecting all the soul plans? Would we get the outline of the Creation plan?

Actually, not at all. That's not how it works.

The plan of all Creation is complex, multifaceted, and completely different from the concepts that humans express and use. It stems from the purpose of Creation itself and leads there. Humans are simply unable to see or understand this, because the expressions of its physical realization are only part, and even not the most important, of the plan; neither can you see them as a complete and comprehensive picture. And if you want to know the truth, even the souls do not...

The number of beings close to the full plan, and having the ability to understand it - even in part, even just certain segments of it - is very small.

Well, in terms of the Creation plan, Mary's life was crowned with complete success and she laid a theoretical, academic foundation for changing the status of women, but the script of her story raises some questions, and I would like to present the whole picture.

The main goal before I was born as Mary was to test my ability as a soul reincarnated in a person who would grow up to be a pioneer and succeed in their mission. As I speak to you, more than two centuries after Mary's death, I can say that the developments have been interesting. Although I could ask you to go and read a little for yourself, I wouldn't do that to you...

So it's like this: After her death, William Godwin named the infant "Mary," after his beloved wife. In her memory, he wrote *Memoirs of the Author of A Vindication of the Rights of Woman*. Godwin intended to portray his wife as he knew her, with complete sincerity, love, and a great deal of compassion, but when he told the story of her illegitimate children, talking about her love life – and especially her suicide attempts – it never occurred to him that British society would not see eye to eye with him. Contrary to his intent, Mary was perceived as a promiscuous, immoral woman who harmed the sacred structure of the British family and society as a whole. Godwin made it even worse when he reinforced opinions that were in her writings that seemed to dovetail with his own thoughts to the point of distortion – for example, when he described her as religiously skeptical, even though this didn't fit reality at all, or when he said she was an emotional woman in whom he, in his rationality, instilled balance.

Godwin's book caused Mary to be slandered and condemned by many writers over the next century. It was said that "no self-respecting woman would read her works." However, not everyone shared this view, and some took the trouble to read her writings nevertheless; they were even reprinted every few decades. A respected writer who made the effort to read Mary's *oeuvre* and take it seriously was George Eliot who, some sixty years after Mary's death, devoted an article to women's roles and rights and compared Mary to an American journalist, critic, and women's rights activist who, like Mary, bore a child out of wedlock.

Ninety years after her death, and with the outbreak of the feminist revolution and the rise of the movement for equal rights for women, Mary Wollstonecraft's work was returned to the center of the public stage and gained wide legitimacy. Her name came up in every forum of the movement, and her books were the foundation on which the movement built itself. Many women have praised her. Virginia Woolf even wrote about her that "one form of immortality is hers undoubtedly: she is alive and active, she argues and experiments, we hear her voice and trace her influence even now amongst the living."

Okay, so what was so urgent for us, in the spirit world, to create Mary's work a hundred years before it was used? And why did she have to be slandered and her reputation ruined?

So here's some perspective, from a greater distance. When formulating the soul plan, I had to select a number of variables with which to craft the story. I chose the parents from a variety of options. I chose the country – England – and I also chose the time. It was important that the author of social theory live in the age of social revolutions and be influenced by them. The French Revolution provided a perfect atmosphere, and Mary believed with all her heart that she could bring her ideas to fulfillment in the new and liberated France. This strong belief of hers, combined with an atmosphere of innovation, served as an excellent platform and impetus for composing her theories.

However, we also knew that human society was not yet ready for change, and that further processes would be carried out by other souls, reaching maturity only a hundred years later. All that remained was to "freeze" the books, but not make them disappear, and there is nothing like a good condemnation to erase a book - for a limited time. When the time comes, it is the very condemnation that can be leveraged to bring its contents back into the public sphere – which was why Godwin wrote his book. But in order for the book to "do the job," it had to be written out of deep pain, suffused with a great deal of emotion and passion, so she had to die when the love between the two was still in full swing and they were still young, which is exactly what happened.

In other words, the Creation plan encompassing many people and many soul plans, worked as efficiently- how would you say it?- as a Swiss watch.

And why did she have to give birth just before she died? Well, that already belongs to another story and a soul contract I signed even before the birth of Mary Wollstonecraft; she had to give birth to her second daughter because that child would play an equally important role.

Little Mary inherited from her mother both her writing ability and her resolution, and she herself became a literary pioneer. At the age of eight, she began to read her mother's writings and was deeply influenced by them, and so it happened that she actually followed in her footsteps. When she was seventeen, she fell in love with a married man, poet Percy Bysshe Shelley; she fled with him to France, accompanied by her stepsister Claire, who fell in love with Percy's friend - the poet George Gordon, Lord Byron - and became his mistress.

The members of this group spent a great deal of time together, exploring literature and poetry. One time, Byron came up with the idea of a contest to create fantastical creatures; this led Mary to write a story which, under Percy Shelley's influence, she developed into a novel. It was a pioneering and trailblazing novel, the first science fiction in the world, and it is renowned until this very day. The book is *Frankenstein*.

CHAPTER FOURTEEN

The New Age

Over two hundred and twenty years have passed since Mary Wollstonecraft's life, bringing us to the third decade of the twenty-first century. If I were a person, I would say that I'm excited. The last journey I made ended about a year ago and was an important period of life that I will immediately tell you about. I need only a few minutes of your time to describe how I have cleansed the imbalance created in my essence due to the life of the shaman Maurier, as well as the great transformation that you humans are in the midst of.

The life periods of the Swiss Johann and the English Mary that came after the end of Maurier's life were important and facilitated the cleansing process I had to go through after the lives of Alfonso and Maurier- in practice, even if indirectly, greatly reducing the damage to my essential character of healing and caregiving. I accomplished the final healing in another period of life as a village blacksmith and horseshoer named Günter, and at the end felt that I had returned to my true essence.

Günter

Günter was born in a Prussian village in 1825 to a poor family, the son of a blacksmith and horseshoer in whose footsteps he was supposed to follow. Günter, however, felt that this path did not need to be his path. From the moment he stood his ground and left his parents' home, he fought against the injustice of the gaps between the classes. When he heard about the *Bund der Kommunisten* (Communist League) and the teachings of Marx and Engels, he joined and became the representative of the communists where he lived.

When the "Springtime of the Peoples" began (the Revolutions of 1848),[30] he decided, as an active and believing communist, to participate in them wholeheartedly. He paid a price for this, as along with seven "rebels," he had the dubious honor of being put on trial, found guilty, and sentenced to three years in prison. When he was released and set free, he discovered, much to his disappointment, that life in the country had changed, as the *Bund der Kommunisten* he loved so much had disintegrated, and so he returned to his parents' house in the small village.

Günter returned as a new man. His time in prison among his ill-fated fellow inmates increased his commitment to every person by virtue of their being a person. Ideology did him no good behind bars, and in its place he discovered spiritual fortitude and a strong desire to help others. The guards recognized these qualities in him and put him to work in the prison's infirmary, where he was first exposed to the world of medicine and nursing. When he returned home, he helped his father in the smithy, but also began to help and take care

---

30   The Springtime of the Peoples was a wave of local uprisings for liberation from the yoke of foreigners and for national unity that took place in Europe for two years, beginning in 1848.

of his neighbors, even aiding the customers who came to shoe their horses. He soon also discovered that horses sometimes needed no less care and medical relief than their owners, and he acquired a reputation throughout the region as a veterinarian for horses as well as a healer for humans. The smithy became famous throughout the land, to the delight of Günter's father and brother, and he himself became a sought-after, well-known veterinarian and healer. He lived a full, happy life until his death at age sixty-eight.

Günter never knew that the lesson I set up for myself in his life was to challenge the routine that would put him on the same track as his father, to learn to make decisions based on inner faith even if they involve risk. Neither did he know that his propensity for involvement in public life stemmed from everything I had brought with me from the lives of Johann and Mary, and that the nature of being a healer was part of the soul plan aimed at correcting and finally stabilizing this trait of mine. It was no wonder that when I finished my days in this incarnation and returned home, I felt like I had been restored to my true self.

Now, before I move on to the story of the last incarnation, I must ask you, dear readers, whether you have noticed that the earth is changing.

"Changing? But it all looks the same," you might say.

No, dear readers. It only seems so to those who are not observant, but for one hundred and fifty years, everything around you has been changing. For one hundred and fifty years, new, unique opportunities have been uncovered; for one hundred and fifty years there have been people among you who sense them, embrace them, and fulfill them. Huge changes are taking place in everything, if you just care to look. New ways of thinking come down, a developed consciousness is assimilated, and all of these elements affect all of your lifestyles.

New theories, never before known, have become a new foundation for your life. Humanity has learned and is still learning to see the invisible. It is now legitimate to ask, "How did life arise, and how did it develop?" Disciplines that address the mind, such as psychology, have appeared on the world stage; physics has introduced new theories that have never before been propounded; abstract art has introduced a new perspective within your lives; and technological advancement has brought about what you could never have imagined.

You don't need to saddle a horse anymore to get moving, nor do you need to harpoon whales to get oil for lanterns to light up the streets of London. Human beings have always dreamed of flying like birds, and now this has come to pass. The world, which was so vast, is now a global village. Everything is close to everything, cultures intermix, and man is already looking for routes to take you off your beautiful planet. The familiar societal structures have been put to the test and transformed, various approaches to government have arisen, spousal and familial ties are being altered, and the entire social structure stands before fundamental changes, the edges of which you are only beginning to perceive.

And the change has only just begun... Future generations will be different from you, and you can already see the first signs of this within children born recently. They are different- more developed, more inclusive, with the love of nature and the love of living things embedded in their being, and with a closer connection to nature and the hidden worlds.

And all this occurs with the biggest change taking place in the background.

Over one hundred and fifty years, humanity has reached a level of evolution that allows humans to connect to the world beyond the veil- to our world, the world of souls- and acquire knowledge, heal, and be healed. No, I am not talking about a substitute for the various religions, and I am not talking about introducing new prayer formulas and rituals; I am talking about the direct connection to us – each person to their soul represented by their higher self, each person to the high Guidance that accompanies their soul, and all in a direct and personal way, without intermediaries.

You probably remember the chapter in which I told you about that stage in human development when man could already grasp and accept the idea of immaterial divinity, a divinity that does not need totems and stone idols to represent it. I said then that 3,500 years ago, we initiated a pilot program of belief in an abstract god, one who has no figure or image. After 1,500 years of this experiment, when human society was already largely ready for it, we began the phase of spreading this thought throughout the world.

And now, about 2,000 years after I was involved in the birth process of John the Baptist, the age of spiritual leadership from those who announce the word of God to man is coming to an end. The important role of priests, rabbis, imams and other clergymen is in its final stages. They founded the great religions and spread them throughout the world, and they served as mediators for the higher worlds, for knowledge and information, and for healing and for divinity, but their important work has now been completed, and for about 150 years the new age has been dawning.

People were constantly looking for the way to what was beyond them, but always within the framework of one religion or another. The direct connection to what is beyond human perception indeed existed, but only among unique individuals. They were called "prophets" or "witches" and "sorcerers" when despised, but now this ability is expanding and being exposed to the entire human population, to the "ordinary" people.

At first it was a trickle in various places in the world as individuals began to talk about it in public and forming groups and associations. So it was with Helena Blavatsky, one of the founders of the Theosophical Society in 1875; so it was with George Gurdjieff, who, in the nineteenth century, developed the Fourth Way; so it was in Germany with Wilhelm Reich, who developed the Orgone theory; so it was, of course, with Rudolf Steiner, who introduced anthroposophy; and so it was with many others. The number of people who espouse the spiritual approach is growing, the number of people who connect to knowledge is growing, and what was considered in the wake of the Scientific Revolution to be vain and useless is taking a wider place in social consensus and beginning to drip into the ranks of scientists.

The transition to the new, current era also began as a "pilot" program, but while then it lasted 1,500 years, now it is advancing very quickly. The number of people connecting, the ones you call "messengers of light" is growing, and very soon it will cross the critical mass threshold, beyond the point of no return, and humanity will fully enter the next stage.

And why did it happen? And how did it happen? You should already know.

According to the plan of Creation, we, the individual souls that have been reincarnated since days of yore, bring with us the change. It reaches the various bodies in which we are realized, creating, as if by magic, tiny changes in your bodily systems. Thus, within a few generations, human beings will be different in that their abilities will improve and change, and their conduct and even behavior will be different.

This massive transformation requires the mobilization of many forces of nature to provide a supportive and enabling environment, and indeed there are many partners. The entire cosmos is organized accordingly, and solar storms that come through sunspots, for example, occur in precise coordination with the process. And this change is happening.

This is neither wonder nor miracle. Humans may disagree and explain it as an inevitable evolutionary process of nature – which is fine – but the change in humans is occurring at a pace unmatched and unprecedented in the history of life across the planet.

At the turn of the twentieth century, I knew I wanted to be reincarnated in a person who would experience the great process of change that humanity was going through, who would know how to see what was hidden from others, connect to the Guidances, transform his consciousness, and become another messenger of light symbolizing the change.

When the soul plan was prepared for me, and possible scenarios for its implementation were presented to me, I chose one that would take place in the Land of Israel. Here was the first pilot program that led man to the knowledge of an external God without a form; here I lived as Tirzah when King Solomon (Shlomo) built the Temple to that abstract God; and here I was Athaliah when his Temple was destroyed. I was here at the end of the pilot program, and even participated in starting the process of spreading faith in that abstract God – and I came back here 1,000 years later, during the Crusader Period.

I decided to return here in the period after the "Great War," the one you later called World War I, and I lived in the body of an Israeli while the mad evil of World War II was eradicated. The same people who had played their part in the pilot program a millennium earlier, who had sent out apostles to spread Christianity, who had almost been exterminated- were rising from the ashes, like a phoenix.

To actually arrive in this country and realize in it the life of a person who knew how to observe, to go through the change and mark upon his body the new process of change for humanity, was exactly what I needed. Indeed, the person in whose body I found form, whose life ended only recently, serves as a great example of one born in an age in which life is conducted in the way of "old energy" (the lifestyle his parents and grandparents are accustomed to), but who senses the change and is intrigued. There are many like him among you today, and you think of them as "spiritual" or as those who "seek themselves." Many more will come and, as the years go by, future generations will already be born into this new way of life.

I invite you to meet Shlomo.

Zichron Ya'akov

"Shlomo, you fool, just harness the mule. Come on! How long does it take to harness that old thing?" Shlomo smiled to himself, wondering when the old man would find a different way to wish him "Good morning!" The only change that had occurred in the past few years was how he related to the mule, who was now "that old thing." He harnessed the animal to the shaft, got up on the wagon, and came out to meet his father, who stood beyond the stable, a cigarette jammed into the corner of his mouth, holding a pitchfork and a hoe. He concluded his greeting the way he always did. "Oh, at last, it's almost noon!"

It was another normal summer morning. The grapes were already ripe and the harvest would soon begin and, as always, these were the days when Shmaryahu ("Shmerele," as his mother and family called him) was under pressure not to miss the exact date when the fruit would be at its best. These were the days when it was best not to get too close to him.

Many years of grief, anger, physical pain, and emotional insult passed until Shlomo learned to recognize his father's idiosyncrasies and accept his behavior with forgiveness and understanding, even though in his heart he knew the slights could not pass without leaving residue and a mark. In his adulthood, he also learned to appreciate the professionalism and rigor of his father, who was a great, self-taught expert in viticulture, and his attitude towards Shmerele softened.

Shlomo was born in 1930 in Zichron Ya'akov. Hilik, his grandfather's father, had emigrated from Romania and was counted among the founders of the settlement. The "distinguished" family had, since that time, earned its keep from growing grapes, thereby maintaining a partnership in the local winepress built by Baron de Rothschild.

Life in the small settlement in those tumultuous days had its ups and downs. The records of the events of the Nili[31] underground movement, which ended only thirteen years before Shlomo's birth, the constant war on malaria, the events of 1929, and the great Arab uprising seven years later had not yet been erased from the minds of the locals. All of this continued to keep the tension high in the settlement and within its families.

The family was Orthodox, and their home, a farmhouse, was imbued with the ideology of building the country. The nature of life and the difficulties of work dictated a rigid upbringing that suited Shmaryahu's personality; at home, words like "softness" or "love" were considered almost rude, the highway to compromise and failure.

Shlomo and his brothers attended the local school, but also had their chores on the family farm. Shlomo, the eldest, was a gentle, small-boned boy who reminded everyone of his grandmother, a pianist and intellectual, and Shmerele did not enjoy this. The gentle boy

---

31   Pro-Britain, Anti-Turkey underground espionage movement that was active during World War I in Israel, and was based in Zichron Ya'akov.

was startled every time his father raised his voice; more than once, he escaped and disappeared, and often, at least in early childhood, he would burst into tears "like a spoiled little girl." When he finished elementary school and reached high school age, his parents sent him to boarding school at the neighboring Meir Shfeya Youth Village, from which he returned home only on the weekends.

Shlomo was very homesick then, missing his brothers, his mother, and even his father, whom he feared but admired. Only some years later, when he completed his studies and became a "man," joining the Palmach[32] at age eighteen and taking part in Israel's War of Independence, was his father able to accept him as "a man in his own right, as eccentric as he might be."

The strongest evidence for this eccentricity was Hemda, the young woman from a kibbutz whom Shlomo met when they served in the same brigade. Shmerele couldn't understand how Shlomo could have become close to the daughter of Socialists, émigrés of the "Second Aliya," who denigrated any rural folk of the First Aliya as a "Boaz."[33] This, he declared, was "the boy's failure." But the years had their effect; the war came to an end, and Shlomo married Hemda and brought her to Zichron Ya'akov, to the family farm.

Gradually, Shmerele realized that his son was no less intelligent than he, no less talented than he and, if not for some eccentricities, he could be considered quite successful.

Hemda's personal history was not particularly satisfactory either.

---

32 "Palmach" was a brigade of combat units fighting in Israel prior to the establishment of the State.

33 Boaz was a land owner in the Land of Israel. He was married to Ruth, who came to be King David's great-grandmother. The full story is taken from the Book of Ruth in the Bible Where is the full story? Why even mention it?

Apparently she would never forget having had to sleep in the communal children's house, those days when she missed her mother terribly and yearned for a hug, for a maternal embrace rather than that of the disciplinarian in charge of the children, whose only concern was making sure the children observed their mandated bedtime.

Shlomo and Hemda found love and friendship in each other and lived their lives in peace. Shlomo joined his father on the farm and learned from him everything that was possible, adding something of his own, and slowly beginning to manage the farm in practice. He developed and expanded it, and their vintage became known for its quantitative and qualitative advantage.

However, there was a fly in the ointment. Without noticing how and when it happened, Shlomo had begun to adopt his father's behavior. Suddenly the farm and vineyard were more important than the household; everything was geared to the needs of the vines and not to the needs of man, and whoever did not accede to his demands suffered from his wrath. Hemda, who stood by his side and saw the importance of the vineyard and its contribution to the fulfillment of their destiny in the country and their economic wellbeing, also showed signs of impatience towards their children, regarding them as "spoiled," or "useless and spineless."

The change seeped in like a thief in the night, without Shlomo's noticing it, and only from time to time did the thought creep into his heart that something was wrong. He saw this in the sadness that had crept into the eyes of his daughter Ilana, and in the attempts of his first-born son Elad to evade an argument or even a conversation with him.

He brought this up with Hemda, and although they both felt that the anger contaminating their home was deleterious, they were unable to put their finger on the source of the problem. Shlomo, coming from an observant family, looked for an answer in the synagogue, but he slowly began to feel like a stranger in that environment – especially when it provided him no answers. Hemda, from a secular home that followed the philosophies of the leaders of the USSR – Lenin and Stalin – also felt that something was awry, but had no idea where to find a solution - "certainly not in a kibbutz education," she said, smiling bitterly to herself.

Hemda was the love of Shlomo's life, and she felt the same way about him. This love allowed them to find a middle ground that enabled them to respect each other and live a satisfying life, but they both felt that they were missing something in their home. They couldn't understand it, so despite the frustration, they just accepted it as a decree from heaven.

One evening, when Elad was about fifteen, he entered the storehouse in the yard at the end of the workday as his father was arranging the tools for the following day and getting ready to go home. The boy wanted to ask permission to attend a performance by the spiritual medium Margot Klausner.

Shlomo gave the child a pitying look. He had of course heard of Mrs. Klausner – because who had not heard of the owner of the Herzliya Film Studios and Carmel Newsreels who called herself a medium and claimed to talk to the dead? But to go to her show? There was a limit!

How surprised he was later, when the family sat down to dinner and Elad brought up the subject again, as Hemda supported him and even suggested that they all go together. Shlomo couldn't help thinking that only those who grew up on a kibbutz and received a communist education could accept and agree to something so foreign to Judaism. But Shlomo loved Hemda, and in the end he accepted her proposal.

Elad, whose gentleness reminded Shlomo of himself in his youth, was delighted and said, "I swear, this will be fantastic for you. I don't understand how you failed to think of it yourselves."

And so Shlomo and Hemda put on their finest clothes and went to the show. The electrifying atmosphere accompanying the performance and the "aura" around the special people on stage amazed them, even if they didn't believe in everything that they saw, and the experience was etched in their memories for years.

Then the Yom Kippur War broke out, and Elad was called to reserve duty. On the eve of Sukkot, five days after Yom Kippur, a delegation arrived at their *sukka*.[34] But it was not the *ushpizin*, the traditional guests of the holiday, rather the least welcome arrivals – those who, when they appeared at the door, darkened the world of Shlomo and his family forever.

The officer was the one who broke the silence. Quietly, and with much respect and empathy, he informed them that their son Elad had fallen in the Battle of Khishniyah in the Golan Heights. He died heroically, he told them, in defense of his comrades-in-arms, his family, and the entire people of Israel.

With these words, the darkness penetrated their house and repelled the light. Everything had lost its importance. Neither the vineyard, nor the settlement, nor the state, were important anymore. They were there alone, only the family amid its unbearable mourning, only the inconceivable absence of Elad.

The week of *shiva* ended, then the thirtieth day of mourning, and Shlomo returned to the vines. There, in the midst of the quiet plants, next to his aged father Shmerele, pruning branches and weeding the beds, usually focused within himself and quiet, Shlomo found a semblanceof peace. There, when he checked the quality of the soil,

---

34   A Jewish ritual, when during the seven days of the Sukkoth holiday, people spend their time in a specially built hut close to their home.

grasping twigs and brushing knots and buds, he could begin to sense the ground again and the tranquility it imparted.

The family members drew closer to one another. Shlomo and Hemda were unwilling to fall back into the arguments and quarrels that had been the background noise of the house previously, and the home that had always been lively but alienating became quiet and connected.

It took six months until Shlomo dared to enter Elad's room to get closer to the boy through his memory and belongings. He sat down on the bed, touched the pillow and the folded blanket, and pictured Elad in his mind's eye. Then he got up, went to the desk and grabbed a pencil, turned the handle of the sharpener attached to the table and straightened a page that had been lying around for quite a while. He raised his head to the shelves above the table and smiled to himself when he saw Rudolf Steiner's *Human and Cosmic Thought* and *A Psychology of Body, Soul, and Spirit*. He recalled conversations they'd had a few years before, when Elad sent them to Margot Klausner's show, then noticed her book as well, *Reincarnation and Other Stories*, and sat down to read.

That night he read parts of it to Hemda, and they were both moved by the experience. Reincarnation? Yes, that had been mentioned in the performance they had all attended, and they even used a medium to raise the dead - but that was all for show, wasn't it? Still, if it were true, might it be possible to speak with Elad? Had Elad, without knowing it, left them a means to communicate with him when he was still alive?

The next morning, Shlomo went to Herzliya Studios and asked to meet the CEO, Margot Klausner. It didn't even occur to him that she might not be there or might be too busy to see him. Very quickly he found himself studying with Margot and her partner, Hanan

Avraham. He was happy that Hemda would also join him from time to time. He discovered an entire spiritual world, and although he didn't like scaring the dead from their eternal slumber, the two participated in many séances and received messages from Elad, messages they had no doubt came from him. How do they describe it in police investigations? There were confidential details that only they and Elad could have known.

At the same time, and as he opened himself up to the world of mysticism, Shlomo began to look for other directions. He soon discovered the breadth of Rudolf Steiner's world of anthroposophy and became a follower of his teachings and the bioenergy technique; this was followed by embracing the ideas of Rafi Rosen, who had developed biorgonomy therapy. Suddenly he also realized that the Bagelmaker[35] of Hadera, to whom they had once taken Shmerele to treat his back pains, had not been some hack drumming up business based on the placebo effect, as he had thought up until then.

Shlomo also managed to sweep Hemda up in his enthusiasm. Although she didn't always see eye to eye with him on the matter, when he decided to open a clinic and treat others with biorgonomy, she joined him – on the condition that these treatments would not impinge on his work in the vineyard.

Shlomo and Hemda discovered the connection to the higher Guidances, to their higher selves, and, without realizing it, their lives

---

35   Avraham Gershkovitz from Hadera, known as the "Bagelmaker," was the first Israeli to heal people by alternative medicine, which gained great publicity in the 1970s. Despite the opposition of local medical professionals, who even appealed to the courts in the hope of forcing him to abandon these (foolish or stupid) pursuits, the court allowed him to continue his activities after hearing testimonials from patients who had recovered thanks to him,.

changed completely.

It all began with one of the many workshops they attended when the instructor put the class into deep meditation, and this led Shlomo to deep-body relaxation and inner peace. Then he suggested to the students to turn to their higher selves as they had learned and to ask a question, so Shlomo said in his heart, "I turn to my Higher Self and would like to know whether I am conducting my life as my soul would like."

This was a surprising question that I, his soul, could not answer. Not long after birth, the part of me in his body had lost the memory of his plan; my other part, the one left out of the body, was prohibited from "exchanging knowledge" with the part in his body. Had these parts of the soul been able to "talk" to each other and convey information, the whole purpose of erasing that memory would have been undermined! Instead, the question went on to my Guide, who immediately sensed the "high frequency" on which Shlomo operated, felt the purity with which the question was asked, and knew that Shlomo was ready for a direct connection - and so appeared before him.

Shlomo indeed felt the connection, and he suddenly saw in his mind's eye a sublime and impressive entity that presented itself as the "high Guidance," coming to respond to his request. The entity began, "You are blessed, Shlomo. You asked a question, but before I answer it..."

The picture before his eyes changed and a figure who introduced itself as Hilik, Shmerele's grandfather, appeared before him. Shlomo did not recognize him at first. The figure appeared as a young bearded man with a skullcap, wearing a sleeveless undershirt and shorts. A few seconds passed before he noticed the striking resemblance to the figure at the center of a framed picture in his father's house: Hilik.

Hilik sought to convey his feelings of love and affection for his grandchildren Shmerele and his sister, expressed his joy at seeing his great-grandchild experience such success in life. He even flooded Shlomo with an intense wave of love that Shlomo had never before experienced. Hilik then noted that this day had been his birthday when he was among the living! He thanked Shlomo and disappeared.

The picture changed again and the high Guide reappeared and said, "Your question cannot be answered. According to the plan, you must discover your destiny while living your life, not because you received information about it. However," he added with a smile, "here in heaven we see you, you and Hemda, in your efforts to do good, and we are satisfied with that."

When the meditation exercise was over and Shlomo regained consciousness, he saw that people were staring at him, and did not understand why. When he turned to Hemda, he saw her in tears. "What happened?" he asked. Then he discovered that the people who had finished their meditation had seen and heard him go through his process. Shlomo turned to the instructor and said, "So I imagined it and spoke aloud without realizing. So what? What's the big deal?"

Then it dawned on him that this was in fact the first time he had experienced direct channeling - not some imaginary pictures, but a full, powerful connection. He had been in a kind of trance, cut off from his surroundings, emotionally and mentally free to receive messages from the Guidances.

This experience initiated a conversation in class, at the end of which the instructor advised him to check at home if it was indeed Hilik's birthday.

Shlomo was impatient to get home, and when he finally parked the car in the yard, he went straight into the east wing of the house, to his father's room, and asked him about Hilik's birthday. Shmerele pulled out an old diary, leafed through and found it. "Strange," he said, "you asked about Grandpa's birthday on the very day. It's today!"

Then he went to the closet, pulled out a bottle of Extra Fine brandy, poured it into two glasses, pushed one into Shlomo's hand and said, "How unfortunate that you never knew him when he was alive. He was head and shoulders above the rest, and it's a great honor to raise a glass in his memory." In one move, he emptied the glass into his mouth and swallowed. "Oh, oh, oh - if only we had some herring in the house," he muttered to himself.

Shlomo smiled at the old man, putting a hand on his shoulder: "It's all good, Dad. I'll send one of the kids to go get some."

The rumors about Shlomo and Hemda's experience spread throughout the small settlement, and people talked about what they were going through. "Poor people... that incident drove them completely nuts."

There were those who tried to provoke Shlomo and said to him, "Enough with the nonsense. Elad cannot be brought back to life, but you're killing yourself. In the end you'll go crazy. Then what"?

No one was willing to listen and accept their words, and so it happened that Shlomo and Hemda slowly moved away from their old friends, but it never occurred to them, not even for a moment, that belief in this way of life had too high a price and that it might be worth abandoning it and calling it quits.

Still, the more they stuck to their views and their path, the more they discovered it had its own advantages. The number of patients who knocked on the door of their little clinic was growing. At first, most of the people came from outside the settlement, but gradually success stories reached even the stubborn locals in the little town; patients began to come from among them as well. Time passed, and people who had initially rejected them came back, one by one, to their home.

The connection to the Guidances and the ongoing counseling they received through them became a way of life for Shlomo and Hemda, and they changed. Everyone noticed that they became softer. "Not soft like rags," explained one of the farmers at a meeting at the agricultural tool shop in the settlement, "but strong people who have a special tenderness that makes you want to be with them."

Shlomo revealed himself to have a capacity for containing and caring that he had never shown before – so much so that his friends all raised eyebrows. They remembered that on the first anniversary of Shmerele's death, they returned from the cemetery and discovered that his room, which had been sealed in the interim months, had been broken into and the door was left wide open. Thieves had tried their luck, and when they found nothing of value, they simply turned around and destroyed everything. Rage flared and Shlomo's blood boiled, as did the blood of his other sons.

Then he saw the picture. On the pile of objects that lay in the center of the room was a picture of Hilik, face up. Shlomo looked at it and saw the figure of Hilik smiling at him as if to say, "I'm proud of you, Shlomo." A wave of compassion suddenly washed over him. Surely the perpetrators were troubled youths, he thought to himself, realizing that this was not an occasion for anger, but for mercy – that he shouldn't get upset, but take positive action instead. Indeed, he soon turned to the settlement's welfare department and began to work among the youth in crisis.

And so Shlomo and Hemda were better people to those around them, and they in turn responded accordingly and loved them back. It seemed that even the vineyard felt this, as its yield increased and the quality of the grapes improved more and more. It wasn't that there were no mishaps – of course there were – and they weren't spared the occasional argument, but they didn't escalate into fierce quarrels as they once had.

Their children grew up and started families, developing in new directions and leaving the nest. Only their youngest daughter, who married a boy from the settlement, stayed close to home; his new son-in-law, whom Shlomo preferred to call "my other son," joined the farm and, with the consent of all the siblings, became his successor. When their eldest son was born and they wanted to name him Elad, Hemda gave her approval.

As the years passed, Shlomo grew old and entrusted the vineyard to his son-in-law. He also visited the clinic less, but he felt that his life was full and that he was living it properly. More than once he remembered his life "before" and once even said to Hemda, "When he left us, our Elad made sure that our lives would be turned upside down, so that we would get on the right path; for that, I thank him so much."

Shlomo became weaker, and his family cared for him, but he responded with a smile and said, "You know that death is not the end, but the beginning of a new adventure. When I go home, I will know that I have fulfilled what my soul so longed to fulfill in this life, and it will be received with cheers of joy and acclaim. So why should you be troubled at the thought of my passing?"

Then one sunny day, halfway through 2019, when Hemda took him out to the yard for a cup of tea, and he sat on a bench in the shade of a weeping willow, he turned to her and said, "My day has come, Hemda. I feel it. No, don't cry," he hushed her, "and don't say, 'What? All of a sudden?' Don't say the things that are usually said at times like these because you, like me, know that this is true.

"Now listen to me, my love. Remember, we have lived a life of honor and love for our fellow man, for the soul, and for Creation as a whole. We must be grateful for that. Remember how we discovered that we are not alone here, that we are continuing on a path that is thousands of years old, and through these few years of ours, we have done all we could to reach our inner truth, to live according to our highest consciousness to teach others and to let our children and grandchildren and perhaps everyone around us know that truth is the way of the soul, that goodness and love are what bring us our highest achievements. I end my life with a great sense of satisfaction, of having reached my potential. I will close my eyes happily, not sadly."

Another moment of silence passed, and Shlomo continued, "I hope to meet Elad there; we never stopped missing him, you and I. Don't take me to the hospital, because I want my life to end here, in the yard cultivated by Grandpa Hilik more than 130 years ago. When I go on my way, I'll wait for you up there, but there is no need for you to hurry..."

CHAPTER FIFTEEN

Epilogue

Quiet.

Silence descended on me at the end of the book, and I, accustomed to the presence of the soul that has accompanied me over the past year and a half, was left alone with a sense of "And what now?"

It all began with a pact we made. I devoted all the time required to the mission, and the soul passed on its story to me. And so it did. It passed on to me everything that could be passed on to a human being, and I wrote it down. It was different from all the other periods of my life, a time when I was connected day and night to this extraordinary soul. Through it, I experienced many people in their moments of pleasure and pain; I was proud of their successes, and I ached at their failures; I was happy in their moments of happiness, and I was angry "with myself" when they acted improperly. And I underwent the routine of their lives.

So now it's over. And now what? That's it?

I tried to write a happy ending for this book. I typed vigorously but it turned to dust in my hand, and I tossed draft after draft into the recycle bin. I felt that I had to turn to the soul that had accompanied me and ask it for help. And it? It was as if it were just waiting for me to ask, and to my great joy the information came in the way the whole book had been told to me - from the mouth of the soul itself:

"The upheaval that Shlomo went through during his life," it told me, "is not unique. In fact, many human beings have connected to their Guidances over the generations, but recently there has been a change, and more and more people across the planet are going through it. And it has grown, as all of humanity is changing. It will not be long now, and the change you experience will have a great impact.

"As you probably already understand, the development of mankind is not just an evolutionary move; it has been directed and moving in a path set by the Creator since the dawn of Creation, bringing human society towards unity. The unmediated connection to the Guidance, to the "higher self," imbues humanity with "cosmic love" whose main expression is in empowering the sense of compassion and empathy for others to become the main value. The day is not far off when the spirit of brotherhood will become overpowering, and hatred and violence will be diminished until they ultimately disappear. Poverty, privation, the disgrace of hunger- all these will disappear and remain only in the history books. In their place will come physical, mental, and emotional well-being.

"This miraculous change will have a great impact on all of Creation, including the spirit world. The book you have written describes the 'higher worlds' as something that has many differentiated entities, as souls that maintain a relationship between them, but that is not the whole truth. The spirit world has no objects, has no 'image description;' there is also no separateness that human beings could understand. Here, we are all one, and we are all separate. We are all energy and we are all one consciousness, but we are all also discrete - even if not in the way you understand. It would not be wrong to say that misunderstanding is mutual, because in fact we, too, can directly understand a person's feeling and their unique vision, so different from ours, only while we are in the body. The imminent transformation of human beings, the unmediated connection with the Guidance and the higher consciousness and even with the Creator himself - all this will have an impact on the spirit world as a whole and on Creation as a whole. We, here, are looking forward to it with eager anticipation.

"I have been with you for 17,000 Earth-years. I have been through hundreds of incarnations, and I was with man at the beginning of the journey when the main goal was only survival. I participated in the growth of the feeling of self-identification, and later in the religious and cultural development. Now it is time to accompany man with great joy to the next stage, the stage of direct connection to divinity, of oneness of heart with Creation, a stage at which people will connect with each other while maintaining the uniqueness within each one. This is the stage that I am happy to call the era of Love Thy Neighbor as Thyself." If I were a human being, I would now feel the great hope of these things and even call aloud, and with great joy, 'Long live humanity! Long live Creation!'"

Quiet.

But this time it is a silence of wholeness, a silence of completion. It is over and done. It has not been easy for me to write this book, or at least not as easy as its predecessor. Here I was given information whose veracity I had to believe in without having in my hands any "evidence," not even the faintest, as to the truth of things; I had to deal, within myself, with the layers of rationality left in me. But as I wrote, I discovered that I was directed by the Guidance that led me; I learned to trust it, and I benefited. I no longer feared that I was fabricating imaginary stories and musings, and I knew that the path the soul described was accurate. I knew that everything I wrote about the existence of the soul in the higher realms is true knowledge, knowledge that I have received from my Higher Guidance, even if it doesn't meet the rules of the scientific truth of empiricism.

The existence of souls in the wondrous spiritual world is eternal. The soul exists forever, and from time to time it is reincarnated in the human body. It experiences its life; it learns lessons and, in the process, it advances humanity and allows it to develop. Dr. Deepak Chopra[36] puts it this way:

Each of us is here to discover our true selves; that essentially we are spiritual beings who have taken manifestation in physical form; that we're not human beings that have occasional spiritual experiences, that we're spiritual beings that have occasional human experiences.

It is difficult for us humans to understand this. But I, who went through a long process at the time of writing, can feel the truth and trust in it. There were quite a few moments in which I wondered, "What now?" or "Is what I write true?" But I turned to the high Guidance, and the answers flowed from it to me.

I am very grateful, even to those with whom we are not familiar and cannot even imagine.

And if we're talking about gratitude, I owe a huge thank-you to my partner, Leora Shachar, who accompanied me throughout the writing period, who awakened, illuminated and deepened in me the knowledge and the sublime sense of connection. Thanks as well to my beloved brother, and to Tamar Wolf for their comments and insights that helped the book reach completion.

---

36   Deepak Chopra is an Indian-American author and advocate of alternative medicine. A prominent figure in the New Age Movement, his books and videos have made him one of the best-known and wealthiest practitioners of alternative medicine... In 1999, *Time* magazine included Chopra in its list of the twentieth century's heroes and icons. (Wikipedia)

Made in the USA
Middletown, DE
15 August 2022

71420526R00166